○ ★ ○ ★ ○ ★ **Full Metal Apache**

Post-Contemporary Interventions
Series editors: Stanley Fish and Fredric Jameson

Takayuki Tatsumi

★○★○★○★ Full Metal Apache

Transactions Between Cyberpunk Japan and Avant-Pop America

Duke University Press Durham and London 2006

2nd printing, 2006

Printed in the United States of America on acid-free paper ∞

Designed by Heather Hensley

Typeset in Monotype Garamond by Tseng Information Systems, Inc.

Library of Congress Cataloging-in-Publication Data appear on the last printed page of this book.

Duke University Press gratefully acknowledges the support of two organizations that provided funds toward the production of this book:

The Japan Foundation

Keio University, through the Keio Gijuku Fukuzawa Memorial Fund

To my parents and Mari

"This historical sense, which is a sense of the timeless and of the temporal together, is what makes a writer traditional. And it is at the same time what makes a writer most acutely conscious of his place in time, of his own contemporaneity."

T. S. Eliot, "Tradition and the Individual Talent" (1919)

"For us, of course, things can change so abruptly, so violently, so profoundly, that futures like our grandparents' have insufficient 'now' to stand on. We have no future because our present is too volatile."

William Gibson, *Pattern Recognition* (2003)

"The twentieth century has thus brought to the fore the hidden link between trauma and law. The aftermath of the events of September 11, 2001, in the United States has dramatized the same connection for the twenty-first century."

Shoshana Felman, *The Juridical Unconscious: Trials and Traumas in the Twentieth Century* (2002)

CONTENTS

FOREWORD Tatsumi Battles the Pink Punk Cadillac Samurai Robot Cat in Space for Control of the Japanoid Reality Studio

'Cause it's hard to say what's real.

—The Flaming Lips, "One More Robot/Sympathy 3000–21," on *Yoshimi Battles the Pink Robots*

Buckle Up!

Greetings fellow Japanoids![1]

As Chief Design Consultant and Systems Analyst for Team Takayuki[2] for over a decade, I've been asked to say a few prefatory remarks about the remarkable journey you'll be taking in just a few pages when you board *Full Metal Apache*, the brilliant, paradigm-smashing study by Japan's hippest literary critic and cultural commentator, Takayuki Tatsumi.[3] Since this is almost certainly going to seem (at least initially) like a pretty wild, high-speed ride over unfamiliar, aesthetically "difficult" cultural terrain, I will focus on providing information about *Apache*'s background and evolution so that readers can make the adjustments necessary to avoid the sense of cultural vertigo, disassociation, info-overload, and other symptoms of dis-orientation.

Incidentally, don't be alarmed by that loud *boom* most of you heard just now—that was just the sound of *Full Metal Apache* breaking through the multicultural equivalent of the sound barrier somewhere over the Pacific as it headed eastward toward our shores.[4] That virtual roar officially confirms that the fastest rising star from the land of the rising sun — my good friend and long-time collaborator, Takayuki Tatsumi — is finally about to make his long-overdue major label debut in America.[5] Clad in black leather and mirrorshades, and accompanied by his wife and cultural navigator, Mari Kotani (a.k.a. the "Queen of Heroic Fantasy"),[6] Tatsumi has been moving in our direction at breakneck speed along the recently completed system of global informational highways connecting East and West that has finally allowed cultural traffic to move freely in both directions.

Fully aware of how easy it is for even major critical studies to get lost amidst the profusion of (mostly forgettable) postmodernist titles being generated by America's corporate-style university press system, Tatsumi and the entire crew of Team Takayuki have made every effort to ensure that his arrival here is a memorable one by having him roll into our neck of the woods *not* in one of those cramped, boxy, fuel-efficient literary vehicles usually associated with Japan[7] but instead in *Full Metal Apache* — which is to say, in the critical equivalent of a custom-built, souped-up Hummer stretch limo.

And, as is true of a Hummer, there's a great deal more to *Full Metal Apache* than mere ostentatious display or aggressive iconography — there's extra "leg room," for example, to allow Tatsumi's restless Japanoid imagination to roam around in, plenty of textual "space" to allow him to comfortably put on the many critical hats he likes to don for special cultural occasions (sample hat insignias: *I'm a hyper-queer cyborg feminist — and proud of it! Caution: deconstruction work ahead*; *I'm a creative masochist — go ahead and hit me!*; and *I was a teenage Japanoid!*).[8]

There's even plenty of room inside *Apache*'s custom-made framework to accommodate the enormous, unruly multicultural crowd of radically innovative writers and artists from both sides of the Pacific who have been hand-picked by Tatsumi to accompany him on *Apache*'s joy-ride into the exotic, previously uncharted regions of Japanoid culture. And it's an eclectic array of passengers indeed (think *Sgt. Pepper's* album cover): fiction writers and poets, folklorists and filmmakers, architects and anime artists, graphic designers and graphic novelists, playwrights, musicians and manga creators, copywriters (as people who write ad copy for television ads are known in Japan), performance artists, and many others working in as yet unclassifiable mixed genre forms. But for all their heterogeneity of background, culture, formal interests, and genre, these passengers do share certain commonalties—an extremity of artistic vision, for example, that typically finds expression in the sorts of disruptive, transgressive stylistic practices formerly associated with the western avant-garde,[9] and a mutual urge to counter the orientalist and occidentalist stereotypes and assumptions by openly and exuberantly appropriating materials drawn freely from East and West from sources both high and low—and then remixing them into new, hopefully liberating combinations.

Moreover, *Apache*'s cast-of-thousands include not only contemporary Japanoid writers and artists, but earlier figures, including several whose careers stretch back to the nineteenth century when Japanese and western cultures first began to interact with one another after Japan's long, 250-year, self-imposed period of isolation.[10] Tatsumi has thoughtfully seated these figures in the first-class compartment next to contemporary Japanoids with whom they share affinities. A few examples of *Apache*'s seating chart will illustrate the sorts of odd juxtapositions that result from this multicultural intermingling:

— Edgar Allan Poe (the subject of Tatsumi's Ph.D. dissertation at Cornell) is seated next to Hungarian composer, Béla Bartók, who in turn is positioned next to the renowned Japanese playwright Shuji Terayama, who in 1977 staged in downtown Tokyo what Tatsumi describes as "a phantasmagoric hyperkitsch musical" entitled *The Miraculous Mandarin*, which incorporated his adaptations of Bartók's 1919 ballet *The Miraculous Mandarin* and Poe's story "The Man That Was Used Up."

— Japanese folklorist Kunio Yanagita (best known in Japan for his enormously popular compilation of Japanese folktales, *Tono Monogatari* [*The Legends of Tono*] 1910) is paired up with Lafcadio Hearn, who had westernized many of these folktales even before Yanagita had been able to compile them.

— Avant-pop author Masahiko Shimada and Paul Auster are seated in a replica of the same Chinese restaurant in Manhattan they used as settings in their novels; joining them is the darling of post–World War II Japanese literary experimentalism, Kobo Abe.

— Japanese emperor Hirohito, General Douglas McArthur, and American presidents Thomas Jefferson and Bill Clinton are seated at the crowded guests-of-honor table, joined by Shozo Numa (author of the legendary Japanese meganovel, *Yapoo the Human Cattle*); Italian opera superstar Puccini; filmmakers Ridley Scott, D. W. Griffith, Tim Burton, and Kiyoshi Kurosawa; American authors

John Luther Long (whose 1898 novel *Madame Butterfly* inspired the Puccini opera), Michael Crichton, Philip K. Dick, Steve Erickson, and Washington Irving; and Japanese avant-playwrights, Yoji Sakate and Hideki Noda.

Finally in keeping with postmodernist collapse of genre boundaries and its blurring of any distinction between art and criticism, Tatsumi has made sure there's ample room for the entire staff of Team Takayuki, whose ranks include nearly all the usual American and European suspects, as well as several Japanese theorists.

While readers may be able to recognize some of these critics and a few of the older figures with established reputations, nearly all of the Japanoid writers and artists (including the Americans) appearing in *Full Metal Apache* are likely to be almost completely unfamiliar to most Americans. Indeed, one of the things that makes it such a landmark work in the fields of postmodern culture generally, and Japanology in particular, is the way Tatsumi's individual commentaries and exhaustive citations of bibliographical information combine to form the first reliable cognitive map of the Japanoid culture that has been thriving and mutating ever since its emergence during the late 1980s.

Of course, it goes without saying that a vehicle carrying a cultural load this "heavy" requires plenty of power—not just intellectual horsepower (though the crew of critics and theorists Takayuki has on board ensures there's plenty of that) but enough electrical juice to power up the satellite dish, CD and DVD players, the laptops and electronic notebooks, and miscellaneous other writing machines that function as a nonstop interface between the protocyborgs Takayuki and Mari and the Japanoid cultural world of the hyperreal. Fueled by a new, high-octane gas that is just one of many practical applications of Tatsumi's discovery of the untapped energy potential contained in "junk" (a key trope throughout *Apache*) and "chaos," *Apache*'s difference engine features Tatsumi's revolutionary paradigm (gear)-shift mechanism, which replaces the outmoded "o(rientalist)/o(ccidentalist)" paradigm, whose basic design flaws became increasingly apparent when they resulted in a series of spectacular critical "flameouts," thus littering the cultural highways with useless (and hazardous) skeleton frames of burned-out critical vehicles. In developing this new paradigm (gear) shift mechanism for use in *Apache*, Tatsumi based his design on two mutually supporting principles that emerged out of the turbulent wake of the rise of hyperconsumerist capitalism in the 1980s, whose logic required an acceleration in the amount of cultural data being exchanged globally, and thus produced an ever tighter feedback loop of mutual borrowings and other forms of cultural interaction exchange between Japan and the West. In *Apache*'s concluding chapter, Tatsumi describes the two components of this paradigm shift as follows:

1. Since the 1970s Japan's own excessive occidentalism has sometimes gone so far as to simulate the most canonical discourse of western orientalism. However, in Japanese postmodern literature, the logic of imitation has been replaced by one of "synchronicity" between American and Japanese works. It is the logic of hypercapitalism that requires us to throw away our bullshit ideas about causal relationship and to be confronted with the multinational synchronicity between "literature" and "paraliterature."
2. The 1980s saw another revolutionary paradigm shift. For the first time since John Luther Long's novel *Madame Butterfly* (1898), Anglo-American writers, through their own logic of mimicry, imitated and reappropriated "Japanesque" images, that is images that at once draw on and distort Japanese culture. At the same time their Japanese counterparts came to realize that writing subversive fiction in the wake of cyberpunk meant gaining an insight into the radically science-fictional "Japan." Thus, the significance of "Japonism" at the fin de siècle is precisely repeated and radically modified by the rise of what we would like to designate "neo-Japonism" around the new turn of the century ("Waiting for Godzilla").

As is also true of a Hummer, *Apache* is a literary vehicle designed to do much more than languidly cruise around the cultural Mainstreets before picking up the kids from soccer practice. To the contrary, it has been constructed so that it's operating at its most ferocious efficiency while crashing through the outdated roadblocks and detours erected years ago by orientalists and occidentalists and then heading "off road" along the confusing trails of historical, economic, political, and cultural circumstances leading into the heart of the heart of the Japanoid desert of the real.

Of course, all vehicles, no matter how superbly designed, have their limitations. Even a greatly expanded, retrofitted Hummer, for instance, is only as good as the person behind the wheel. Fortunately, in the case of Takayuki Tatsumi, you've got an experienced driver with a "track record" so impressive that it has made him . . .

Big in Japan . . .

There may be other Japanese scholars with more established reputations, or who have been around longer, but there is probably no other figure that has had a greater impact on the postmodern literary and cultural scene in Japan than Takayuki Tatsumi. Currently a professor of American literature at Tokyo's prestigious Keio University, Tatsumi (b. 1955) received his Ph.D. at Cornell in 1987, where he studied with such theory luminaries as Jonathan Culler (who chaired his thesis on Edgar Allan Poe), Cynthia Chase, Henry Louis Gates Jr., Gayatri Spivak, Mark Seltzer, and (probably the figure having the greatest long-term impact) gay, black American SF innovator and theorist Samuel R. Delany. Upon his return to Japan, Tatsumi immediately established himself as a major player within Japan's vital American studies community, when his very first book-length critical study, *Cyberpunk America*, was selected as the recipient of the 1988 Japanese-American Friendship Award. Part meticulously researched historical overview, part highly personal (and often playful) commentary, and part theory-driven critical study, *Cyberpunk America*'s eclectic methodology and its focus on art existing on the margins of the avant-garde and pop culture (particularly SF), established the template Tatsumi would be using in the barrage of critical texts he would publish during the next dozen years. In this veritable tsunami of publications, which includes everything from academic essays, interviews, reviews, dialogues (highly popular in Japan), translations, anthologies, manifestos, and commentaries, up through (at last count) sixteen major book-length critical studies, Tatsumi draws upon insights from nearly all the leading critical methodologies—Jamesonian and Baudrillardian Marxism, the semiotic approaches of Barthes, Foucault's cultural archeology, feminism and postfeminism (especially Haraway's "Cyborg Manifesto," whose influence is everywhere apparent in *Full Metal Apache*), queer theory, Said's orientalism and other postcolonialist approaches, new historicist, and miscellaneous theorizations of postmodern literary production such as "paraliterature" (Samuel R. Delany), "slipstream" (Bruce Sterling), "posthumanism" (Katherine Hayles), and "avant-pop" (Larry McCaffery)—to explore the entire range of postmodern literary and cultural production.

This flurry of activity has gained for Tatsumi not only the attention and respect of his academic peers, but a level of popular recognition that rivals that of some of the literary celebrities he writes about; just as important, the steady stream of publication in Japan's leading newspapers and magazines, not to mention the personal contacts he has developed with writers and other artists from both sides of the Pacific, has thrust him into a prominent position of influence within the Japanese publishing scene, which increasingly began to rely on his insights and recommendations concerning what works should be translated and published, and which trends were worthy of being introduced and promoted in Japan.

Why Tatsumi Was Born to Run

Even the sketchiest outline of Tatsumi's personal and educational background reveals the degree to which the multicultural perspectives he relies on throughout *Full Metal Apache* have always been less a theoretical abstraction than simply part of his daily reality matrix. Tatsumi grew up as the only son in a privileged, intellectually sophisticated family environment headed by his father, Tatsumi Toyohiko, a distinguished professor of British literature whose academic specialty was the work of Cardinal Newman. Both his father and his mother had likewise been raised in families that had been deeply influenced by western culture—and for which the importance of travel and the value of being educated abroad were simply givens.

Such values were reinforced by anecdotes Takayuki was told as a child by his great-aunt, Wataruko Kawase (1900–2003), about the fabulous voyage she had taken as a young woman of twenty when she departed from Yokohama as part of the second wave of foreign travel undertaken by Japanese artists, educators, and intellectuals just after World War I; sailing through the Suez Canal, she arrived in England, where she studied literature at University College of London. The indelible nature of the impact that her stay abroad would have on her life was evident not so much by the degree she returned with, nor by her impressive command of written and spoken English, which she spoke utterly fluently with a slight British accent still evident when I met her seventy-five years later, but by her deep understanding and appreciation for western culture.

Creative Masochism

By the time Tatsumi entered high school in the late sixties, he had blossomed into a bookish youth already displaying features of his father's intellectual rigor and appreciation for the monuments of western high culture. But he was also developing a prodigious appetite for rock music, jazz, American TV shows, cheap paperback genre novels, and other western pop forms that initially began trickling into Japan during the American occupation after the War and whose flow by the late sixties had reached the flood stage. As was the case with so many other members of this generation, the source of Tatsumi's fascination with western pop culture was considerably more complex than the obvious enjoyment of consuming the exotic other (though this was certainly involved). True, American subculture was appealing to Japanese youths from this period due to its novelty, its exoticism, and of course its ready availability; but equally important was the way it provided a kind of masochistic thrill of willing subordination to a dominant other.

The masochistic streak runs very deep within Japanese culture, and its real sources lay not in the reactions to events following World War II but in several deeper factors ranging from childrearing practices and rigid gender relations, to a sense of national identity containing several radically opposed components—that is, hyperinflated egotism and sense of racial and cultural superiority *and* equally pervasive sense of abjection, cultural inferiority, and insecurity[11]—whose irreconcilability lead to maladjustment. But as has been perhaps most memorably depicted in Tanizaki's novels, however we locate its sources, the masochist nature of the Japanese relationship to western culture has been evident throughout the twentieth century. At any rate, the impact these masochist impulses have had on contemporary Japanese culture recurs throughout *Full Metal Apache*, often via Tatsumi's optimistic concept of "creative masochism."

Irrespective of whatever psychosexual appeal it might have, the growing appetite on the part of Japanese youth for western pop was also clearly rooted in more immediate circumstances. Its conspicuous consumption became a means for this post-postwar generation of proto-Japanoid youths to signify their break from the past and to establish their own identity—a newer, hipper, hybrid identity freed from the old-fashioned occidentalist attitudes and values of their parents. This consumption also became an expression of the spirit of renewal and change that was brewing within a Japanese youth eager to connect up with the sense of rebellious cultural energy and radical utopianism that was becoming so visible in the West during the sixties.

Meanwhile, Tatsumi's deepening fascination with western pop forms began to manifest itself in more personal, creative ways. An accomplished piano player, trained since childhood to play western classical music, Tatsumi began to jam with several other jazz aficionados, and by the time he was in college he was playing keyboard for a jazz band whose repertoire included the Beatles, R & B, western classical, and jazz fusion.

Portrait of the Japanoid Critic as a Young Cyborgian Otaku

But it was another distinctly American form of pop culture—that is, SF—that was to have the most decisive long-term impact on Tatsumi.[12] Although the impact of technological change on Japan had been of central concern to pre–World War II Japanese writers and artists from Soseki to Ozu, the American brand of SF that had been emerging in the United States—first as the pulpy space opera forms of Doc Smith and Buck Rogers in the thirties and later as the more sober, speculative forms that rose to ascendancy under editor John Campbell—had never been practiced in Japan. This began to change during the late forties and early fifties, when the thousands of cheap SF paperbacks left behind by American servicemen began to circulate among Japanese youths via the black markets operating in Tokyo and other major cities. The rise of SF to prominence was given an enormous boost in the late fifties with the release of several classic Japanese SF films, including *Mothra* and especially the camp classic *Godzilla*, whose portrayal of a radiation-spawned monster wreaking havoc on the streets of Tokyo tapped into the deeper societal fears on both sides of the Pacific (so much so that *Godzilla* remains the most recognized Japanese cultural artifact ever imported to America). By the late sixties when Tatsumi first began reading widely in SF, Japanese SF was beginning to mature, and Tatsumi was able to find a sense of personal and intellectual connection with the legions of similarly geeky, disaffected youths who comprised the active and vital community of Japanese fandom.[13]

This early immersion in SF was something Tatsumi would draw upon later when he began exploring postmodern culture more systematically.[14] By the mid-eighties when he was studying at Cornell, Tatsumi was also attending numerous American SF conventions, including several that helped launch the cyberpunk movement. Recognizing that cyberpunk authors shared a number of important thematic concerns and formal impulses with postmodernist authors such as Burroughs, Pynchon, and DeLillo, Tatsumi attended the 1986 SFRA Conference held in San Diego that featured a number of panels dealing with cyberpunk. It turned out that the director of that conference was someone who shared Tatsumi's conviction that American SF had not only recently emerged as a major literary form, but that in many ways the cyberpunk movement in particular could be seen as representing a kind of apotheosis of postmodernism. The director also gave Tatsumi an early draft of the entry he was writing about contemporary American fiction for *The Columbia Literary History of the U.S.*, an essay entitled "The Fictions of the Present" that used the opening lines from Gibson's *Neuromancer* ("The sky above the port was the color of a television tuned to a dead channel") and whose central thesis was that only SF and quasi-SF authors were dealing with the most crucial aspect of contemporary American life—that is, the growing impact of technological change on the lives and imaginations of ordinary Americans. Two years later, Tatsumi devoted the concluding chapter of *Cyberpunk America* to this conference director—which is how I came to be one of the first Americans to join Team Takayuki.

Two Side-Trips Conclude this Prefatory Detour

Just as even the most elaborately retrofitted Hummers have their limitations, so, too, do introductory critical analogies that rely on them. The truth is that no automobile analogy, no matter how rich and ingeniously worked out is capable of accurately modeling a critical sensibility as complex and richly nuanced as Tatsumi's, or of adequately suggesting what readers are going to encounter once they take off with Tatsumi in *Apache*. I will therefore now turn off the ignition to my Hummer analogy, leaving the car motif to recede, like an image in a rearview mirror, and conclude my preface with two brief side trips—after which: you're on your own. Sayonara!

Prefatory Side Trip No. 1: A Selection of Haiku and Poetry Inspired by Full Metal Apache

The postmodern pond
A "frog" jumps in
The "sound" of the "water."
The silkscreen door slams

Mari's kimono
Waves.
On the young shoots of the leaves
appearing on the computer screen
A spider's web lies suspended
The World Wide Web.
To what shall I compare
this so-called "real world"?
To the white wake behind
A rocket ship that has roared away
At dawn!
The cries of the sim-insects
are buried in the coded roots of
the sparse pampas grass program—
The end of humanity's autumn is in
The millions-of-colors prints of the last leaves.
To bird and butterfly
it is unknown, this "flower" here:
the autumn sky above the port
The color of a television
tuned to a dead channel.[15]

Prefatory Side Trip No. 2: Final Coda: It's all over now . . .

Take what you have gathered from coincidence . . .

—Bob Dylan, "It's All Over Now, Baby Blue"

Takayuki begins most of his individual discussions by citing purely random coincidences, and I will conclude my foreword in a similar manner by asking readers to consider the curious set of synchronicities involved in the U.S. publication of a book about Japanoid culture that has a concluding chapter whose humorously ominous title—"Waiting for Godzilla"—raises expectations that seem to be directly answered by the simultaneous arrival on our shores of an actual Godzilla, the great Japanese slugger Hideki Matsui; this new, appropriately Japanoid incarnation of Godzilla then proceeds to once again take center stage in a large metropolis, amidst thousands of screaming citizens, who react to his appearance not in the clichéd, panic-stricken manner we expect from the orientalist paradigm but in the typical Japanoid three-step process: appreciation, appropriation, remixing.

I'm not sure what conclusions Tatsumi would draw from this improbable set of coincidences, but I suggest that it provides another demonstration of the validity of the highly unorthodox, argument-from-random-coincidences methodology Tatsumi employs throughout *Full Metal Apache*. More fundamentally, it also literalizes Tatsumi's underlying point that as far as Americans are concerned, the waiting is finally over. Japanoid culture isn't threatening to arrive, it's already here. Japanoids are not creatures spawned from the orientalist paradigm representing the exotic other who are adept mimics capable of imitating us. Japanoids are people just like me. Japanoids are our next-door neighbors. Japanoids are our closest friends, our wives, our children.

Indeed, as Tatsumi convincingly argues throughout this marvelous, eye-opening study, Japanoids are already . . . you.

Larry McCaffery

ACKNOWLEDGMENTS

This book is a critical intervention into the myth of origins in the wake of literary and cultural theories such as deconstruction, cyberpunk, and avant-pop. Nevertheless, every book is required to start by reinventing the myth of its own origins—an irony from the outset, since this questioning and reinventing of origins must necessarily be in conspiracy with each other. Yet without this conspiracy I could not have meditated upon the theory, history, aesthetics, performance, and representation peculiar to what I call “full metal Apache.”

With this irony of origins in mind, let me here locate, reinvent, and “acknowledge” my own primal scene. As a child in downtown Tokyo in the mid-1950s and 1960s, I was shocked by the destruction and reconstruction of the Institute for Nature Study, a unique botanical garden that sat just in front of my house, right in the path of construction for the Tokyo Metropolitan Expressway. This primal scene starts with the beautiful garden that had been my favorite playground, and the ugly construction machinery that deformed its landscape. However, I very soon found myself enjoying the in-between atmosphere of the construction, discovering a new playground in the chaotic and chimeric fusion of the natural forest with the high-tech expressway. What is more, I was to discover later that the Institute for Nature Study had always already been more cultural than natural, especially in the way its “educational garden” reproduced plant communities from earlier days. Undoubtedly, it is the scene that I have just located and reinvented that paved the way for the post-Foucauldian, Derridean, Ballardian, Gibsonian, and Harawayan sensibility of this book.

This image enabled me to perceive a number of radical things occurring simultaneously across different cultural fields in the 1970s and early 1980s, especially in critical theory and postmodern fiction. It was this sense of coincidence—not only between poststructuralist insights and postcyberpunk innovations, but also between Japan and the United States—that induced me to study American literature and literary theory in North America. Therefore, my deepest gratitude goes to my North American mentor Jonathan Culler of Cornell University and my collaborator Larry McCaffery at San Diego State University. My time at Cornell between 1984 and 1987 fostered my understanding of disfiguration and my involvement with cyberpunk, while my days at San Diego State in the summer of 1993 helped me elaborate my own theory of comparative avant-pop. Here I would also like to acknowledge a deep debt to the Fulbright Foundation, the Japan Foundation, the Japan Society, the Japan Society for the Promotion of Science, and the Office of Research Administration at Keio University (especially the Keio Gijuku Fukuzawa Memorial Fund for the Advancement of Education and Research), for the financial support they have generously provided over the last two decades. Without their assistance, I could not have completed this project.

I would also like to express my appreciation to a number of scholars and editors who helped me publish earlier articles and interviews and books, whether solo or collaborative, the fruits of which were revised and openly or secretly incorporated into this book: Henry Louis Gates Jr. of Harvard University (*Diacritics*), Donald Hassler of Kent State University (*Extrapolation*), Ronald Sukenick of the University of Colorado (*American Book Review*), Daniel Pearlman of the University of Rhode Island (Council for the Literature of the Fantastic), Robert McLaughlin of Illinois State University (*Review of Contemporary Fiction*), Tadashi Uchino of the University of Tokyo (*Theater Arts*), Nobuo Kamioka of Gakushuin University (*Japanese Journal of American Studies*), Joan Gordon of Nassau Community College (Science Fiction Research Association), Veronica Hollinger of Trent University (*SF Studies*), Steve Brown (*SF Eye*), David Pringle (*Interzone*), Helen Strang (*Critique: Studies in Contemporary Fiction*), Yuji Shimahara (Misuzu Publishers), Hiroaki Sakashita (Heibonsha Publishers), Koishiro Hoshino (Iwanami Publishing), Kenichi Kawai (Treville Publishers), Masatoshi Izaki (Chikuma Publishers), Shingo Ishii (Chikuma Publishers), Mayumi Shimizu (Chikuma Publishers), Sugawa Yoshiyuki (Netto Kobo), Etsuko Hosoi (Hayakawa Publishing), Yoshihiro Shiozawa (Hayakawa Publishing), and Yutaka Yano (Shincho Publishers). I have also been lucky to receive frank feedback and invaluable suggestions from a number of good friends and colleagues: Mari Kotani, Mary Knighton, Kiyooka Charles, Kazuko Behrens, Doug Anderson, Sinda Gregory, Paul Williams, David Blair, Mark Amerika, Mark Driscoll, Dianne Nelson, Brett deBary, Barton Levi St. Armand, Samuel Otter, Kyoko Hirano, Michael Keezing, Christopher Bolton, Thomas Lamarre, Livia Monet, N. Katherine Hayles, and Yasuko Nakaegawa. I am most indebted to the book's external reviewers, including Anne Allison of Duke University and Susan Napier of the University of Texas at Austin, as well as to my brave and skillful editor Reynolds Smith at Duke University Press.

In retrospect, the book had its own origins at an exciting symposium on cinema and representation held at Rikkyo University in Tokyo on June 18, 1994, where Fredric Jameson and Peter Fitting were my co-panelists. It was at the reception immediately after the symposium that Fredric Jameson suggested I submit a proposal for my own book, though at the time I am sure he did not guess that because of my transpacific situation, it would require more than a decade to complete the project.

At this point, let me provide some bibliographical data. Parts of chapter 1 were published in Hayakawa Publishing's monthly *Higeki-Kigeki* [Tragedy and Comedy] (May 2000) and Seidosha Publishing's monthly *Yuriika* [Eureka] (June 2001). An earlier version of chapter 2 was published in *Critique* 39.1 (fall 1997). Chapter 3 first served as the preface to *Future War Novels of the 1890s* (London: Routledge/Thoemmes, 1998). Chapter 4 was first printed in the *Geibun-Kenkyu* [Journal of Arts and Letters] 71 (December 1996) and *The Newsletter of The Council for the Literature of the Fantastic* 1.5 (1998). An earlier version of chapter 5 was published in the special J. G. Ballard issue of *Interzone*, no. 106 (April 1996). Parts of chapter 6 first appeared in *SF Eye*, no. 9 (November 1991), and *SF Eye*, no. 12 (August 1993). Earlier versions of chapter 7 were included in *SF Eye*, no. 1 (March 1987) and *Storming the Reality Studio: A Casebook of Cyberpunk and Postmodern American Fiction*, edited by Larry McCaffery (Durham: Duke University Press, 1991). The first version of chapter 8 appeared in *Para*Doxa* 2.1 (1996). Chapter 9 grew out of an article in issue no. 15 of *SF Eye* (December 1997), the final issue of my primary critical playground. Chapter 10 was first published in *Theater Arts*, no. 5 (April 1996) and expanded and delivered at the 1999 International Edgar Allan Poe Conference in Richmond, Virginia, on October 19, 1999. Chapter 11, the title essay of this book, was first printed in *The Japanese Journal of American Studies*, no. 7 (1996). The prototype of the conclusion was delivered at a conference entitled "The American Impact on Germany, France, Italy and Japan, 1945–1995: An International Comparison," held at Brown University on April 13, 1996; it was later printed in *American Book Review* (June–July 1996). This version was substantially revised for the Japanese Subculture conference "Visions, Revisions, Incorporations," held at the University of Montreal on March 27, 1998, and was finally included in *Transactions, Transgressions, Transformations: American Culture in Western Europe and Japan*, edited by Heide Fehrenbach and Uta Poiger (New York: Berghahn Press, 2000). Appendix 1 was first published in *SF Eye*, no. 12 (August 1993), and won the 1994 Pioneer Award sponsored by the Science Fiction Research Association. Appendix 2 was produced in 1998 but has never before appeared in print.

Last, but certainly not least, I would like to thank my family, especially my great-aunt Wataruko Kawase, an impeccable bilingual and bicultural intellectual, who lived to see the paradigm shifts of three centuries (1900–2003) but who did not live to see this publication; my father, Toyohiko Tatsumi, who has studied John Henry Newman and the Oxford movement for a long time; my mother, Chizuko Tatsumi, whose humorous misperception of *Hayakawa's SF Magazine* as an immoral and subversive monthly ignited my deep and enduring interest in this literary subgenre; and my wife, Mari Kotani, insightful critic, accomplished costume player, and a perpetually refreshing influence.

INTRODUCTION Anatomies of Dependence

Born in a Christian family in 1950s Tokyo, I grew up in a naturalized Anglo-American culture. Unaware of the political and racial and ontological impacts of the occupation period, I never questioned the Americanisms incorporated into my way of life in Japan. Indeed, I must have imagined it always to have been that way, basically the same as in the United States, and likely to remain so. It is not that I was ignorant of my own culture; rather, I could not conceive then of "culture" as the effect of pan-Pacific negotiations, as an end product of never-ending intercultural oscillations between Americanization and Japanization. As an innocent and careless Japanese boy, of course, I simply took up American culture as my own, never "seeing" it per se as the biased and deformed and exaggerated result of crosscultural transactions. But with the advent of Japan's high-growth period in the late 1970s, I had my first chance to visit North America; that was when I began to notice that culture has always been a comic effect of transculturation.

For instance, traditional Japanese ghosts that I learned about as an elementary school student through the book *Kwaidan* (1904) appear to have been overlaid with the esoteric culture of African American voodoo and zombies, which the author Koizumi Yakumo (a.k.a. Lafcadio Hearn) had researched during his New Orleans years from the 1870s through the 1880s. In an intriguing avant-le-siècle parallel, early twentieth-century Europe welcomed the Italian composer Puccini's orientalist opera *Madama Butterfly* based on the American lawyer John Luther Long's novel published in 1898, while the early twenty-first century saw the completion of the Japanese postmodern trilogy *Infinite Canon* (2000–2003) by Masahiko Shimada, itself in part inspired by Chinese American playwright David Henry Hwang's transvestite drama *M. Butterfly*, staged on Broadway in 1986. Even today, while we enjoy the neoorientalist representations of Japan that we readily find in films such as the pre-cyberpunk masterpiece *Blade Runner* (1982) or the hardcore avant-pop film *Kill Bill* (2003–2004), appealing North American cultural icons such as Anne of Green Gables and Audrey Hepburn—whom we once believed constituted essential aspects of American culture—have turned out to be the mere effects of Japanese occidentalism. It is this critical exoticist ethos, entertained at the nexus between Americanization and Japanization, that fascinated me and led me into my current interest in the postmodern phase of comparative culture and literature.

Yet this new approach alone was not enough. Despite my Cornell years in the mid-1980s, when as a literary Americanist I fully imbibed the methodologies and ideas of deconstruction and cyberpunk and cultural studies, all of which gave me tremendous inspiration for reexamining pan-Pacific transcultural dynamics, none of them inspired the writing of this book.

To explain how this book came into being requires a brief digression by way of an anecdote deeply lodged and cherished in my memory. Back in August of 1997, I had invited my friend Paul Williams, the famous poet, rock 'n' roll critic, and administrator of the Philip K. Dick estate, to my summer cottage in Fujimi, a town in the Japanese Alps of Nagano Prefecture. While taking a casual walk on the street of this resort one beautiful Sunday, we ran by chance into Dr. Takeo Doi, the distinguished psychiatrist and philosopher well-known for his bestseller *Amae no Kozo* (1971; translated by John Bester as *The Anatomy of Dependence*, 1973). Of course, I promptly moved to introduce the two men, assuming that Paul was unfamiliar with Dr. Doi's work. At this point, however, something wonderful happened: Paul eagerly took over his own self-introduction, saying to Dr. Doi, "I have long admired your work. You have been my spiritual guru." To me, this was truly a fantastic encounter, the contact of cultures between a typical modernist theoretician and a typical postmodern baby boomer.

As such, this trans-Pacific and transgenerational encounter immediately called to mind the final chapter of *The Anatomy of Dependence*, where Dr. Doi already had analyzed the significance of the counter culture's flower children:

> It is only recently, it seems, that parents began to spoil their children in the Japanese sense (the well-known words of Dr. Spock are probably highly significant here). The Western sensibility where children are concerned has been drawing closer to the Japanese in recent years: but parallel with this has been an increase in the number of children who never grow up. . . . The phenomenon of childishness is seen in its most acute form in the hippie cult. . . . In practice, the present tendency to shelve all distinctions—of adult and child, male and female, cultured and uncultured, East and West—in favor of a uniform childish *amae* can only be called a regression for mankind, yet it may prove to be a necessary step towards the creation of a new culture of the future, since it is recognized that in the individual the creative act is preceded by a kind of regressive phenomenon. (164–165)

The Japanese idea of *amae*, roughly translated here as "dependence," refers to the feeling originally experienced by all normal infants at the breast of the mother—the desire to be passively loved, or the unwillingness to be separated from the warm mother-child circle and cast into a world of objective "reality."[1] When I first read this book as a freshman in 1974, I understood the concept of *amae* only abstractly; but now, after more than two decades, the word had become flesh. That casual encounter between Dr. Doi and Paul afforded me insight into a splendid case history of transcultural crossings between Japan and the United States.

Isn't it rather ironic that while the United States constructed itself in the late eighteenth century as the first democratic nation by making its declaration of "independence," now Japan in the postmodern era exerts powerful cultural influences on the globalized post–flower children of the United States and elsewhere with a philosophy of "dependence"? This irony enables us to read from a different perspective not only Japanese writers such as Shozo Numa, Ryu Murakami and Haruki Murakami but also American writers like Thomas Pynchon, Philip K. Dick, and Steve Erickson. It is my contention that a kind of "creative masochism" (an important cultural concept pervading this book), emerged, in part as a result of Dr. Doi's theory. Although "creative masochism" certainly hints at the postwar political unconscious of Japan in the wake of defeat—along with other contemporary concepts such as "creative defeat" (Shigeto Tsuru), the "mental history of failure and defeat" (Masao Yamaguchi), and "the strategy of being radically fragile" (Seigo Matsuoka)—it also delineates the aesthetic effect achieved by being passive and dependent, updating perhaps a certain Keatsian romantic concept of "negative capability." Thus, it was the miraculous encounter between the Japanese psychiatrist and the American flower child that first emboldened and motivated me to write this book.

Since the turn of the last century, the semiosis of things Japanese has been radically consumed and disseminated by Anglo-American writers. But recently, postmodern Japanese artists have become ever more ambitious in their creative attempts to disrupt, defamiliarize, and queer the conventionally drawn boundaries between orientalism and occidentalism. Just as Anglo-American representations of the Japanese other have long derived from received stereotypes of Fujiyama-geisha-sushi-harakiri, so too have Japanese people long modeled America on the basis of stereotypes of Kennedy-Apache-*Gone-with-the-Wind*.

Yet, at this turn into the new millennium, we have plunged into mostly chaotic and transculturally infectious negotiations between orientalism and occidentalism, between the western belief in eternity and the Japanese aesthetics of the moment, between a western, production-oriented, idealistic sensibility and a Japanese high-tech consumerist, posthistorical mentality. Take a glance at Japanese postmodern literature; you might be amazed to see how the kingdom of excessive transportation is basically just another name for a network of synchronicity, where anything and all things can happen simultaneously, overcoming any limit and exceeding any colonialist or imperialist intent. The post-cyberpunk and globalist milieu we all inhabit will undoubtedly precipitate a reconsideration of the creative masochism inherent in postwar Japanese mental history, and may even prophesy the advent of a new exoticism for our alien planet in the coming millennium.

This book is divided into five parts and a conclusion. Part 1, "Theory," concentrates on the potential of literary theory in the globalist age, spells out the cyborgian making of postwar Japanese subjectivity based upon "Mikadophilia" and "creative masochism," and details the discipline of comparative metafiction that informs my work. In this part, I offer a reinterpretation of John Luther Long, Philip K. Dick, Thomas Pynchon, William Gibson, Bruce Sterling, Steve Erickson, and Tim Burton, along with their Japanese counterparts Shozo Numa, Yasutaka Tsutsui, Masahiko Shimada, Hideki

Noda, Yoji Sakate, Kiyoshi Kurosawa, and t.o.L (tree of Life). These rereadings develop a poetics of postmetafiction, whose origins could well be located in my 1992 collaboration in the form of a dialogue with Larry McCaffery, entitled "Toward the Frontiers of Fiction: From Metafiction and Cyberpunk through Avant-Pop" (reproduced in appendix 1).

Part 2, "History," pursues the way of queering the oriental, restructuring the historical space in which images of the Far East intersect with those of Anglo-America. In Anglo-American culture, the turn of the last century saw a boom in "future war" novels foregrounding the "yellow peril," a phenomenon I consider through works by H. G. Wells, M. P. Shiel, Jack London, and others. In Japan, meanwhile, the turn of the last century saw the rise of "Deep North gothic," which exaggerated the fear and allure of the absolute other. I discuss this period as reflected in Lafcadio Hearn (a.k.a. Yakumo Koizumi), Kunio Yanagita, and Ryunosuke Akutagawa. The resulting culture clash of western orientalism and Asian occidentalism affords access to a queer reading of the works of several contemporary English speculative fiction writers: J. G. Ballard's masterpiece of the technoscape, *Crash*, as well as his mainstream bestseller *Empire of the Sun*, illuminate the dynamics between ethnicity and sexuality, while Richard Calder's Dollscape series, including his novel *Dead Girls*, comprises yet another radical reinterpretation of Madame Butterfly, this one from the viewpoint of technoexoticism. My email interview with Richard Calder (reproduced in appendix 2) will undoubtedly deepen your understanding of this nanofash technogothic genius.

Part 3, "Aesthetics," starts with a consideration of the Japanese reception of the cyberpunk movement in the 1980s, then examines the signifier "Japan" as consistently reappropriated and creatively deformed by post-cyberpunk avant-pop writers. My interest here is focused not only on the structure of the exoticist unconscious but also on the postapocalyptic humor of canonical cyberpunk novels such as William Gibson's 1990s trilogy *Virtual Light*, *Idoru*, and *All Tomorrow's Parties*. Here my argument ends by paving the way for the theory of new exoticism, as is clear in the two works written in 1996, Allan Brown's Japanophilic novel *Audrey Hepburn's Neck*, and Michael Keezing's avant-porn short story, "Anna-chan of Green Gables."

Part 4, "Performance," investigates how the cultural clash delineated thus far contributed to the reengineering of postwar Tokyo, particularly during the high-growth period. Through a discussion of the playwright Shuji Terayama's avant-garde magic musical "The Miraculous Mandarin," I explore how Terayama incorporated both Edgar Allan Poe's tale "The Man That Was Used Up" and Béla Bartók's opera *The Miraculous Mandarin* into his own work, as well as how Terayama's play determined both the geography and the psychogeography of 1970s Shibuya, Tokyo, where the play was first performed.

Part 5, "Representation," includes the title essay and constitutes the essence of this book. Here, I situate the Japanese director Shinya Tsukamoto's *Tetsuo* diptych in the tradition of postwar "Apache" fictionists such as Ken Kaiko and Sakyo Komatsu. In exploring the impact of American captivity narratives on the creative masochism of the Japanese cyborgian identity argued in earlier chapters, this chapter goes a step further and posits what I like to call the "Mikadophilia syndrome."

The conclusion, "Waiting for Godzilla," closely analyzes the metaphorics of the well-known Japanese monster Godzilla, exposing a fascinating intersection of orientalism and occidentalism. Other monster movies and postmodern and postcolonial texts also serve to shed future light on this intersection, including Sakyo Komatsu's best-selling *Japan Sinks* (over four million copies sold), Mark Jacobson's cult novel *Gojiro*, Erika Kobayashi's "Neversoapland," and Genpei Akasegawa's pop art manifesto, *Thomasson*. This last section should underline the fact that my literary and cultural interests throughout the book circulate around the indeterminate, unpredictable, and even chaotic dynamics between the orientalist gaze and the occidentalist one, without which we could not have constituted our own reality.

PART 1 *Theory*

CHAPTER 1 Mikadophilia, or The Fate of Cyborgian Identity in the Postmillenarian Milieu

In the wake of cyberculture, multiculturalism, and postcolonialism in the 1980s, we cannot help but notice the tremendous impact of hyperreality (that is, of a media-saturated reality in the sense of Jean Baudrillard) on the discursive status of "orientalism" as a western stylization of the East and of "occidentalism" as an eastern stylization of the West. For multinationalist hypermedia have helped to blur the distinction between reality and fiction as never before. At the same time, the western concept of logocentric reality has proved to be no more than a dominant narrative. Let me illustrate this point by reconsidering the recent relationship between the United States and Japan, exploring the three stages in the development of "mimicry": the essentialist myth of originality and imitation, the late capitalist synchronicity between different cultures, and the multicultural and transgeneric poetics of chaotic negotiation.

The Three Stages in the Development of Mimicry

There is no doubt that, since its reopening to the outside world in the early Meiji era, that is, in the 1860s, Japan has persistently westernized, modernized, and especially "Americanized" itself by closely "imitating" Anglo-American styles and obediently following the example of modern, white, western civilization. And yet until recently, few critics have fully examined the political nature of Japanese mimetic desire. Recent postcolonial theory can help us in this project. Japan was of course never formally colonized by a western nation, and indeed it became a colonial power itself. However, Japan's status as one of the objects of western, including American orientalist, imaginations and Japan's efforts to emulate western and American examples make it useful to draw on concepts developed in postcolonial theory, such as mimicry, in order to understand the complex interactions between Japan and the United States. As Homi Bhabha points out in his essay "Of Mimicry and Man: The Ambivalence of Colonial Discourse" (1984), it is in the comic turn from the high ideals of the colonial imagination to its low mimetic literary effects that "mimicry" becomes visible as "the desire for a reformed, recognizable Other, as a subject of a difference that is almost the same, but not quite" (*Location of Culture*, 85–86). It has long been assumed that although the colonized respond to colonial domination via a complex "mimicry," this mimicry can never succeed in effacing the difference between the western original and the colonized copy. Western thinking on Japan has much in common with attitudes toward the (formerly) colonized. Thus westerners have both admired and denigrated the Japanese as adept mimics, who are good at copying but lack in originality.

Postcolonial theorists, however, have exposed the concept of originality as a western ideological invention, and in turn they see mimicry not as a failed attempt to achieve originality, but as a counterstrategy that radically problematizes the very origin of originality. Using these insights, Marilyn Ivy, in her provocative book *Discourses of the Vanishing* (1995), has explained the myth of "imitation" with regard to Japan: "It is no doubt Japan's . . . entry into geopolitics as an entirely exotic and late modernizing nation-state instead of as an outright colony that has made its mimicry all the more threatening. As the only predominantly nonwhite nation to have challenged western dominance on a global scale during World War II . . . Japan, in its role as quasi-colonized mimic, has finally exceeded itself: now it is American companies, educators, and social scientists who speak of the necessity of learning from Japan in the hope of copying its economic miracles, its pedagogical successes, its societal orderliness" (7).

Following Ivy, an innovative reconsideration of mimicry can thus provide us with a powerful device for analyzing U.S.–Japanese relations from a postcolonial perspective.

Ivy's reformulation of Japanese mimicry has direct and persuasive applications for literature. Modern Japanese writers, whether prewar or postwar, started their careers by imitating and assimilating the works of Anglo-American precursors. One example is *The Legends of*

Tono (1910), an apparently original collection of Japanese traditional myths, legends, and folklore compiled by the father of Japanese nativist ethnology, Kunio Yanagita. Yanagita's text focused on the town of Tono in the Deep North of Japan where people still encountered difficulty in telling fact from fiction and the actual from the imaginary, just like the inhabitants of Sleepy Hollow in Washington Irving's tale. Yanagita modeled his work on the author of the famous short story collection *Kwaidan*, Lafcadio Hearn, a.k.a. Yakumo Koizumi. Thus, it was not the Japanese nationalist Yanagita but the multinational author Hearn/Koizumi who established a Japanese sensibility for folklore at the turn of the century, when the popularity of "Japonism" in Europe and the United States reached its peak. While Yanagita himself believed this supernaturalist anthology to be antithetical and even "antidotal" to modern westernization, his project was in fact not imaginable without the western orientalist Hearn. In a sense the search for "originality" turned out to be the result of "imitation," revealing how problematic both concepts are.

In the 1950s and the 1960s, it became almost inevitable for Japanese writers to adopt much from the latest translated Anglo-American fiction and to follow American examples produced in the Pax Americana climate. Thus the Japanese tried to import a huge number of Anglo-American cultural products and unwittingly misread their own occidentalism as a genuine internationalism. And Japan's excessive occidentalism has sometimes gone so far as to simulate the most canonical discourse of western orientalism.

Representations of the ethnic other, whether correct or incorrect, have long enchanted talented writers who are ambitious to incorporate the most avant-garde images into their fiction. Just as Anglo-American representations of the Japanese still seem to derive from the stereotypes of Fujiyama-geisha-sushi-harakiri, so we Japanese (including intellectuals) have long modeled America upon the stereotypes of Kennedy-Apache-*Gone-with-the-Wind.* In her provocative essay "Imaging the Other in Japanese Advertising Campaigns," Millie Creighton carefully analyzes the way in which advertisements in Japan invoke foreigners of several sorts, especially white occidentals who are referred to as "gaijin": "In ways parallel to Western orientalism, Japanese occidentalism also involved a sexual projection of the other, particularly the allure of the occidental woman. However, as a response to the increasing impact of Western culture on Japan, Japanese occidentalism involved more than attraction to and exoticization of the Western other. The creation of *gaijin* as a social construction of Japanese occidentalism also mirrored a need to assert control over the moral threat of an intruding outside world" (144).

Japanese commercials of the mid-1990s are perfect examples of such an occidentalist strategy for domesticating and naturalizing the other. In a Kirin beer campaign, Harrison Ford is depicted not as a glamorous celebrity but as an ordinary "salaryman" working for a typical Japanese company. As David Lazarus reports, a number of A-list Hollywood stars can still be seen pitching Japanese products in more traditional I-use-this-and-so-should-you endorsements. "Jodie Foster sells cars. Madonna and Sean Connery sell liquor. Arnold Schwarzenegger sells energy drinks. . . . Demi Moore sells shampoo. Sharon Stone sells cosmetics. And, of course, there's Sylvester Stallone, who seems a particularly apt choice for commercials that sell ham" (Lazarus, "Harrison-San!," 58). Thus the traditional discourse of Japanese occidentalism has at once exoticized and domesticated gaijin; it has tried to overcome its hidden Anglophobia, which is caused by the essentialist myth of originality and imitation. The result has been a certain synchronicity of Japanese occidentalism and American orientalism.

One significant aspect of postwar Japanese history has been the metamorphosing of masochistic imitation into the principle of technocapitalist recreation. In his splendid book *Suicidal Narrative in Modern Japan*, Alan Wolfe has described the sensibility that shaped thinking on postwar Japan: "If there is a metaphorical paradigm that best characterizes historical writing about the 1940s in Japan, it is that of death and rebirth. . . . The resulting combination of marginal deprivation (buffeted by American rations and black marketeering) and relative freedom seemed to produce a mood of heady optimism and expressive vitality" (167).

The way the Japanese responded to the disastrous earthquake that struck the Osaka-Kobe district on January 17, 1995 (the beginning of the fiftieth anniversary of the end of World War II), illuminates how a distinct form of memory has developed out of the postwar history of Japanese reconstruction. This form of memory represents, assimilates, and domesticates the earthquaking other. Just as economic recession in the 1980s seduced Americans to revive the discourse of Japan bashing, so the Osaka-Kobe earthquake carried some Japanese religious fanatics to renewed anti-Americanism. Both sides of the Pacific made every effort to erase their respective national trauma.

Thus it is notable that immediately after the earthquake, Shoko Asahara, the charismatic leader of the doomsday cult Aum Shinrikyo (The True Teaching of Aum), attributed the disaster to a conspiracy of the United States, whose "mysterious Great Power had set off the earthquake either with a small, distant nuclear explosion or by 'radiating high voltage microwaves' into the ground near the fault line" (Sayle, "Nerve Gas," 68). No matter how fanatic this death cult is, its response to disasters is very typically occidentalist and has a longer history.

Back in the 1950s, the monster Godzilla represented the similarly sinister effect of nuclear devastation brought about by the United States. The figure of Godzilla as the ultimately disastrous other helped the postwar Japanese reconstruct a national identity by making themselves into victims of and resisters against an outside threat. The occidentalist Godzilla of the 1950s helped postwar Japanese writers develop the prophetic imagination of a creative masochism based on what William Kelly has designated "the absence of moral panic" in the panel on "Hollywood and the Media" at the conference "The American Cultural Impact on Germany, France, Italy, and Japan, 1945–1995: An International Comparison" (Brown University, April 1996). What is more, in the mid-1960s, the weekly Japanese TV series *Ultra Q*, featuring a variety of post-Godzilla monsters, accelerated the alteration between destruction and reconstruction. However fatally Tokyo gets destroyed by brand-new monsters, you will find the very same city reconstructed quickly and beautifully next week. Armageddon happens once a week, Resurrection the following week. This is the two-beat jazz that Japan was dancing in its high-growth period.

Like Henry Adams, who saw the turn of the century as the transition from the time of the Virgin to that of the Dynamo (*Education of Henry Adams*, chap. 25), I could well reconsider postwar Japan's rehabilitation as a paradigm shift from the emperor as the feudalistic demigod to Godzilla as the postnuclear semigod. As if witnessing this paradigm shift, the mainstream novelist Shichiro Fukazawa published in the November 1960 issue of *Chuo Koron* an anti-imperialist and blasphemous short story "Furyu Mutan" (The Story of a Dream of Courtly Elegance), and unwittingly incited a right-wing terrorist to murder, on February 1, 1961, the family maid of the president of the publishing company. Since this story narrates the fantasy of a popular revolt that not only overthrows the Japanese government but also executes the imperial family in a series of intimately described decapitations, it is no wonder that the murderer, a member of the Aikokuto (Great Japan Patriotic Party), got angry enough to attack (indirectly) the writer or the publisher. What matters here, however, is that, as John Whittier Treat has pointed out, Fukazawa's story disclosed the paradox of "the emperor's status as both reified symbol and reigning symbolist," and that his rhetoric made the text "anathema to many right-wing activists and left-wing intellectuals alike" ("Beheaded Emperors," 106). Put simply, by unveiling the limit of ideology with the paradox, Fukazawa skillfully offended "the political orthodoxies of progressive intellectuals and imperial absolutists alike" (111). It is through this aporia of ideological struggle that a brand-new paradigm becomes visible.

Thus, taking the place of the emperor as well as caricaturing the mechanics of the emperor, Godzilla as the new paradigm came to be followed by similar images in the 1970s. Examples include Shozo Numa's far-future speculative fiction *Kachikujin Yapoo* (Yapoo the Human Cattle), completed in 1970; Isaiah Ben-Dasan's *Nihonjin (Nipponjin) to Yudayajin* (The Japanese and the Jew), published in 1970; and Sakyo Komatsu's four-million-copy bestseller *Nippon Chinbotsu* (Japan Sinks), whose amazing book sales coincided with the 1973 oil shock. As I will discuss in more detail elsewhere in this book, while the ancient Jews experienced the original diaspora (597–598 B.C.) in Babylon as an ontological predicament, Komatsu radically reconfigured the very notion of diaspora into a powerful engine of Japanese capitalism in the high-growth period of the 1970s. What is more, let us note that, symptomatic of the oil shock and the end of the Vietnam War, the year 1973 saw the astonishing coincidence between *Japan Sinks* and Thomas Pynchon's *Gravity's Rainbow*, neither of which could have been written without the kind of nuclear imagination that is represented by Godzilla. Komatsu and Pynchon undoubtedly meditated upon what would happen to the postapocalyptic junkyard and how we should react to the age of reconstruction. This is how they both in equal measure predicted postdiasporic and globally networked space in the posteighties reality, in which everything is connected with everything else, mostly as if through a web of conspiracy. And it is this postwar historical background that enables us to witness the paradigm shift from the logic of imitation to the logic of synchronicity between Japan and the United States in the 1980s, and the advent of chaotic negotiations between orientalism and occidentalism in the 1990s, as I will show in the conclusion.

Into the Abyss of the Pan-Pacific: Why the Obsession with *Blade Runner*?

Now take a comparative glance at a pair of magic trees that intruded menacingly into the cultural deep forest of 1999: Tim Burton's "Tree of the Dead" and Kiyoshi Kurosawa's "Charisma." The first of these trees is featured in *Sleepy Hollow*, a film by the quintessential cult artist Tim Burton based on "The Legend of Sleepy Hollow" by the nineteenth-century American romantic Washington Irving. Modeled roughly on the enormous and fearful "tulip tree" that Irving depicted in the original story, Burton's "Tree of the Dead" is a sort of monster. When attacked, it bleeds copiously and vomits out the human corpses it has swallowed. It also serves as a way station through which a headless rider passes en route between the real and other worlds.

The second tree appears in *Charisma* ("Karisuma," as the Japanese title is transliterated), a film by the young Japanese cinematographer Kiyoshi Kurosawa (no relation to Akira Kurosawa), which is based on a story he wrote after ten years of planning. Kurosawa's "Charisma" tree is a kind of cyborg that generates pollutants. Although the people of the forest have cared generously for the tree, considering it part of the law of the world and maintaining it through a high-tech process, the tree creates a biohazard and requires them to confront the aporia: should they choose this tree or the whole forest?

The symbolic as well as synchronic representation of trees has a familiar literary heritage, spanning from the trees of William Faulkner and Katherine Anne Porter to those of Kenzaburo Oe. Yet the critical difference between the Tree of the Dead, a kind of organic, self-willed intelligence, and Charisma, a tree that influences and controls everything in the woods around it but is itself devoid of substance, serves as an especially telling sylvan reflection of the cultural contrast between the United States and Japan at the turn of the new millennium. Indeed, these trees offer near perfect allegories of the construction of their respective national identities.

To interpret these allegories, let us begin by considering how the authority of the American president corresponds not to that of the Japanese prime minister but rather to that of the emperor. In the early republican era, the people of the United States wanted George Washington to be their emperor, disclosing and naturalizing the contradictory structure of what might be termed "democratic imperialism." At the conclusion of the revolution, George Washington occupied a position of unchallenged authority in the thirteen former colonies, and there was strong sentiment in the Continental Army for crowning him king. Washington was appalled by the idea and angrily rejected it when it was broached to him by Colonel Lewis Nicola, a Frenchman who had served under Washington and who is reported to have had a great deal of influence with the officers in the army (Roberts, "Stubborn Washington"). The presidential campaign of 2000 found this feudalistic American tradition alive and well; as Andrew Sullivan has pointed out ("Counter Culture," 24), both George W. Bush and Al Gore were inheritors of hereditary power within a vibrantly nepotistic cultural milieu.

In contrast, Japan has been forced to live with what might be called "imperialistic democracy," enjoying the contradictory but peaceful coexistence of the emperor and the prime minister. While the American president can be characterized as a responsible, accountable individual who mimics the heroic role of Superman, the Japanese emperor is a weirdly chimeric cyborg, who has always first and foremost been required to preserve and prolong his own life, even under inhuman conditions, in order to secure the integrity of the nation.

In this light, consider that whereas Burton's Tree of the Dead convincingly signifies an organic and democratic individual, Kurosawa's Charisma represents the cyborgian life of a Japanese charismatic figure, prosthetically empowered both to threaten and demand respect from a nation at once.

Hence it was in 1989 that Kiyoshi Kurosawa first made up his mind to shoot *Charisma*; he was keenly conscious of the death of the Showa emperor in January of that year. In the latter half of 1988, the Japanese people had been troubled not so much by the high-tech medical treatment to which the dying emperor was subjected as by their vision of the emperor as both the emblem of the vanishing traditional Japanese culture and as the ultimate cyborg who had constituted the essence of postwar Japanese body politics. It was not that the Japanese emperor had maintained the body of crypto-imperialism within himself, but rather that although he had always been afflicted with ontological contradictions, the entire nation had consumed his exis-

Fig. 1 See how the Emperor gets metamorphosed. Photographic triptych. © Nippon Eiga Shinsha Co.

tential problem as a sort of enjoyable spectacle, revealing itself to have been gravely infected with what might be designated "mediamania," a symptom of our late capitalist media-saturated society.

Next, let us recall September 27, 1945, the day that the Showa emperor, as defeated general, had his first formal negotiation with General Douglas McArthur. On that day, the emperor bravely proclaimed his complete responsibility for the actions of his nation during World War II, surrendering himself personally to the final judgment of the General Headquarters of the Allied powers. Through this personal surrender, Emperor Hirohito persuaded McArthur to spare Japan from further ravages of war. With this regenesis under the occupation, the defeated nation was deprived of the myth of radical innocence, reluctantly accepting its paradoxical fate of maintaining the emperor as its ultimate symbol while promoting a simultaneous democratic hybridization.

It is in the shadow of this fate that, even in twenty-first-century Japan, Ridley Scott's cult movie *Blade Runner* (1982) continues to win an ever increasing number of admirers, regardless of whether its viewers are science fiction fans. Unstable as the postwar Japanese emperor system remains, its deep structure bears the imprint of a false memory of democratic ideology; it is a system that revived the Japanese nation as one that had already developed a consistent, hardcore, democratic body politic, and as such it allowed the Japanese to survive the occupation peacefully. Corresponding beautifully to this postwar scenario, the narrative of *Blade Runner*—based on Philip K. Dick's novel *Do Androids Dream of Electric Sheep?* (1968)—centers on the false memories

Fig. 2 Tamala against the shadow of her doppelgänger Tatla. Frame from t.o.L.'s anime *Tamala 2010: A Punk Cat in Space*. © Tamala2010 Project.

with which runaway "replicants" must implant themselves in order to pass for human beings and outwit the bladerunners, that is, the bounty hunters who threaten their lives.

It is no wonder therefore that in 2001, two decades after *Blade Runner*, the Japanese designers t.o.L (tree of Life) skillfully digested the artistic fruits of *Blade Runner* and created the brilliant anime *Tamala 2010: A Punk Cat in Space*, featuring a one-year-old but extremely coquettish female kitten, Tamala, who survived a terrible fire designated "The Red Night of Edessa," which had taken place on the planet of Edessa in the constellation of the Hunter (Orion) in 1869 of the CatEarth calendar. This fire killed 200,000 newborn kittens, and only Tamala is allowed to flee the planet of Edessa for CatEarth, where she comes to be raised by a stepmother, "Anaconda Bitch," who lives on the Gonnoske-zaka slope in Meguro Ward, Tokyo. The chain-smoking kitten Tamala keeps searching for her origin in the Hunter, but the Pynchonesque network of the interstellar megacorporation Catty &

Fig. 3 Tamala's doppelgänger Tatla on the escalator. Frame from t.o.L.'s anime *Tamala 2010: A Punk Cat in Space*. © Tamala2010 Project.

Co. forces her to remain one year old forever and repeat the mythopeoic cycle of death and rebirth endlessly. Tamala's desire is fated to be interrupted by her own fate. Yet it is her fate that guarantees the peace of cosmos. This logic makes us reconsider the cyborgian construction of Japanese identity. Just as the replicants in *Blade Runner* cannot surpass the limit of their programmed endurance, Tamala is destined to remain a one-year-old, thereby perpetuating the rhythm of destruction and resurrection. This plot invites us to recall that in May 1951 General Douglas McArthur stated that "if the Anglo-Saxon was say 45 years of age in his development, in the sciences, the arts, divinity, [and] culture . . . [the] Japanese . . . in spite of their antiquity measured by time, were in a very tuitionary condition. Measured by the standards of modern civilization, they would be like a boy of 12." If General McArthur, for colonialist reasons, found it convenient to make the Japanese remain twelve years old forever, we could well re-

Fig. 4 The Civil Information and Education Section have a heated discussion with the Japanese directors. Scene from Yoji Sakate's *The Emperor and the Kiss*, 1999. © Rin Ko Gun Theater Company/ Good Fellows Inc., photo by Syugyo Ohara.

define him not as the new emperor but as the political engineer of new replicants.

Blade Runner was welcomed in Japan because it reenacted for viewers both their own false memories of democracy and the hybrid construction of their postwar selves. Viewing *Blade Runner* comforts and relaxes the Japanese. With its profoundly convincing rationalization of hybrid subjectivity, it offers a kind of catharsis. In contrast to the superathletic hero that a series of American presidents have played for their people, the cyborgian superstar exemplified by the Japanese emperor had a tremendous impact on the self-realization of the postwar Japanese. Without the cyborgian mental/historical structure that I have termed "creative masochism"—discussed at length below—postwar Japan could not have succeeded in its rapid reconstruction.

Even as postmodern Japan basks in "mediamania," the Japanese people show no sign of recovering from their deep obsession with the emperor. Moreover, even as the media prolong and consume the emperor's life as a sort of spectacle, the emperor continues to secretly extend the deep structure of his paradoxical authority by appropriating the very media on which this structure is founded. It is ironic that in 1885 William Gilbert and Arthur Sullivan staged a hardcore orientalist operetta, *The Mikado*, which featured an emperor as the dictator of a never-never land: a dictator, moreover, who is diabolic, necrophilic, and enthusiastic about capital punishments. Despite its deep prejudice, this typical Savoy Theater operetta gives sharp insight into the Japanese imperialist structure in which the emperor gains more and more dignity by merging himself with the very structure invented by his people. The Victorian scenario that the operetta presents, though, will make it clear why the Japanese emperor is essentially in conspiracy with the postmodern media. This conspiracy is a form of mediamania that I call "Mikadophilia," which helped develop director Kiyoshi Kurosawa's symbolic representation of the magic tree Charisma, in such sharp contrast to Tim Burton's Tree of the Dead, as described earlier.

The concept of Mikadophilia allows a strong interpretation of a pair of postmodern Japanese plays that premiered in 1999, and to which we will now turn: Yoji Sakate's *Tenno to Seppun* (The Emperor and the Kiss) and Hideki Noda's *Pandora no Kane* (Pandora's Bell).[1]

The Millennia of Mikadophilia: *The Emperor and the Kiss* and *Pandora's Bell*

At first glance, Yoji Sakate's *The Emperor and the Kiss* (which ran at Theater Suzunari in Shimokitazawa, Tokyo, from November 13 to December 12, 1999) and Hideki Noda's *Pandora's Bell* (performed at Setagaya Public Theatre in Sangenjaya, Tokyo, from November 6 to December 26, 1999) would appear to share little beyond a historical moment. *The Emperor* is a kind of realistic campus narrative, based on Kyoko Hirano's 1992 book *Mr. Smith Goes to Tokyo* (originally her English-language 1987 doctoral dissertation, subsequently revised and translated by the author). In contrast, *Pandora's Bell* is a highly surrealistic historical romance written by Hideki Noda, but showcasing the performances of a pair of dramatists simultaneously: dramatist Yukio Ninagawa's take on the play's subject as well as Noda's own.

Nevertheless, both Sakate and Noda employ a strikingly similar trans-spatiotemporal dramaturgy, ambitiously remixing past and present in their respective works. Sakate's *The Emperor* pursues a narrative plot that unwinds in the occupation period, in which the Civil Information and Education Section (CIE) of the occupation government repressed any cinematic representation of either the emperor or the emperor system, instead promulgating "American democracy" and American cultural norms by promoting the act of kissing in the movies. At the same time, the narrative incorporates a plot set in the high-growth period, in which postmodern high school kids attempt to produce a film *about* the occupation period.

Pursuing a similar intertemporal strategy, *Pandora's Bell* foregrounds a tale of prewar Nagasaki in which Pinkerton Zaibatsuary encourages archeology professor Kanakugi and his assistant Oz to excavate such ancient artifacts as "Pandora's Bell," while simultaneously unfolding another plot line set in a mythic ancient past. In this second plot, which Noda presents as alternative and anachronistic Japanese history, Queen Himejo inherits her elder brother's throne, but news of his survival makes her the target of a coup d'état and leads to her witnessing the explosion of a new sun via Pandora's Bell. What matters here is that a careful glance at the bell will reveal its top to be the tail assembly unit of a huge missile, that is, the wreckage of Fat Man, the atomic bomb dropped on Nagasaki on August 9, 1945, three days after Little Boy was dropped on Hiroshima. Pandora's Bell is nothing but an inverted missile. Of course, you may be puzzled by this anachronism. Why is the atomic bomb discovered in the prewar years or in the ancient times? However, as you become more and more familiar with this playwright's strategy, you will be convinced that it is through this kind of creative anachronism that Hideki Noda brilliantly represents Pandora's Bell as the atomic bomb literally and figuratively.

As the name Pinkerton Zaibatsuary suggests, Noda is keenly conscious of Puccini's opera *Madama Butterfly*, which was based on the novel *Madame Butterfly* (1898) by John Luther Long. In both the novel and the opera, an American gentleman named B. F. Pinkerton marries a Japanese ex-geisha named Cho-Cho-san (Madame Butterfly). Their interracial marriage ends tragically with the heroine's honorable suicide. It is interesting to consider how an American novel written at the turn of the nineteenth century came to have such a powerful influence on a Japanese play performed at the turn of the twentieth century, and how the Japanese play in turn further investigates Japan–U.S. transcultural politics by itself reappropriating the motif of Madame Butterfly.

Whereas *The Emperor* offers a complex mise-en-scène to accommodate a Chinese-box narrative of postmodern high school students narrativizing the Japanese cinema of the occupation period, *Pandora's Bell* comprises a mobius strip, one inscribed with a worm hole across which prewar Nagasaki and mythic ancient times dramatically intersect. And whereas *The Emperor* reconstructs the history of modern Japan obscured by the blindness of the historicizing dilemma of cinematographers, *Pandora's Bell* more ambitiously revises postwar Japanese history by staging a clash of civilizations, that is, of ancient and

Fig. 5 Mizuwo, King of the Funeral, and Queen Himejo. Scene from Hideki Noda's *Pandora's Bell*, 1999. © Noda Map Theater Company, photo by Tsukasa Aoki.

modern civilizations. Yet despite their differences, these plays share a deep interest in interrogating the concept of history structured by the presence of the emperor.

The question remains as to what led Sakate and Noda to mount their respective challenges to the very structure of history? Consider the following from a speech by Yoshiya, an employee of the film company Shin-Nippon in *The Emperor and the Kiss* (unconventionally, this character is not given a full name): "People often complain about having been deceived. Being deceived is proof not of your virtue but of your vice. Simply put, it exposes your faithlessness or inconstancy. If a people carelessly continues to complain about having been deceived, they will not learn anything, and will doubtless be deceived again and again. Even now, it seems they are being taken in by another liar. No dictionary tells us that the deceived is any better than the deceiver" (β 12).

This passage is analogous to a speech made by Hiiba, an old nurse in *Pandora's Bell*, played in the original production by Noda himself; here she suggests the national necessity of mock funerals in which conspiracy and irresponsibility are intertwined very closely: "Queen Himejo was cajoled by Mizuwo into seizing the crown of her elder brother. It was this guy Mizuwo, nicknamed 'King of the Funeral,' who skillfully seduced Queen Himejo into replacing the former king. He held sway over Her Majesty. Thus was this country forced into concentrating on performing a variety of funeral services" (129).

In Noda's conception, royal authority is made possible through deception, which defines the deceived as evil. Whoever assumes the throne must continue to deceive his or her people, otherwise he or she will either be displaced by someone else or will have to commit harakiri. To put it another way, the structure of deception will remain intact regardless of who holds royal authority.

With this understanding in mind, it becomes clear how the Japanese emperor retained sovereignty after the war by skillfully concealing the nature of his identity and role, which had been deprived of responsibility by the occupation. As the plays of Sakate and Noda reflect, naturalizing and prolonging the politics of irresponsibility are essential to the cyborgian identity of the Japanese emperor.

For further insight into this paradox of ultimate authority and basic irresponsibility that determined the framework of the postwar Japanese mind, consider Kyoko Hirano's *Mr. Smith Goes to Tokyo*, which inspired Sakate's dramatic imagination. In an essay on the film director Mansaku Itami, Hirano illustrates this paradox with a quote from Itami, who felt uneasy with the alacrity with which 100 million Japanese people converted from prowar activism or silent support to pacifism as soon as the war ended. Itami questioned how everyone claimed to have been deceived by others during the war, but no one took responsibility for having done the deceiving: "If you are so naïve as to believe that you are exempt from responsibility upon claiming that you were deceived," Itami wrote, "and that thus you now belong to the right causes, you must wash your face (and wake up)" (quoted in Hirano, "Japanese Filmmakers," 222).

Pursuing Itami's insight that the act of allowing oneself to be deceived is in itself an act of complicity, Hirano wrote the following:

> In a broader sense, complicity is symptomatic of a lethargic national culture that has failed to remain conscious, reflective, and responsible. The result is a kind of servility that allows deceit. Itami finds the roots of this problem in Japanese history: The feudal system and the isolationist policies of Japan had not been overturned by the Japanese themselves. Rather, it was foreign forces that brought the era of feudalism to a close. The Japanese had never grasped the notion of basic human rights. Itami believes that it is the servility of the Japanese people that allowed such a tyrannical and oppressive government to exist. (Ibid.)

Hirano argues convincingly that a mental history of servility helped naturalize the paradox of the emperor's ultimate sovereignty and limitless irresponsibility in Japanese culture. General McArthur did not arrive on the scene and strip the Japanese emperor of responsibility; on the contrary, the Japanese emperor had always enjoyed authority without responsibility.

Most significantly, the essential paradox of the emperor came to encompass his people. It is for this reason that the Japanese tend to shift responsibility upward, only to arrive at an emperor who is radically exempt from all responsibility. At this point, the Japanese usually start playing dominoes in the other direction, blaming not their superiors but junior petty officials. Thus the emperor's paradox of sovereignty and irresponsibility naturally gave rise to the Japanese people's dilemma: the symbolic emperor system combined with liberal democracy. And just as the emperor has survived postwar life as a cyborgian chimera, so too have the Japanese people all become cyborgs—what I refer to as "Japanoids"—transforming a once divine nation into a monstrously hybrid one.

As I have explicated it here, this cultural history clarifies why it is becoming increasingly difficult to distinguish the logic of the emperor from that of his nation. Postmodern as it may sound, the cyborgian identity would not have been possible without the defacement of our modern sense of individual responsibility. Illustrating this point, Sakate's *The Emperor* features Yukiko, a foreign-born Japanese girl who has returned to Japan. Yukiko points out that despite the postwar emperor's claims to be a man, not a god, he and the royal family are deprived of basic human rights, including the right to refuse to be photographed. It is ironic that by renouncing divine authority, the royal family became not humans but cultural signifiers to be loved, admired, and consumed through the capitalistic media. The less substantial the royal family became, the more Mikadophilic became the nation as a whole. It is not that existence precedes essence, but that signifier precedes ideology. I regard this phenomenon not as a revival of the emperor system but rather as an effect of cyborgian nationality.

Looking back, an early work of Yasutaka Tsutsui, one of Japan's major metafictionists, has proven prophetic in this regard. Deeply influenced by Daniel Boorstin's *The Image*, Tsutsui's first novella, *Tokaido Senso* (Tokaido Wars) (1965), entailed the author's reinterpreting the "pseudo-event" as a new god, and mass communication as a contemporary cult in the McLuhanian sense. This formulation remains intriguing today. It is not that the near-divine emperor was replaced by a pseudo-event, but that his irresponsibility transformed him into an all-seeing spirit, Emerson's all-seeing eye, engendering a brand-new cult of spectacular capitalism within the cultural context of situationism.

In view of this understanding, it is clear how the respective senses of responsibility for war converge in Noda's *Pandora's Bell* and Sakate's *The Emperor*. In *Pandora's Bell*, Queen Himejo the deceiver enters the Bell, the wreckage of the nuclear missile, which she believes to be an inverted vessel, but which turns out to be a nuclear missive dispatched from the future. In *The Emperor*, a deceived people, discontented with the status quo, resolve to enter true history.

Fabulous, Formless Madness

Beyond questions of responsibility, *Pandora's Bell* and *The Emperor and the Kiss* also afford deep insight into the structure of madness. In paradoxical Japan both the deceiver and the deceived are to blame. However, as Shoichi Inoue has pointed out (*Kyoki to Oken*, 250–255), royal authority has invariably been intertwined with madness. Historically, anyone who commits lèse majesté in Japan is condemned as insane. Yet it must be noted that if the Showa emperor, whose father, the Taisho emperor, had suffered from mental illness, had opposed the war-era military bureaucracy, he too would immediately have been confined to a mental hospital.

It is well known that at the first meeting of the Showa emperor and General McArthur on September 27, 1945, McArthur was deeply impressed by the emperor's dignity and decency. Finding the emperor prepared to accept any fate, McArthur realized that the emperor might be useful to the occupation. The general was keenly aware of the potential for a violent uprising against occupation forces and a subsequent communist takeover if the emperor were prosecuted for his role in the war (Hirano, *Mr. Smith*, 110–111). McArthur therefore decided to keep Emperor Hirohito alive, inaugurating the general's skillful remixing of American democracy with the emperor system.

Most germane to our discussion here is what inspired the general to appropriate the emperor rather than kill him. Asked by McArthur why he could not have stopped the war, Emperor Hirohito explained that despite his self-professed pacifism, "my people love me very much. Therefore, if I had protested against the war or taken a pacifist position, my people would undoubtedly have confined me to a mental hospital or something like that, looking after me there until the war was over" (Inoue, *Kyoki to Oken*, 171). As Ian Buruma acutely pointed out, the imperial institution had been used until the end of the war to quash free speech and political accountability; "Without examining his part in the war, the 'system of irresponsibilities' could not be properly exposed, which made it likely that, in one form or another, it would continue" (Buruma, *The Wages of Guilt*, 176). Right here we are convinced that the (pseudo-)diagnosis of madness had been very closely intertwined with the system of irresponsibility.

Although no emperor or emperor-like figure appears on stage in Sakate's *The Emperor*, the representation of madness in the play bears closely on the emperor's reasoning with McArthur. *The Emperor* foregrounds a symbolic encounter between Emiko Kurimoto, increasingly mentally ill after being violently attacked, and her boyfriend Ueno, leader of the high school filmmaking club. When the memory of violence leads Emiko to pretend to be blind and dumb, Ueno begs her, "Stay here, and just believe, believe what the reels of our film say to you. For our film is the ultimate device linking you and me in darkness" (19). Emiko's response to violence offers a perfect allegory for how—in order to remain individually liberal in an age of occupation and censorship—the postwar Japanese pretended to be unable to see, hear, or speak. Whether in prewar or postwar Japanese society, anyone out of sync with the national consensus is quickly dismissed as mad; Emiko's feigned madness thus offers a highly political example that even the Showa emperor could have followed. Conscious of Inoue's close reexamination of the complicity of sovereignty and madness, Sakate thus vividly illustrates the ambivalence between madness and the violence of censorship, which cannot help but recall the image of the emperor as fearing the diagnosis of madness and representing the system of irresponsibility, as I examined above.

Hideki Noda creates what seems like a more straightforward perspective on this issue. *Pandora's Bell* presents a complete cultural/anthropological milieu in which its tale of regal upheaval is set. What is relevant here is that when the former king turns out to be alive, he is diagnosed as mad, and therefore illegitimate. As the Showa emperor explained to McArthur, when a king transgresses the military bureaucratic national consensus, the nation is always happy to diminish or erase his presence, even to the point of relegating him to the ranks of the mentally deranged.

Yet through the Pandora's Bell artifact the deep structure of the emperor system is rendered visible. Queen Himejo states: "Everyone in this country knew very well that my elder brother was alive and well. . . . But people have also pretended not to see him, much as we are usually unaware of breathing the air. Probably people have hesitated to reveal the nature of the air as madness they have insistently breathed in. This kingdom has remained secure by repressing madness and defeat. Yet the sound of Pandora's Bell will make everything visible and audible" (130). With this declaration, Queen Himejo offers a cogent redefinition of Mikadophilia, in which Mikadophilia—love for the emperor—now conceals the essence of the emperor, which is discovered to be "madness and defeat."

Now let us note the creatively anachronistic setting of the play. That is, a mythic ancient kingdom succeeds in unearthing "Pandora's Bell," which proves to be a missile (inverted) that could not have been invented without post-Einsteinian nuclear technology. The discovery of this "ancient" artifact is thus inconsistent with modern notions of linear temporal progression. Yet today we know that almost 60 percent of artifacts unearthed in archeological digs transgress existing understandings of history in some way. These unexplained artifacts are called "ooparts" (out-of-place artifacts) by some in Japan. If this sounds like outrageously implausible pseudoscientific theory, I would argue that on the contrary, it is more plausible that a history of several hundred years' worth of knowledge amassed in the natural sciences has succeeded in brainwashing and censoring humankind while concealing its own madness through the mechanism of media discourse.

Mikadophilia took shape in a similar manner, naturalizing madness within the cyborgian subjectivity of Japanoids. In considering the contemporary Japan–U.S. intersection, it is necessary to begin with an understanding of this unique construction of chimeric, heterogeneous, postimperial identity. It is this identity that has engendered and embraced the sensibility of what I would like to call "creative masochism," a sensibility across which the cultural clash of orientalism and occidentalism plays out.

Toward a Poetics of Comparative Avant-Pop

Against the background of this cultural history, a post-comparative-literary perspective serves to illuminate the contemporary transcultural problematics. As I have illustrated with reference both to plays such as *M. Butterfly*, *The Emperor and the Kiss*, and *Pandora's Bell*, and films such as *Blade Runner*, *Sleepy Hollow*, and *Charisma*, the interracial identity exemplified by Madame Butterfly at the turn of the nineteenth century developed into a cyborgian identity exemplified by Anglo-American replicants, as well as by the Japanese emperor himself at the turn of the twentieth century. The advent of cultural studies in the last two decades of that century—especially the work of theoreticians such as Gayatri Spivak, Donna Haraway, Trinh Minh-ha, and Homi Bhabha—further enabled the rediscovery of a creolian hybrid identity that is closely related to this chimeric cyborgian identity. The technology of race reflects race produced by technology, suggesting a chiastic logic that illuminates the late capitalistic literary and cultural crossroads that not only link Japan and the United States but also replace the logic of causal influence with that of global synchronicity.

Consider a critical watershed of the early 1990s: the death of Kobo Abe on January 22, 1993, at the age of sixty-eight. Indisputably, Abe was one of the greatest avant-garde writers of postwar Japan; his novels include *The Woman in the Dunes* (1962), *The Face of Another* (1964), and *The Ruined Map* (1967), all known internationally at least through their highly praised film adaptations. To some Japanese intellectuals, the death of Abe signified the death of the avant-garde itself.

In retrospect, however, Abe's radicalism had begun to diminish as early as the 1970s. Abe won renown in the mass-productionist age, an era during which he could imagine the writer only as a *producer* of fiction. Yet most readers today feel a stronger affinity to younger writers such as Paul Auster, who wrote *The New York Trilogy* as an act of re-reading, updating, and in this sense, *consuming* such precursors as Poe, Hawthorne, Kafka, and Abe himself. However authentic Abe may have been, and however similar their approaches to the urban maze may appear, contemporary readers prefer Auster to Abe for the simple reason that Auster is up to date. Herein lies the logic of the ironic relationship between art and business: while anything is permitted in avant-gardism, everything becomes *dated* in a hyperconsumerist society, where consumerism has run rampant so that virtually everything is a commodity. The irony here is particularly useful in considering what has come to pass in our pan-Pacific transculture in the last decades of the last millennium.

In this regard, Abe's literary philosophy offers an interesting subject of inquiry. Famous for totally rejecting all forms of ritual, Abe said in a speech at the International PEN conference in Manhattan in

January 1986 that he so hated any form of ritualistic convention that he had skipped the wedding of his own daughter. Ritualistic as this kind of conference sounds, this anecdote provides the key to understanding Abe's literary decline. In the 1960s, Abe became a charismatic figure of the avant-garde by utterly victimizing literary convention as he focused entirely on *creative production*. Abe in the 1980s became out of date for the simple reason that this decade saw the astonishing escalation of the hyperconsumerist society, an escalation that transformed the most radical renunciation of literary convention into a major literary convention in itself.

Every contemporary artist must come to terms with this paradox, but how can the theory of postmodern avant-gardism account for it? One of the most potent strategies for doing so is what Larry McCaffery calls "avant-pop,"[2] a concept that springs from the recognition that "the blurring of the traditional distinctions between 'high' and 'pop' art has become a central, defining feature of postmodernism itself" ("The Avant-Pop Phenomenon," 216). McCaffery points to rock videos by Madonna, Peter Gabriel, and Laurie Anderson; cyberpunk novels such as William Gibson's *Neuromancer*; and television shows such as *Max Headroom*, *Saturday Night Live*, and *Twin Peaks* as examples of art informed by the avant-pop tendency toward deconstructing the difference between high art and junk culture.

I first came across this concept in the spring of 1991 in McCaffery's essay "Post-Pynchon Postmodern American Fiction," which appeared in the Japanese literary magazine *Positive*, no. 1. At the time, "avant-pop" helped me to understand the apparent degeneration of such established avant-garde artists as Kobo Abe, as well as the international emergence of a number of post-Abe postmodern writers. To be more precise, Abe did not so much degenerate as become dated by the logic of hyperconsumerism, in which the most avant-garde, the most anticonventional, and the most artistically aggressive are assessed, restylized, and reconfigured within the ongoing globalization of pop culture.

The metaphorics of sadomasochism offer a penetrating angle on the avant-pop phenomenon. While avant-garde artists used to be producers who were prevented from being too sadistic to their audiences for fear of losing their interest, the rise of hyperconsumerization reversed the role playing such that by yielding to the desire of hyperconsumers, that is, ultramasochists, the most creative artists become the real masochists; they must empathize with the masochistic desire of their audiences, in a sense embodying these desires in a way that resembles John Keats's concept of negative capability.

Thus, "avant-pop" serves to clarify the collapsing distinctions between avant-garde and pop culture, production and consumption, and sadism and masochism—indeed, to deconstruct them completely. My discussion of avant-pop furthermore will reveal that with the act of deconstruction naturalized in our times, deconstruction itself emerges simply as another form of ideology—a prodigy of consumerist discourse—rather than as any postideological tactic.

Reinterpreting avant-pop as a form of creative masochism in this sense encourages us to confront the possibilities of an S&M reading of the dynamics of international politics, in particular the politics of the Japan–U.S. relationship, as I will discuss below. For now, let me provide a good example of avant-pop, rather than speculating further on it as abstract theory.

If a Cyborgian Butterfly Flaps Its Wings in Beijing: Abe, Shimada, Hwang, Faulkner, Erickson, and Crichton

Compare Kobo Abe, who was born in 1924, and a younger Japanese writer, Masahiko Shimada, who was born in 1961. Both share an interest in urban self-fashioning, but the father-and-son-like generation gap that separates them engendered significant critical differences as well. The contrast between Abe's famous play *Tomodachi* (Friends), written and first performed in 1967, and Shimada's 1989 novel *Yume-tsukai* (Dream Messenger) illustrates these differences clearly.

In Abe's *Friends*, a young man is visited one day by a strange family, the members of which all claim to be friends who are trying to save him. These strangers gradually take over his apartment, torture him mentally, and eventually deprive him of everything—his housing, fiancée, and job. Abe's themes in this play are existential by definition: the fear of the other, the loss of identity, and the alienation of an individual.

In contrast, Shimada's *Dream Messenger* begins not with loss of identity, but with the capitalization of identity. The main characters of the story are "rental children," who earn money by acting as blood children for people who are infertile or whose children have died. Readers familiar with Shimada's quasi-cyberpunk 1990 novel

Rococo-cho (A Town Called Rococo), which was heavily influenced by both William Gibson's cyberspace trilogy and Ridley Scott's *Blade Runner*, might assume that this concept of a rental family is based in science fiction. However, the heroes of *Dream Messenger* are not replicants inhabiting the near future, but real, contemporary human beings—or to be more precise, representations of cyborgian Japanese subjectivities.

In fact, the publication of *Dream Messengers* coincided with the birth of an actual "rent-a-family" industry in Japan around 1990. This industry became a popular topic in a number of Japan's major weeklies in the early 1990s, made its way into a soap opera, and was taken up in Misa Yamamura's hardboiled detective fiction *Mysteries of a Rental Family* (1993).

The concept of a rental family may amaze and even disgust many Americans, especially those who were born and raised during the mass-productionist age of the Pax Americana, which became visible in the wake of World War II. At first glance, the idea may seem to insult human dignity, degrading people by sadistically selling them the inalienable along with the alienable.

But on further reflection, one might come to find the idea appealing, at least in the consumerist sense. If you are obliged to join a family reunion on some ritualistic occasion like a wedding or a funeral—and if you don't feel like attending unaccompanied—you need only ask a rent-a-family company for a rent-a-child, rent-a-spouse, rent-a-fiancé, or an all-purpose rent-a-sweetheart. A 1993 article on one rent-a-family company, the name of which might be translated as "Japan Social Improvement Society," reports that if one can afford the three-hour fee of 120,000 yen (approximately $1,000), the company will supply a professional "entertainer" trained in psychology, conversation, and social relations. One of the male entertainers quoted in the article hopes that the day will come when rent-a-family businesses restore human relationships so skillfully that no one will need them anymore ("Rentertainers," 87).

To reiterate, this is not a fabricated science fiction scenario but a typical, realistic fragment of postmodern Japanese life that not only naturalizes the loss of identity but also *capitalizes* on this loss.

Hence, the difference between Abe's *Friends* and Shimada's *Dream Messenger* corresponds to that between the avant-garde and the avant-pop. From the 1940s onward, Abe described the ontological predicament caused by the rise of consumerist society from the viewpoint of writer-as-producer. In the 1990s, Shimada created a narrative of rental children in which the consumerization of identity is self-evident, writing from the perspective of writer-as-consumer—a consumer who resembles his own readers to a great extent.

This difference leads us naturally to consider the contrast between Abe's anticolonialist communism and Shimada's postcolonialist communism. Born in Manchuria in the imperialist era, Abe could not help but criticize the mother country—and all conventional political systems—with the example of his own diasporic being, as radically allegorized in such novels as *The Woman in the Dunes*. Shimada, born during the high-growth period in the greater Tokyo suburbs (in the Yokohama area), in contrast promoted racial hybridization and canonical transgression as a challenge to the emperor system. Shimada's new trilogy, called *Mugen Kanon* (Infinite Canon) and consisting of *Suisei no Junin* (Inhabiting the Comet), *Utsukushii Tamashii* (Beautiful Soul), and *Etorofu no Koi* (Lovers in Turup Island), not only deconstructs the Long-Puccini paradigm of Madame Butterfly, but also reappropriates David Henry Hwang's Broadway play *M. Butterfly* (1986), a pseudo-queer romance between a transgender prima donna of Kyo-geki (classical Chinese opera) and a French official attracted and deceived by exoticism, who ends up committing honorable suicide.[3]

Subsequently, Shimada wrote a brilliant postmodern Japanese version of a *Gone with the Wind*–like soap opera, featuring the forbidden romances that a fictional crown princess conducted prior to her royal marriage. Regrettably, the birth of the real crown princess's first child in December 2001—which excited the whole nation—coincided with the completion of this second novel in Shimada's trilogy, and the author and publisher (Shincho-sha) were forced to postpone publication.

The relationship between Abe and Shimada is analogous to that between William Faulkner, the avant-garde writer, and Steve Erickson, the avant-pop visionary. Where Faulkner's Yoknapatawpha saga focuses on America's multiracial predicament from an existentialist viewpoint, Erickson's nocturnal novels—deeply influenced by David Griffith's film *The Birth of a Nation* (1915)—envisioned both pseudo-slavery in the context of contemporary romantic love (*Days between Stations*, his first novel), and pseudoconsumerism within republican slavery (*Arc d'X*, his fourth novel).

Despite the influence of Faulkner, Erickson the late capitalist avant-pop artist offers in *Arc d'X* (1993) an alternate portrait of

Thomas Jefferson, in which Jefferson ends up selling himself to his own house slaves, becoming by the end of the novel a slave of the slaves. Guarded by armed slaves and with the shackles on his wrists, this naked white man Thomas Jefferson tells President John Adams: "It's the final resolution of the dilemma of power . . . to be at once both king and slave. To at once lead an army and be its waterboy. To command every man and woman within miles, and be subject to the whim of any little colored child who wanders in and orders me to dance like a puppet, or make a funny face, or wear something silly on my head such as the peel of an orange or an animal turd" (289). It was interesting to witness the postmodern, or avant-pop, simultaneity between the marketing of *Dream Messenger*, Shimada's narrative of rental children, in the United States in 1993, and the publication of *Arc d'X*, Erickson's representation of Thomas Jefferson as the slave of slaves, in the same year. Despite their different nationalities, both authors share the perverse logic of creative masochism, which informs their deep concerns with the capitalization of identity.

Regarding Erickson, one might interpret his alternate portrait of Jefferson as being simply the product of a purely surrealistic imagination. However, it is likely that this imagination was engendered by the author's keenly international consciousness of politicoeconomic reality—specifically, of the post-1980s hyperconsumerist society of the Pax Japonica, when Japan's economic power grew exponentially, as prophesied by the American sociologist Ezra Vogel in his best-seller, *Japan as Number One* (1979). Rather than remixing Kobo Abe (in the manner of, for example, Paul Auster), Erickson offers a perspective on today's multiethnic tensions—an insight drawn not along the black-white contours of Thomas Pynchon's *Gravity's Rainbow* (1973), but rather according to the S&M metaphorics observable in the recent revival of Japanese and American nationalism.

More specifically, this revival is evident in the ideological conflict between the discourse of Japan bashing (which repudiates the rise of Japanese capitalism) and the discourse of posthistory (to employ Francis Fukuyama's term), with its totalizing appraisal of Japanese economic hegemony as the effect of Japanese Buddhism repeating the scenario of Protestant capitalism in Europe. Whether or not Japan should be bashed depends upon whether or not one accepts its hyper-consumerist development. Whereas the mass-productionist age made it possible to liken the U.S.–Japan relationship to that of husband and wife, our own hyperconsumerist age encourages a different comparison: to that between man and femme fatale.

It was precisely this analogy that Michael Crichton employed in his best-selling novel *Rising Sun*: "Japan is like a woman that he [John Connor] can't live with, and can't live without, you know?" (34). However, it seems evident not that the United States and Japan have exchanged their respective S&M roles, but rather that exposure to hyperconsumerism has led nations to deconstruct the difference between creation/production (writing) and consumption (reading), thereby opening the way to becoming both creative and masochistic at once. "Avant-pop" holds tremendous potential for elucidating this development in the field of comparative literary cultural studies.

Constructing a Theory of Creative Masochism: Kojève, Michaels, and Numa

To explore the perspective of creative masochism further, let us reconsider several critical texts, beginning with a work by Alexandre Kojève, a key precursor of posthistorical philosophy. Kojève originally published his *Introduction to the Reading of Hegel* in 1947, then annotated his study after several trips abroad between 1948 and 1959.

Kojève's travels led him to conclude that posthistory had been realized in the postwar way of life of the American people, who seemed to him to have returned to a state of animality in their inattention to teleology. However, after a voyage to Japan in 1959, Kojève revised his views radically. Regarding Japan as a country that "has for almost three centuries experienced life at the 'end of History,'" but finding Japanese people "anything but animal," Kojève wrote the following:

> "Post-historical" Japanese civilization undertook ways diametrically opposed to the "American way." . . . The peaks . . . of specifically Japanese snobbery—the Noh Theater, the ceremony of tea, and the art of bouquets of flowers—were and still remain the exclusive prerogative of the nobles and the rich. But in spite of persistent economic and political inequalities, all Japanese without exception are currently in a position to live according to totally formalized values—that is, values completely empty of all "human" content in the "historical" sense. . . . This seems to allow one to believe that the recently begun interaction between Japan and the Western World will finally lead not to a rebarbarization of the Japanese but to a "Japanization" of the Westerners. (161–162)

In responding to this well-known passage, some Japanese intellectuals have boasted of the "historical" predominance of Japanese postmodernism. However, with the advent of the age when the difference between creation/production (writing) and consumption (reading) gets blurred, as suggested in the previous section, a more accurate reading of Kojève's notion of the "Japanization of the Westerners" will convince us that it comprises a form of hyperconsumerization in which, producers-as-writers are unable to be sadistic enough to spank masochistic consumers-as-readers satisfyingly. In the state of postmodern consumption, even producers-as-writers are transformed into metaconsumers whose response to new commodities such as the rental family is always masochistic, but is also highly creative. It is in this sense that the Japanese people have accepted ritualistic values "completely empty of all 'human' content in the 'historical' sense."

It is tempting to locate a similar understanding of postmodern society in Walter Benn Michaels. In *The Gold Standard and the Logic of Naturalism*, his new-historicist study of American naturalist authors, Michaels writes: "What the masochist loves is only the freedom to be a slave. . . . To put it another way, the masochist loves what the capitalist loves: the freedom to buy and sell, the inalienable right to alienate. In this respect, the masochist embodies the purest commitments to laissez-faire" (132–133). Michaels arrived at this insight through his close reading of Frank Norris's *McTeague* (1899). However, if one considers this passage in conjunction with the quotation from Kojève above, it becomes obvious that Michaels is addressing this typical turn-of-the-century naturalist novel not as a traditional Marxist but as a hyperconsumerist, one who must have been keenly conscious of the Pax Japonica of the 1980s, and one whose own most masochistically creative tool of consumption was a literary criticism capable of reading the S&M metaphorics into capitalism as such.

We are confronted with a paradox: to promote Japan-bashing discourse emotionally is to accelerate creative masochism logically within the hyperconsumerist society represented by Japan; and to believe in the advent of posthistory in the post–cold war era is to endorse the rise of global hyperconsumerization—what Kojève called the "Japanization of the Westerners"—in which Japan will continue to be creative enough to the extent that it remains content with the economy of masochism.

In the face of this paradox, one of Japan's most idiosyncratic writers, Shozo Numa, continues to write and revise his one and only meganovel, *Yapoo the Human Cattle* (1956–2000), which I will discuss in greater detail in chapter 2. Far more inventive than Michael Crichton's *Rising Sun*, Numa's *Yapoo* had already begun almost forty years ago to envision a far-future Japan-bashing utopia in which orientals, especially the Japanese, are re-figured not as *Homo sapiens*, but as *Simias sapiens*; not as human beings, but as cattle called Yapoo. From our contemporary vantage point, *Yapoo the Human Cattle* can be seen to have predicted the fate of postmodern society: the further our consumer-capitalistic society advances, the more difficult it becomes for us to distinguish between ideology and sexual sadomasochism.

It is in this type of hyperconsumerist atmosphere that the concept of avant-pop becomes most convincing. When the logic of economics has demolished the distinction between aesthetically radical, politically subversive art (the traditional domain of the avant-garde) and MTV pop songs, as well as between what is realistic and what is antirealistic, it becomes necessary to rethink how art might resume its important "sadistic" role of "punishing" its audience in order to reawaken it to a life of "real" pleasure and fulfillment.

At such a juncture, Mark Poster's remarks in his article "The Question of Agency: Michel de Certeau and the History of Consumerism" offer direction. However objective one's analytical approach may seem, Poster argues, we must recognize the myth of objectivity as another rhetoric, another metadiscourse fashioning our sense of "reality." Although avant-gardism has long been believed to be a metafictional rhetoric displacing reality, we must not forget that it is a framework of reality that has been constructed rhetorically—whether its rhetoric is ontological or consumerist or creative-masochistic.

It follows that, before engaging in any further speculation on the fate of avant-pop arts and literature, we must first examine the current historical status of antirealism and progressive metafiction, attempting to discern whether these now function as liberating devices or as mere instruments of style or marketing that employ images of rebellion or radicalism to encourage continued hyperconsumerism. With its call for new methods of countering the deadening forces of pop culture and hyperconsumption, McCaffery's conception of the avant-pop makes it clear that "Storming the Reality Studio" may be more difficult than storming the "antireality studio."

CHAPTER 2 Comparative Metafiction: Somewhere between Ideology and Rhetoric

The appearance in 1990 of Thomas Pynchon's fourth novel, *Vineland*, coincided with that of William Gibson and Bruce Sterling's collaborative novel *The Difference Engine*; to me, this coincidence offers an ironic but illuminating point of departure for considering everything that would influence the fate of postmodernism in the 1990s. In *Vineland*, Pynchon, the guru of the late sixties—historicizing the revolution of the flower children as a sacrament of contemporary pilgrim fathers—offers a nasty take on his successors of the eighties, mocking post-Pynchonesque high-tech, hyperorientalist discourse. In contrast, in *The Difference Engine*, the hardcore cyberpunks Gibson and Sterling—pursuing an alternate history of a Victorian Britain revolutionized by steam-driven information technology—persist in their devotion to cutting up, sampling, and remixing the metafictional treasury of the great master Pynchon, whom they had admired for so long.

At least in Anglo-American literary history, the hegemony of metafiction had gained such a hold by 1990 that its gimmicks—the play of floating signifiers, self-reflexive obsession, and Chinese-box structures, among others—had become completely self-evident, and post-Pynchon postmodern writers such as William Vollmann, Kathy Acker, Steven Millhauser, Julian Barnes, and Peter Ackroyd all seemed to take such metafictive devices for granted. Moreover, a series of critical achievements around the year 1980, including Robert Scholes's *Fabulation and Metafiction* (1979), Linda Hutcheon's *Narcissistic Narrative* (1980), and Larry McCaffery's *The Metafictional Muse* (1982), valorized the genre, enabling the location of the metafictionists within a broad context, and encompassing archetypes such as Cervantes, Stern, and Gide; precursors such as Conrad, Joyce, and Faulkner; and contemporary experimenters such as Borges, Lem, and Calvino.[1]

A question of particular interest to my discussion is, what could have led so many prominent critics to devote their attention to the framework of metafiction? In *High Resolution* (1989) Henry Sussman argues that the Anglo-American "will to literacy" ignited a deep interaction between the establishment of metafictional literature and the academic institutionalization of deconstructionist criticism from the 1960s to the 1980s (197–228). In the latter half of the twentieth century, no other immanent forms of writing and reading better satisfied the pedagogic need to redefine English as a multinational language rather than an imperialistic one. The more universal the metafictionist and deconstructionist imperatives grew in capitalist countries, the more apparent the ideological aspect of English literacy became.

Though consumed and exhausted by the varied critical discourses it has encountered—or as an ironic effect of such hyperconsumption—metafictionism is now embedded within the texture of our political unconscious. Seeking insight into this unconscious, let us therefore consider the following questions pertaining to the genre: Why do Anglo-American metafictionists prefer totalitarian figures? What does their appropriation of Japanesque imagery mean? And in which direction does the horizon of Japanese postmodern literature lie?

A Portrait of the Hypermodern Scheherazade

Taken together, *Vineland* and *The Difference Engine* reveal the orientation of postmodern literature. First, one witnesses in these two novels examples of at least three characteristic aspects of late-eighties American fiction: North American magic realism, as described by Norman Spinrad; the slipstream, as described by Bruce Sterling; and the avant-pop, as described by Larry McCaffery.[2] New maximalism might be added to this list, except for a problem that these unfamiliar concepts confront: that in the age of hypercapitalism, every binary opposition—including magic realism as ethnic fantasy/magic realism as WASP nightmare, mainstream fiction/science fiction, and avant-garde experimentation/popular culture, among others—must be deconstructed and exposed as a product of human subjectivity positioned to narrate metaliterary texts, that is, as a metadiscursive effect of a grand narrative.

Patricia Waugh, noting the complex relationship between ideology and formalism, has questioned the "*politically* 'radical' status of *aesthetically* 'radical' texts." Metafiction and deconstruction used to be considered the most progressive of cultural tools, possessing the power to deconstruct the totality of ideology, but now this pair have taken the place of ideology, becoming ideologies themselves, which can afford to rewrite the history of postconsumerist society even as they expose ideology as always having been metafictional.[3]

As Terry Eagleton implies in *Ideology: An Introduction* (1991), the framework of ideological "hegemony" is itself a circular, self-referential affair, which "like a work of literary fiction secretly fashions the reality it claims to be at work upon" (215). If metafiction is recovering its importance now, it does so less as the experimental form born out of the 1960s that it has been appreciated as being than as an ultraconservative ideology that was in general circulation throughout the 1980s. As such, there is the sense that the genre might as well serve to rebuild many of the hitherto familiar representational figures of literature.

That repetition produces difference was the (credo and/or first and last) refuge of the typical deconstructionists of the 1970s, unwitting promoters of hypercapitalist ideology. And yet, once ideology demystified itself in the late 1980s, it became clear that difference is a product of the upheaval of ideological struggle, which is itself nothing but the simultaneous product of rhetorical strategy.

What brought me to this view is Raymond Federman's understanding of metafiction vis-à-vis an understanding of former U.S. president John F. Kennedy as a new form of media signifier:

> By the time President Kennedy took office, America was ready to receive the kind of electrifying and electronic image he projected through the mass media and that quickly lodged itself in the American consciousness. . . . The message and the image that Kennedy presented offered themselves as the defenders of a rational discourse that had finally triumphed over the irrational discourse that had led to Nazi and Fascist politics. . . . Thus when Kennedy smiled that meant that he was happy, and America was happy. When he spoke in a grave tone of voice and announced that the country could be destroyed in an atomic blast coming from Cuba, the entire nation changed mood. . . . This is why the assassination of John F. Kennedy (public and televised as it were) had such a traumatic impact on the American consciousness. . . . Suddenly the American

> people were doubting the very reality of the events they were witnessing, especially on television. It took certain blunders of the Johnson administration, and subsequently the manipulations and lies of the Nixon administration, and of course the Vietnam War, and the Watergate debacle to awaken America from its mass-media state of illusion and optimism. Suddenly there was a general distrust of the official discourse whether spoken, written, or televised as images. . . . The self-reflexive novel that takes shape during the 1960s in a way fills the linguistic gap created by the disarticulation of the official discourse in its relation with the individual.[4]

Among theories of the origins of Anglo-American metafiction, Federman's explication of its emergence at the intersection of ideology and rhetoric is one of the most eloquent. By his logic, the process of fragmentation that we survived between the 1960s and the 1980s—in which the discourse of totality represented by President Kennedy (among others) was detotalized—can be understood to have induced hordes of talented writers to experiment with metaliterary devices.

The assassination of Kennedy by Lee Harvey Oswald in 1963, specifically, represented a critical point between the fall of rationalism and the rise of deconstructionism, one that complicates the reading of literary critical history. It was not simply an influential lecture by the then unfamiliar French philosopher Jacques Derrida at a Johns Hopkins symposium in 1966 that launched the deconstruction movement in the United States, but also the longing of the American unconscious—reeling in the aftermath of the terrifying assassination in 1963—for a reliable scheme such as that represented by Derridanism to which it might resort. Though deconstructionist ideology excels at problematizing binary oppositions, what the deconstructionists believed to be binary oppositions were, as far as the American context is concerned, invented very recently—more precisely, around the historical point of the John F. Kennedy assassination.

Federmanian historicization as explicated above sheds light on the question of why the figure of President Kennedy has so frequently haunted the works of Anglo-American postmodernists, including John Williams's *The Man Who Cried I Am* (1967), Philip Roth's *My Life As a Man* (1974), Neil Ferguson's short story "The Monroe Doctrine" (1983), Derek Pell's *Assassination Rhapsody* (1989), Oliver Stone's film *JFK* (1991), and—of particular relevance to my discussion—Don DeLillo's *Libra* (1988). It is noteworthy that the central topic of DeLillo's novel is not the subjectivity of Oswald the assassin, but rather the construction of this subjectivity by historical contingency, which led him inevitably to assassinate Kennedy. Though the story foregrounds the many biographical coincidences that linked the murderer and the president, what DeLillo aimed to depict was not so much the mournful feeling that gripped Dallas in March 1963 as the textuality of the high-tech information culture that was emerging throughout the 1960s, a culture that not only tightly controlled both Oswald and Kennedy, but also semiotically constructed their subjectivities. However existential their political decisions may sound in DeLillo's depiction, the Kennedy and Oswald of *Libra* convey subjectivities that are woven from the linguistic texture of ideology. Thus, if one reads *Libra* as a typical metafiction, Oswald's act seems not simply to deconstruct the totality of "American dream" ideology, but also to unveil no less than the ideological effects of deconstruction.

Hence, with "the science of literature" as their common background, metafiction and deconstruction—the most progressive modes of writing and reading of the latter half of the twentieth century—helped revive the teleological doctrine of manifest destiny, attempting to expand the frontiers of the field of textuality.

Accordingly, I find it not accidental that some of the greatest masterpieces of metafiction have rendered imaginary universes built around Orwellian, technototalitarian bureaucracies; for instance, let us examine the postmodern fate of Scheherazade. In the early 1960s, John Barth revived Scheherazade, admiring her as a divine incarnation of the "literature of exhaustion" in the course of his attempt to theorize the way to reincarnate "narrativity," as such, in the wake of the "death of the novel."[5] However, just before the dawn of the 1970s, Michel Foucault sentenced Scheherazade to the grave, proclaiming the "death of the author" and privileging the semiotic thanatos of "writing" over the narrative eros of "voice."[6] The discourse of the 1980s, however, seduced Jean Baudrillard into a close analysis of the political appropriation and reappropriation of electronic media during the Gulf War period, on the basis of which he redefined Saddam Hussein as the greatest reincarnation of Scheherazade in our times; in Baudrillard's understanding, Hussein-as-Scheherazade entertained TV audiences both by prolonging the end of the narrative of the war as long as possible and by effacing his own identity.[7]

Thus, what came to be at stake is not the boundary between reality and fiction in the sense that Barth described, but that between reality and *metafiction*, from the viewpoint of the hypermodern Scheherazade. Although metafictional devices have certainly been used to decentralize the ideology of literature, our postdeconstructive, postcybernetic culture, in which reality itself is transformed into metafictionality, reveals that metafiction has fundamentally exerted a new sort of totalitarian ideology.

Turning to a related phenomenon, consider how the discourse of Vietnam War reporters influenced the narratology of Hollywoodish war movies in general, even as the discourse of Hollywood film determined the narratology of Gulf War cameramen. No longer does metafiction overturn reality: reality has come to be mass-produced, mass-marketed, and mass-circulated as metafiction. It is for this purpose that American postmodern writers have repeatedly addressed the Kennedy assassination as the historical moment at which the mirror-stage relationship between fiction and reality was broken into pieces.

Pax Britannica, Pax Americana, Pax Japonica

The more our society goes high-tech, the more omnipresent the hypermodern Scheherazade becomes; by the 1990s, she was everywhere.

The perspective of David Porush is suggestive in this regard. Porush observed a deep connection between the development of metafiction and the rise of cybernetic culture, in which metastructure or self-referentiality is a defining characteristic. In developing this understanding, Porush skillfully reinterpreted a number of metafictional masterpieces as "cybernetic fiction," a form that anticipated the cyberpunk boom to come.[8]

Historically, cyberpunk emerged in the early 1980s from a literary subgenre generally known as science fiction. In the December 30, 1984, issue of the *Washington Post*, science fiction editor and writer Gardner Dozois first picked up the term "cyberpunk" from the title of Bruce Bethke's short story, redefining it as "a self-willed aesthetic school," the members of which included Bruce Sterling, William Gibson, Lewis Shiner, John Shirley, and Rudy Rucker—all "purveyors of bizarre hard-edged high-tech stuff." Among other works, Dozois had perhaps foremost in mind Gibson's award-winning first novel, *Neuromancer* (1984).

To further clarify Dozois's definition of this new subgenre, one need only point out the essential similarity between *Neuromancer* and Ridley Scott's film *Blade Runner* (1982), a similarity that paved the way

—despite Gibson's denial of any audiovisual influence on his works—for cyberpunk to prevail. That is, much as *Blade Runner* depicts androids in punk fashion haunting a Japanesque Los Angeles in 2019, *Neuromancer* represents neurotic cyborgs in punk mode within an extremely dead-tech Japanese cityscape.

To confirm the literary impact of cyberpunk, one need look no further than *The Columbia Literary History of the United States* (1988), edited by Emory Elliott, in which Larry McCaffery, a prominent scholar-critic of metafiction, compares William Gibson with mainstream writers such as Raymond Carver, Joyce Carol Oates, and Leslie Silko, rather than other science fiction writers such as Ursula K. Le Guin, Harlan Ellison, and Thomas Disch. McCaffery writes, "Gibson's *Neuromancer* describes a punked-out, high-tech world of cyber realities, tribal jungles operating on society's marginalized fringes, and dizzying labyrinths of images reflecting human desires that are endlessly replicated in mirrors and computers; yet for all its exoticism, *Neuromancer* offers a compelling vision of the way technology has *already affected* our lives."[9]

If metafiction tried to restore the ideology of the Pax Americana, cyberpunk—having digested its precursor's metaliterary implications within its artful depictions of cybernetically networked culture—promoted the then-rising ideology of the Pax Japonica. Thus did Bruce Sterling, cyberpunk chairman, bid goodbye to the "old stale futures": the cyberpunks no longer found far-future civilizations intriguing, but rather considered the cutting edge of contemporary culture to be the most science-fictional setting imaginable. In Sterling's view, what is of interest now to science fiction can be found neither in space travel (that is, in outer space) nor in drug trips (that is, inner space), but rather in the high-tech power structure already networked "under our skin"—that is, in cyberspace.[10]

To grasp the possibilities of comparative metafiction, it will be useful here to reinvestigate the postorientalist structure of feeling that informs the achievements of William Gibson. In his cyberspace trilogy, which comprised *Neuromancer* as well as the sequels *Count Zero* (1986) and *Mona Lisa Overdrive* (1988), Gibson created an underworld of computer hackers who "jack into" custom cyberspace decks that project their disembodied consciousnesses into the "consensual hallucination" of the "matrix," a global computer network (*Neuromancer*, 5). This direct connection linking the human body and the computer evokes the effect of a kind of collage or bricolage, which representative Dadaists such as Marcel Duchamp and Joseph Cornell could have invented.

A more remarkable aspect of Gibson's fiction, however, is its repositioning of the science fiction genre from its traditional Earthside geographic locus. As brilliantly expressed on his early short story "The Gernsback Continuum" (1981), Gibson is keenly aware that "the Future had come to America first, but had finally passed it by" (37). The age of the Pax Americana has ended, Gibson implies, and that of the Pax Japonica has come into blossom.

Another Gibson story, "The Winter Market" (1986), is also germane in this regard. In this story, Gibson deconstructs the sense of temporal sequence through a reinterpretation of Japanesque fragments, in the process skillfully sampling the essence of what is cyberpunk. One of the main characters of the story, Rubin, is a virtual junk artist with the Japanese nickname "Gomi no Sensei" ("Master of Junk," in English). The narrative explicates a Japanese history of "gomi" (junk) within which Rubin is contextualized:

> Where does the gomi stop and the world begin? The Japanese, a century ago, had already run out of gomi space around Tokyo, so they came up with a plan for creating space out of gomi. By the year 1969 they had built themselves a little island in Tokyo Bay, out of gomi, and christened it Dream Island. But the city was still pouring out its nine thousand tons per day, so they went on to build New Dream Island, and today they coordinate the whole process, and new Nippons rise out of the Pacific . . . He [Rubin, the Gomi no Sensei] has nothing to say about gomi. It's his medium, the air he breathes, something he's swum in all his life. (128)

In short, the Gomi no Sensei transforms whatever deserves the name "Gomi" into sculpture.

Rubin is a friend of the narrator and protagonist of the story, Casey, who is himself a kind of junk artist in that his job is to make cybertapes of other peoples' unconsciouses. One day Rubin throws a party at which Casey meets Lise, a severely handicapped girl with a prosthetic, cybernetic exoskeleton that allows her to function. Casey and Lise fall in love, and—instead of making love—Casey snaps an optic lead into the socket at the spine of Lise's exoskeleton. What he finds in her unconscious is so fabulous that Casey brings an edited tape of fragments of it to market. The tape, entitled *Kings of Sleep*, is a million-seller.

Both Rubin and Casey, finally, are junk artists, one deconstructing the gomi of Tokyo's junkyards, and the other exploiting the semiotic ghosts of the junkyard of the unconscious. The narrator offers the following insight into their essential similarity: "Sometimes it looks to me like nobody in particular lives there (in the living room). . . . I have these times when the place abruptly gives me a kind of low-grade chill, with its basic accumulation of basic consumer goods. . . . [T]here are moments when I see that anyone could be living there, could own those things, and it all seems sort of interchangeable, my life and yours, my life and anybody's" (145).

Here Gibson suggests that not only inanimate objects but also human beings have become as interchangeable as gomi. Junk artists like the late box artist Joseph Cornell modify gomi into up-to-the-minute artworks, but postmodernist logic demands that the retrofitter himself is likely to be retrofitted.

This logic also informs the hero of *Neuromancer*, who is named Henry Dorsett Case and is known as an "artist." A skillful computer hacker, Case earned his living prior to the opening of the novel by stealing data over the matrix. However, Case made a terrible mistake that disgraced his former employer, who arranges for his nervous system to be altered—so as to prevent him from ever again "jacking-in"—as punishment. *Neuromancer* opens with a down-and-out Case combing Chiba City, Japan—a dead-tech zone of outlaw technologists—for a black-market physician who can restore his cybernetic function. Deprived of the ability to access cyberspace, "the body is meat" to Case, who feels he has fallen into "the prison of his own flesh."

In view of these circumstances, Case's name can be decoded literally: to the cyberpunk sensibility, the human body, stripped of cybernetic prosthesis, is nothing more than a suitcase. At the opening of the story, Case is a piece of junk, and he comes to Chiba City, a junkyard, in search of someone who can retrofit him in the manner of a junk artist creating junk art. Gibson here explores the logic by which the junk artist himself becomes the raw material of junk art directly. Remarkably, Gibson narrativized this epitomically postmodernist logic strictly on the basis of his own dream fragments of Japan—his personal imaginings of Dream Island and Chiba City; at the time he wrote these stories, Gibson had never visited Japan.

How, then, are we to understand the role of Japan in cyberpunk literature? Prior to the emergence of cyberpunk, novels such as Jessica Amanda Salmonson's *Tomoe Gozen Saga* (1981–1984) and Somtow Sucharitkul's *Starship and Haiku* (1981) had already offered futuristic Japanese iconography for American consumption, but the mass market ironically ignored these precursors. Moreover, only with the formation of cyberpunk literature did such Japanesque imagery begin appealing to Japanese audiences; then, such imagery could not help but refresh the Japanese sense of reality.

Consider the following examples of Japanesque cyberpunk imagery: Lewis Shiner's first novel *Frontera* (1984) posits a tremendous Japanese conglomerate called Palsystems that holds global political sway; Bruce Sterling's masterpiece *Schismatrix* (1985) begins with a description of a geisha bank and kabuki theater located in space; Michael Swanwick's *Vacuum Flowers* (1987) describes a huge, high-tech multinational corporation called Deutsche Nakasone. Although some reviewers condemn such material as being based on misperceptions of the real Japan, such cyberpunkish discourses seduce the reader into understanding Japan as a semiotic ghost country, one that has already been liberated from the Hegelian metaphysical system of history.

This positioning of Japan reflects a deeper understanding of its relation to the West. Whereas western metaphysics has striven to encompass the ontology of human affairs, Japanese culture has been ruled from the outset by a formalistic snobbery well suited to the end of history in the Hegelian sense, as well as to global capitalism, our future way of life.[11]

I am not boasting, as have some Japanese intellectuals, that Japan has remarkably preceded *postmodern metafictive deconstructionism*. I am rather endorsing the mundane view that there have always been people such as Hegel or Kojève who locate the end of history in the times in which they live. My interest resides in the way certain representational figures, in the metafictional context, have been modified by the historical imperatives of ideology, including the ideologies of posthistory, posthumanity, and postimperialism.

George Orwell's *1984* (1949) and Margaret Atwood's *The Handmaid's Tale* (1985), to compare two relevant examples, share both the common setting of a totalitarian society and similar metanarrative voices. However, protagonist Winston of *1984* displays a typically modernist concern with *reading* and *writing*—witness the functions of the secret book of oligarchic history and Winston's diary—while Offred, the heroine of *The Handmaid's Tale*, embraces the typically postmodernist act of *cutting up* the cassette tapes on which she has recorded a secret history of the theocratic dictatorship that rules her society.

To clarify the function of totalitarianism in regard to this point, let us consider the radical transformation of the representational figure of Adolf Hitler in a series of metafictional alternate histories—Philip K. Dick's *The Man in the High Castle* (1962), Norman Spinrad's *The Iron Dream* (1972), and Steve Erickson's *Tours of the Black Clock* (1989). Dick's novel depicts Hitler as the political symbol of Nazism, the leader under whom the Axis powers won World War II, then divided up an occupied United States. Spinrad's novel recasts Hitler as an implied fictionist amid the authors emigrating to the United States in the 1920s, whose anti-Semitic philosophy is crystallized in a science fiction in which mutants are repressed in the name of human purity. Erickson's novel portrays Hitler as an implied reader of fiction within the fiction, who hires as his personal pornographer a talented writer, Banning Jainlight, to create images that remind the dictator of his incestuous love for his niece Geli Raubal. As these three novels clearly reveal, metafictional structure is itself incestuously intertwined with the ideology of totalitarianism, but the figure representing totalitarianism is doomed to transfiguration as the historical sense of what comprises the totality changes.

Hence, in the early 1960s—before the Kennedy assassination—Dick could still position the Hitlerian totality as the political negative of the Pax Americana in his metafiction. In the early 1970s—in the wake of radical relativism—Spinrad could attempt to recover the Pax Americana in his meta-SF. Finally, in the late 1980s—with the rise of hyperconsumerist desire, Erickson succeeded in reviving the Pax Americana in his metaliterature. Thus, it was the capitalist passage from the postproductionist 1960s through the hyperconsumerist 1980s that had a disfigurative impact upon the literary status of Adolf Hitler. What the metafictionists Dick, Spinrad, and Erickson shared was a common interest in at once Americanizing Hitler and recollecting the American Golden Age. The metafictional figuration of totalitarianism thus enables a rediscovery of the profoundly global dream of American capitalism.

The high-tech, postorientalist mode of cyberpunk writing was offered and widely accepted as a literary breakthrough because it took for granted both metaliterary gimmicks and the metafictive nature of capitalist ideology (an ideology in which, that is, the hyperconsumerist media network enables the very subjectivity that recognizes junk art to become junk art, as described above).

Here let us return to the novel *The Difference Engine*, Gibson and Sterling's 1990 collaboration. Although this novel is set in an alternate Victorian England—where the steam-driven but computer-like "analytical engine" invented by Charles Babbage has transformed British society—and although the novel has been associated with James Blaylock, Tim Powers, and J. K. Jeter, *The Difference Engine* can be seen as cyberpunk that transcends the limitations of old-fashioned metafiction, achieving a sophistication that brings it to the verge of slipstream literature. *The Difference Engine* traces not only the archeology of the computer and the computer hacker, but also that of computer virus, with the help of which the steam-driven computer described in the novel turns out to have described the entire novel itself. Recalling David Porush's ambitious reformulation of metafiction as cybernetic fiction, *The Difference Engine* emerges as one of the greatest literary vindications of the metafictional, self-referential, and *mise-en-abyme* structure of cybernetics as such.

From the viewpoint of our times—and against the backdrop of Kurt Gödel's "Incompleteness Theorems" (1931) and the "Cybernetics" (1948) of Norbert Wiener that Gödel encouraged—this thematics will make perfect sense. Superficially, the Gibson-Sterling team seem to postmodernize the British history of the computer. In the early development of mathematics and cybernetics a central figure was Lady Ada Byron—a disciple and collaborator of Babbage and a genius of mathematics, gambling, and fashion who eventually succumbed to illness and alcoholism. Thus *The Difference Engine*'s steam-driven computer virus "Modus" ends up going out of control, closely reflecting Lady Ada's hysteria.

Yet this alternate history of the era of the Pax Britannica reflects not simply Americanization but also the postmodernization of history. Gibson and Sterling do not necessarily reconstruct history, but rather provide a postmodern rehistoricization of the conspiracy between technology and ideology. The novel thus makes reference to the illness of the traveler Lawrence Oliphant, defined in the then extant pseudoscientific discourse as "railway spine" but, by the end of the 1880s, reclassified as "traumatic neurosis";[12] *The Difference Engine*, however, characterizes Oliphant's disease as "symptoms of advanced syphilis" (354). The development of technology hence necessitates the invention both of new vocabulary and new diseases.

However, it is also noteworthy that a certain sort of ideology gives birth to new technology as a new representation. In this sense, the greatest postmodern irony of the novel is that Babbage's difference engine would not have been constructed without the ideology of the industrial revolution radicals, but that this engine—infected with a steam-driven virus—comes to enact the ideology of the Luddites, the radicals' principal adversaries.

A similar irony also informs Thomas Pynchon's *Vineland*, and Gibson and Sterling must have found specific inspiration for *The Difference Engine* in Pynchon's article "Is it O.K. to be a Luddite?," which appeared in the fall of 1984. In this article, the author provides a brief history of the Luddites that included numerous quotations (such as a poetic reference to "King Ludd" by Lord Byron, father of Ada) and a measure of esoteric speculation:

> Machines have already become so user-friendly that even the most unreconstructed of Luddites can be charmed into laying down the old sledgehammer and stroking a few keys instead. Beyond this seems to be a growing consensus that *knowledge really is power, that there is a pretty straightforward conversion between money and information*, and that somehow, if the logistics can be worked out, miracles may yet be possible. . . . If this is so, Luddites may at last have come to stand on common ground with their Sovian adversaries, the cheerful army of technocrats who were supposed to have the "future in their bones." It may be only a new form of the perennial Luddite ambivalence about machines, or it may be that the deepest Luddite hope of miracle has now come to reside in the computer's ability to get the right data to those whom the data will do the most good. (41; emphasis mine)

If Gibson and Sterling interpreted this passage as suggesting a paradoxical relationship between technocrats and Luddites, it is no surprise that their inspiration would take the form of an alternate history of Victorian Britain in which Lord Byron, champion of the Luddites, is refigured as Lord Byron, prime minister and chairman of the technocratic radicals.

Moreover, it is noteworthy that both Pynchon and the Gibson-Sterling team speculate on the future of technology from the perspective of the Pax Japonica. *Vineland* presents a fascinating group of feminist Luddites called the Kunoichi Attentives, whose ninjutsu technology includes a "Ninja Death Touch" (the "Vibrating Palm") that immediately transforms an adversary into a "Thanatoid," as well as an oriental medical device called a Puncutron capable of resurrecting that Thanatoid. Gibson and Sterling not only describe the Babbage engine as the most paradoxical example of techno-Luddites, but also predict the possible usurpation of its technology by Japanese adherents of Meiji ideology.

The authors explore this possibility through Japanese characters like Meiroku-sha people (the members of the first academic society in Japan), including Yukichi Fukuzawa, Arinori Mori, and Koan Matsuki, who visit Victorian Britain with the aim of importing the difference engine to Japan. These ambassadors of Japan meet with Oliphant and his nephew Edward Mallory, and during the meeting demonstrate a Japanese-made female automaton that pours drinks. This "tea doll," the Japanese "karakuri," inspires Oliphant to make the following remark to his nephew: "The Japanese power their dolls with springs of baleen. . . . They haven't yet learned from us the manufacture of proper springs, but soon they shall. . . . *Their mechanical appliances are presently inferior, due to their lack of knowledge in the applied sciences. Some day, in futurity, they may lead civilisation to heights yet untold.* They, and perhaps the Americans" (*Difference Engine*, 333; emphasis mine).

Comparing Oliphant's conception of "knowledge" as the basis of "civilization" with the italicized passage of "Is it O.K. to be a Luddite?" quoted above ("knowledge really is power"), you will note that just as technological development is now appreciated as a sign of national economic growth, the Victorians—whether British or Japanese—appreciated it as a symptom of military power.

It is for this reason that the character Arinori Mori in *The Difference Engine* (who is based on the Meiji-era genius of the same name who served as Japan's minister of education from 1885 to 1889) says to Oliphant: "Far better, for example, if all Japanese were taught English. Our meagre tongue is of no use in the great world beyond our islands. Soon power of steam and the Engine must pervade our land. English language, following such, must suppress any use of Japanese. *Our intelligent race, eager in pursuit of knowledge, cannot depend on weak and uncertain medium of communication*" (323; emphasis mine).

Mori is seduced into his determination to abolish the Japanese language by the Meiji ideology embodied in the radically militaristic "fukoku-kyohei" ("rich country, strong army") credo, to which Japan owed virtually all of her initial success in the early stages of modern economic growth.[13]

In short, whereas Pynchon, the genius of the post–Pax Americana, mockingly represents the ideology of the Pax Japonica through white American Ninjettes who appropriate Japanese esoterica—and assassinate and resurrect a Japanese fellow named Takeshi Fumimota—Gibson and Sterling successfully set up a three-layer Chinese box in which the Pax Britannica is reviewed through the Pax Americana, which is itself reorganized by the Pax Japonica.

Even at the cutting edge of the Anglo-American literary imagination, Japan thus performs—among other functions—the ideology of technoconsumerism that came to global dominance during the last decade of the twentieth century. In this sense, the signifier "Japan" might best be understood to represent the paradoxical ideology of techno-Ludditism that produced the Modus virus and the Puncutron feminist-orientalist machine. Recall that during the escalation of Japan bashing that followed Toshiba's transgression of Cocom in April 1987, televised images were broadcast of American technocrats destroying electronic consumer goods bearing the Toshiba label, exactly in the manner of Victorian Luddites. From that point on, Japan came to signify at once a subject of technocracy and an object of Luddites. Thus was the essential paradox between technocracy and Ludditism once again revived.

Is there a basis for radically criticizing such stereotypical western conceptions of what Japan signifies? To answer this question, let us turn to Japanese slipstream literature, and in particular to its greatest masterpiece, recently completed by a reclusive writer, in which metafictional and cyberpunkish strategies lay bare the discursive structure not only of the Japanese but of the human being as such.

Rereading *Yapoo the Human Cattle*

The year of 1991 saw the publication of several collections of postmodern short stories, but in regard to Japan, the coincidental publication of two in particular—*Positive*, no. 1, edited by Emiko Saito, and *Monkey Brain Sushi*, edited by Alfred Birnbaum—are of particular interest. *Positive*, no. 1, included cutting-edge American avant-pop tales by such writers as Mark Leyner, William Vollmann, Harold Jaffe, and Marianne Hauser, whom I tentatively designate "post-Pynchonesque." *Monkey Brain Sushi*—which covered comics as well as fiction—showcased the best contemporary Japanese metaliterary/cyberpunkish experiments of such writers as Masahiko Shimada, Gen'ichiro Takahashi, Yoshinori Shimizu, and Kyoji Kobayashi, who are representatives of the age following Yasutaka Tsutsui, the Japanese equivalent of John Barth, John Fowles, David Lodge, Malcolm Bradbury, and Italo Calvino all rolled into one.

The guru of Japanese metafiction, Yasutaka Tsutsui, bears close consideration as a primary architect of the context in which I will locate the author whom I would like to introduce. Tsutsui began his career in the mid-1960s as a science fiction writer, came to transgress the generic boundaries between serious and popular fiction in the 1970s, and won numerous major awards from both the science fiction and mainstream literature communities by the early 1990s. In early works including "Tokaido senso" (The Tokyo-Osaka War; 1964), "Vietnam kanko kosha" (The Vietnam Tourist Bureau; 1967), and *Dasso to tsuiseki no samba* (Samba for Runaways and Chasers; 1972), Tsutsui so fully embraced Daniel Boorstin's theory of the pseudo-event that he prophesied the coming acceleration of hypermedia that would transform identities into computer programs, battlefields into amusement parks, and fictions into realities. Tsutsui's recent major work, the diptych comprising the novels *Asa no Gasupaaru* (Gaspard of the Morning; 1991–1992) and *Paprika* (1993), offers radical reconsiderations of our reality as a version of hyperfictionality, of everyday life as an effect of the political unconscious, and of the boundary transgressor as the ultimate survivor of natural selection. Deeply informed by Darwin, Freud, and the Marx Brothers, Tsutsui has relentlessly deployed his postsituationist poetics of "Cho-kyoko" (hyperfictionality) to expose the conspiracy between reality and fiction that characterizes a late-capitalist age haunted by spectacles and pseudo-events—a milieu that Larry McCaffery, following William Burroughs, might call the "reality studio."

Explaining the parallel evolution of his poetics and world literary forms, Tsutsui wrote: "I do not find it accidental that in the 1960s and the 1970s, just as postsurrealist modes of writing nurtured British New Wave, North American metafiction, and Latin American magic realism, I was making every effort to develop my theory of hyperfictionality, though I had no knowledge of those western literary innovations."[14]

Tsutsui also unwittingly rivaled scholar-critics such as David Lodge and Malcolm Bradbury by experimenting with avant-garde literary criticism. Tsutsui's *Bungaku-bu Tadano Kyoju* (Hitoshi Tadano, Professor of English; 1990), a novel disguised as a series of lectures on contemporary literary theory, became a national bestseller.

Thus Tsutsui's long career from the 1960s to the 1990s maps the gradual acceptance of the hybridization of metafiction and science fiction as the fate of postmodern literature that has characterized Japanese literary history. Whereas the Tsutsui of the 1960s–1980s has been considered analogous to hardcore metafictionists such as John Barth, John Fowles, and Italo Calvino, the Tsutsui of the 1990s may better compare with the godfather of American hyperfiction, Robert Coover, who has promoted the hypertextual reorganization of the metafictional imagination in the wake of the emergence of cyberculture. Let us recall the way he first defined hyperfiction: "hypertext presents a radically divergent technology, interactive and polyvocal, favoring a plurality of discourses over definitive utterance and freeing the reader from domination by the author."[15]

What I would like to discuss, however, is not so much the "Tsutsuistic" coincidence between Japanese literature and Anglo-American literature, as the uniquely Japanese case of a literary work that succeeds most idiosyncratically (if ultimately too dangerously) in questioning the discursive framework of what Japan signifies. In contrast to Tsutsui—a consistently visible presence in the literary market—the author of this work has been reclusive to the point of invisibility. Moreover, whereas Tsutsui has questioned the logocentric framework of western fiction by adopting the narratological heritage of the French nouveau roman, new fiction, and magic realism, this mysterious writer has deconstructed the very narratological framework that makes contemporary sexual-geopolitical identity possible. The name of this writer is Shozo Numa, and his radically significant (and only) novel is entitled *Yapoo the Human Cattle.*

Yapoo appeared first in serial form in *Kitan-Club* magazine in 1956, was first published in book form from Toshi-Shuppan Publishers in 1970, then revised and expanded for the Ohta Publishers edition in 1991, and radically reedited for the final, "definitive" version that appeared in five volumes from Gentosha Publishers in 1999. Comparable to works of Jonathan Swift and the Marquis de Sade—and highly regarded by Yukio Mishima and Tatsuhiko Shibusawa—*Yapoo* describes a stunningly imagined, white-dominated, matriarchal, deep-space-faring, and time-traveling nation of the fortieth century—called the Empire of a Hundred Suns (or EHS). In EHS, blacks are content with their status as slaves and game, and orientals—particularly Japanese people—are considered to be not *Homo sapiens* but rather *Simias sapiens*—that is, they are regarded not as human beings, but as cattle.

Fig. 6 A Yapoo enjoying the fate of living as a sofa bed. Illustration of a scene from *Yapoo the Human Cattle*, the revised and expanded edition (Tokyo: *Sukora*, 1991) by Shozo Numa. Drawing © Akira Uno.

In this far-future society, Japanese people are surgically or biotechnologically transformed into living furniture appliances, and food stock generically called "Yapoo." Among other uses, Yapoo serve as walking lavatories ("secchin"), walking vomitories ("vomitora"), and walking cunnilingual vibrators ("cunnilinga"). Yapoo that have been shrunk to the size of bacteria are used as contraceptives ("tunnel boys"). Bio-mobiles are driven by the cattle's psychic power (Psy-Yapoo). Carpets are made from Yapoo hair ("live carpet"). And of course, Yapoo are eaten by a number of virtuous people of EHS.

The story begins with a ruling-class EHS time-traveler named Pauline Jansen making a forced landing on twentieth-century Earth, where she encounters an Aryan girl named Clara and her Japanese fiancé, Rin'ichiro. Pauline takes Rin'ichiro to be Yapoo, and decides to rebuild his body, transforming him into Clara's personal domestic animal. The events of this meganovel—which center on the transformation of Rin'ichiro from a human being into a human domestic animal—transpire in only a few days, though Numa labored over *Yapoo* for thirty-five years.

To a certain kind of audience, of course, elements of *Yapoo* as reductively described here—or even the entire novel—will sound offensive in the extreme, but regardless of this, Numa's idiosyncratic narrative disfigures the limits of postmodern literature in at least three significant ways.

First, Numa deconstructs such Japanese origin myths as *The Kojiki* or *Nihongi* in *Yapoo*, portraying primordial Japanese mythological figures as artifacts of Yapoo culture transplanted from the far future. For instance, the Japanese mythological river monster known as kappa is recast in *Yapoo* as the tenth (*kappa*, the tenth letter of Greek alphabet) of a new model of hydrobicycle produced in an experimental Yapoo production process; this kappa was subsequently transported from EHS to the ancient Earth: the mythic kappa is no more than a variant form of Yapoo. Note that if it is ethnic mythos that makes national fiction possible, *Yapoo* can be identified as a rare example of truly Japanese metafiction, in the strictest sense.

Second, whereas Gibsonian cyberpunk—exploring how western people in the oriental near-future context will become pieces of junk art—appropriates an end-of-(human)-history-type discourse typical of the western grand narrative, Numa ironically declares the beginning of the history of human cattle by describing an ultraracist society that radically reorganizes evolutionism. In this new history, Japanese people become neither existential beings nor useless junk, but rather *multipurpose domestic animals and/or cattle*, in sharp contrast to Gibson's (as well as Kojève's) redefinition of Japan not as a breeding place but as the world to come. More precisely, the ideological upheaval characterizing the mid- to the late twentieth century demanded the radical disfigurement of the rhetorical status of the Japanese as such, just as we did such figures as Kennedy, Scheherazade, and Hitler. Numa's ironic attitude can thus be construed as a critical assault on the Foucauldian construction of the "human being."

The third disfigurement effected by Yapoo is best approached in light of the major works of Arthur C. Clarke—from *Childhood's End* (1953) through *2061: Odyssey Three* (1987)—all of which depicted some highly imperialistic alien race making human beings their own cattle. And yet, the most essentially cattle-like figures in Clarke's works are not humans but rather beings like the Monolith as a variant of the Overlords; such figures serve as medium or midwife to the future superevolution of human beings and possess stupendous intellectual powers, but their cosmological status is not necessarily higher than that of human beings. In short—and this is the key point—they possess superior intelligence and inferior status.

The impact of Clarke's *Childhood's End* (published in 1953) upon Numa's *Yapoo* (first serialized in 1956) cannot be doubted. First, Clarke's fictionalization of his straightforwardly imperialistic ideology almost certainly provided the dialectic inspiration for Numa's transfiguration of his personal racist-ethnocentric dystopia into a literary utopia:[16] biographically speaking, Numa was deeply ashamed of the Showa emperor's submission to the occupation—which essentially viewed the Japanese royal family as an honorable clan of Yapoo—and deeply insulted by the racism of a British woman with whom he was having a sexual relationship. Hence, in constructing his own dystopia, Numa inverted Clarke's ideology, reexamining the implications of imperialism for gender, class, and race from the Japanese perspective: whereas Foucault viewed these categories of the human condition as inventions arising from the impact of the process of modernization on the western discursive space (and thus, as phenomena of only the past few centuries), Numa has persistently tried to create the other as the very inventor of modern western discourse, subverting the mirror-stage relationship between the Anglo-American and the Japanese.

Western humanism is likely to discover its other, something posthuman, beyond the limit of postmodern technoculture, but Numa's Yapooism locates the radical other growing within the limiting, disciplinary technology of erotoaristocratic discourse; herein lies the critical difference between Clarke and Numa, despite the possible analogy between the Overlord/Monolith and Yapoo, both of which are intelligent but lower-class. What Clarke's superevolution of humanity represents is an ideology of productionist imperialism in which the mirror of production survives intact; in contrast, Numa's biological degradation of the Japanese foresaw the self-referential, metastructural logic of consumerist masochism, in which the subject consuming new technology enjoys being disciplined, whipped, and finally consumed by technocracy itself. Hence, the American ideology of Japan bashing for Numa reflected the American grasp of the Japanese as human cattle that could not be taught through logic but only through physical correction.

The Yapoo of Numa's conception, finally, prove not only handy and edible, but also useful as objects of blame for the abuse that occurs in human history. It emerges in the novel that a revisionist German historian in EHS has successfully attributed the Holocaust to the psychic control of twentieth-century Yapoos over Hitler and the Nazis. In contrast to Dick's, Spinrad's, and Erickson's figures of Hitler, Numa's is thus displaced by the ideology of perverted masochism.

Postmodern metafictionists such as Pynchon may well expect to see within the metafictive frontier the birth of the other. Postmodern science fictionists such as Gibson and Sterling could not help but create the other within cyberspace. Writers of both movements thus conclude that postmodern subjectivity is constructed through techno-networks. In contrast, Numa asserts through fierce irony that it is, rather, ideological bias and that leads to the viewing of specific gender, class, or racial identities literally as technological signifiers rather than ideological entities; one character in the novel thus composes the axiom that the more loyalty a Yapoo develops toward its master, the more delicious its meat becomes (2:545–546).

But is not *Yapoo the Human Cattle*, in the final analysis, ultrasexist, hyperracist, and supertotalitarian? In 1970, when the novel was first published in book form, the answer would surely have been yes on all counts, and it is little wonder that *Yapoo* was received as perverse, weird, frightening, and disgusting. The history of the subsequent thirty-plus years, however, saw the ideology of the Pax Americana supplanted by that of the Pax Japonica, and the ideologies of metafiction and cyberpunk reproduced wholesale by our consumer society. In light of these developments, Numa's work merits a more nuanced reconsideration. We have come to understand that, as Walter Benn Michaels has implied, the more advanced our consumer-capitalist, postmodern society becomes, the more difficult it will be for us to distinguish its ideology from sexual masochism.[17] Furthermore, postmodern discourses make it easier to reinterpret the technomagic orientalism represented by writers such as Numa, even as Numa's novel convincingly shows that postmodern criticism has been surgically transformed into a radical critique of the postmodern itself—that is, into a postmodern version of the frontier spirit in search of techno-imperialist "freedom." From this perspective, Yapoo emerge as both the intelligent subjects and the low-class objects of technocracy, and Numa emerges as not merely attempting to reinvestigate the metafictive ideology of the Pax Japonica but as affording insight into the masochistic construction of consumerist subjectivity as having always been *Yapooized*, rather than "Japanized" in the sense of Kojève or Gibson and Sterling.

Although Shozo Numa has long remained reclusive, underground, and literally slipstream—one of the most unknown (if one of the greatest) contemporary writers, his brave new world has proven sufficiently enchanting that it has been reprinted more than twenty times since 1970 and adapted musically by the 1980s punk rock group the Yapoos. The novel has thus been disciplined, disfigured, and recreated—like the Yapoo themselves—by the avant-pop logic of the cultural materialism of the 1990s, according to which the most inalienable, subcultural, and esoteric is easily and quickly made alienable, commercial, and natural.

PART 2 History

CHAPTER 3 Virus as Metaphor: A Postorientalist Reading of the Future War Novels of the 1890s

Since the turn of the century the image of the "future war" has repeatedly revived itself in fiction and cinema, conquering our media-saturated reality time and again, most recently with Hollywood films such as *Independence Day*, *Mars Attacks!*, *Men in Black*, *Starship Troopers*, *Alien: Resurrection*, and *The Postman*. However, the more popular the future-war narrative gets in the late twentieth century, the more urgent it becomes for us to reevaluate the origin of this narrative in the late nineteenth century, that is, in the masterpiece *The War of the Worlds* (1898) by British father of science fiction, H. G. Wells, a book that inspired other writers to rewrite it in their respective ways and complete their own future-war novels. The most significant of these fictions are collected in *Future War Novels of the 1890s*, which I co-edited and which was published in a handsome edition by Thoemmes (1998).

What exactly has Wells's impact been? As Brian Stableford has pointed out, *The War of the Worlds* is, among other things, the first text to feature aliens in a role that would eventually become a cliché: that is, as monstrous invaders of Earth, competitors in a cosmic struggle.[1] The story is simple—so simple, in fact, that whoever reads it feels encouraged to create his or her own version. The aggressive Martians came to earth riding on meteor-like spaceships. Their superweapon easily overwhelms our weapons. An unexpected accident takes place, however: earthly bacteria, benign to humans, annihilate the Martian invaders, who lack immunity to them. The story is powerfully driven by two narratological devices, which will powerfully influence its fol-

Fig. 7
A postoriental technoscape of Iturup Island. Scene from Mamoru Oshii's *Innocence*, the sequel to *Ghost in the Shell*. © 2004 Shirow Masamune/ KODANSHA·IG, ITNDDTD.

lowers: two paramount clichés—the most formidable invasion and the most unpredictable resolution. In the early years of the new millennium, I would like to focus not only on the ingenuity of Wells the father of future-war fiction, but also on the way his invented science-fictional clichés have been transformed and appropriated by several latecomers—self-proclaimed or crypto-Wellsians who faithfully observe the logic of sequelology, especially in the age of advanced capitalism.[2] The latest Hollywood special effects films of future war can all be reconsidered as sequels to *The War of the Worlds*. From the postmodern "ironical" perspective, the text of *The War of the Worlds* itself seems to be one of those twice-told tales. Back in the 1880s, when the novel was written, it already had several precursors, which I will take up later. But the essence of Wells's revolution in *The War of the Worlds* lies in his brilliant construction of the "nodal point" that sharply distinguishes pre-Wellsian and post-Wellsian literary discourses. To put it simply, in Wells we rediscover the edge of chaos where the cult of advanced technology transforms itself very naturally into the cult of nationalistic ideology.

Let me start with an archaeology of future-war fiction. As I. F. Clarke has argued, the archetype of future-war novels could well be a six-page fantasy about the English Civil War called *Aulicus His Dream of the Kings Sudden Comming to London* (1644), by the seventeenth-century Puritan fanatic Francis Cheynell. We do not find Cheynell's name in any encyclopedia or literary biography of science fiction; he secures only a minor place in the *Dictionary of National Biography*. Cheynell's fantasy, however, represents a striking, fearful vision of King Charles I, triumphant over Oliver Cromwell and the forces of Parliament. Since in May 1644 it was still thought possible that the king could prove victor in the Civil War, the readers of the short story must have been aware of the author's message: "Act now before it is too late."[3] Thus the genre of future war fiction started with the keenest awareness of the "present," as is the case with the best science fiction today.

Cheynell's message about a time after a failed Puritan Revolution should make us reconsider the significance of Robert Fulton (1765–1815), the great pioneer of undersea warfare in the American republican period, as the major prophet of Reagan's American SDI (Strategic Defense Initiative), or Star Wars plan. In the years before the American Revolution, Fulton—a talented inventor, engineer, and artist—devised a rocket and a hand-propelled paddle-wheel boat and showed an aptitude for gun making. Notorious though he was for his hunger for fame and fortune, Fulton was undoubtedly one of the representative men of American republicanism, incarnating what H. Bruce Franklin designates "ideological contradictions" inherent in the transition from mercantile to industrial capitalism.[4] Indeed, while he was eager to achieve "perpetual peace" in republican America in 1797, Fulton simultaneously attempted to invent a weapon to end war, "a curious machine for mending the system of politics," that is to say, a submarine vessel of war designed to destroy the main obstacle to free trade and revolutionary republicanism: "the British navy."[5] It is radically paradoxical that the pursuit of republican peace demanded that Fulton end war by inventing a superweapon to exterminate the enemy. But let us also note that Fulton's paradox is to be shared by another of the all-American heroes, Thomas Edison. This genius of technology was doubtless another representative man of the United States, who billed himself sometimes as a man of peace, at other times as a master inventor of marvelous weapons that could destroy whole armies with the push of a button. Just like Fulton, Edison became a living expression of the paradox in American military potential, which requires us to accept peace as the effect of an atomic deterrent. Edison appears in Garret P. Serviss's *Edison's Conquest of Mars* (1898), one of the future-war fictions collected in *Future War Novels of the 1890s*. As George Locke lucidly spells out in his introduction to that collection, Serviss's novel is one of the great Yankee sequels to Wells's *The War of the Worlds*. Thus, from our viewpoint in the early

2000s, Fulton in the republican age and Edison in the postbellum age seem to join forces, if anachronistically, to reinvent the Cheynellian imperative "Act now before it is too late," thereby anticipating the all-American paradox of the Pax Americana and SDI–Star Wars in the advanced capitalistic age.

With these precursors in mind, we can safely define the status of future-war novels that flourished in the late nineteenth century. The period around the turn of the century saw the rise of two phenomena: the perceived increasing menace of the so-called yellow peril and the rapid development of Japanese military power. Of course, western culture—as Charles Vevier has noted—had long cultivated the theme that the barbarian hordes of Asia—the "yellow" races—were always on the point of invading and destroying Christendom, Europe, and western civilization itself. And it was precisely this radical prejudice that infected the fin-de-siècle United States. The Burlingame Treaty with China in 1868 ignited the yellow peril, for the treaty encouraged Chinese "coolies" (a source of cheap labor) to enter the country to help construct the Pacific railroads. Murder, personal and social humiliation, and physical brutality became the lot of the Chinese workers on the Pacific coast, particularly in California and in the mining camps of the mountain states. In the 1870s in San Francisco, the demagogue Denis Kearny heaped political abuse upon the Chinese and invoked boycotts in the name of the American working man. The specifics of the yellow peril mania are evident in the Chinese Exclusion Acts, passed between 1880 and 1904.[6]

It is not very difficult to find, therefore, especially in the late nineteenth century, a number of future-war fiction works alluding to the yellow peril, works such as: Pierton Dooner's *Last Days of the Republic* (1879), Lorelle's "The Battle of the Wabash" (1880), Robert Wolter's *A Short and Truthful History of the Taking of California and Oregon by the Chinese in the Year A.D. 1889* (1882), William Ward Crane's "The Year 1899" (1893), Otto Mundo's *The Recovered Continent: A Tale of the Chinese Invasion* (1898), and, M. P. Shiel's *The Yellow Danger* (1898), the last of which coined the term "yellow peril" and popularized its use.

Invasion from Asia could well have been perceived in fin-de-siècle English-speaking countries as their greatest danger, and the one most keenly felt. This is the cultural historical context that induced H. G. Wells to write *The War of the Worlds* (serialized in 1897 and published in 1898). Bruce Franklin remarks that the Wellsian Martians, "with their armoured war machines, poison gas, flying machines, and heat beams, are invaders not so much from the neighboring planet as from the approaching century" (65). Another notable work in this tradition is C. L. Graves and E. V. Lucas's *The War of the Wenuses* (1898). But notwithstanding this future other, since the mid-nineteenth century, when Edgar Allan Poe revealed his fear of African Americans and Asiatics in "The Murders in the Rue Morgue" (1841), the image of the other in the West has been strongly entangled with that of people of color.[7] Look at Wells's description of the octopus-like Martians with "no nostrils," "a pair of very large dark-coloured eyes, and just beneath it a kind of flesh beak" (127), and you will recognize the racial prejudice running through it. But I am not interested in attacking Wells's sense of ethnicity. For without this fear of the other *The War of the Worlds* would not have been the literary masterpiece it was. Immediately appealing to the Caucasian audience, the novel became so influential that it generated many literary variants, the Wellsian "by-products" as George Locke calls them in his introduction to *Future War Novels of the 1890s*.

Rereading *The War of the Worlds*, however, we become aware of the irony that while Wells's Martians end up being felled by the earthly germs, elsewhere it is the earthly non-Caucasian others who have invariably been conceived as a sort of fatal virus. The plot line of *The War of the Worlds* coincides wonderfully with the threat of germ warfare, dramatized at the climax of M. P. Shiel's *The Yellow Danger*, which was published in the same year. Cheynell's old imperative "Act now before it is too late" has become obsolete. Instead, Wells has set up a homeopathic or inoculative (Jennerian?) imperative: "Don't act until a virus is slaughtered by another virus."[8]

In the wake of the Russo-Japanese War in 1905, the year that saw the shocking defeat of Russia by Japan, yellow peril literature in fact expanded its scope and started attacking not only the Chinese but also the Japanese; a classic example is Jack London's treatment of the theme in his short story "The Unparalleled Invasion," written in 1906 and published in 1910.[9] In a further development, Roy Norton's novel *Vanishing Fleets* (1907) represents Americans' fear of the red menace, that is, the fear not of American Indians but of Russian communists. At the height of the Russo-Japanese War, the all-American humorist Mark Twain—undoubtedly influenced by future-war novels—provided us, in his pseudo-fairy tales "Flies and Russians" (1904 or 1905) and "The Fable of the Yellow Terror" (1904–1905), vividly satirized this American xenophobia.[10]

The anti-Asian and anti-Russian discourse prevalent around the turn of the century gives us a context for reconsidering the significance of Frederick Robinson's 1914 novel *The War of the Worlds: A Tale of the Year 2000 A.D.* among the many literary variants on Wells's *The War of the Worlds*. In this novel, a Russian prince, maddened by an American woman's rejection of his courtship, organizes a grand alliance of Asians, Africans, and Latin Americans, as well as Martians, to contain and defeat the United States.[11] What interests us here is that Robinson, like other later Wellsian writers, represents "Martians" not as a specific race, but as whatever the term "other" specifies in their respective periods of history, that is, the other as such. In the late 1890s, when Wells completed his archetypal future-war novel, the Martians embodied the other from Asia in general. In the late 1900s, however, Martians became the omen of the yellow, black, and red perils. Likewise, in the late 1930s, especially when Orson Welles produced (on the day before Halloween, 1938) his American radio broadcast version of *The War of the Worlds*, which the audience believed to be true, he must have aroused the fear of fascism represented by Nazi Germany.[12] In the early 1950s, when Byron Haskin's film version of *The War of the Worlds* was first shown, the Martians, in the years of McCarthyism, must have amplified the fear of Russian communism. It is, however, the American xenophobic discourse that paradoxically has constantly cultivated American xenophilia, expanding the possibility of representative arts and narratives.

With this cultural historical background in mind, we can safely enjoy the postmodern narratives of future war. The greatest tribute in the 1990s to *The War of the Worlds* is the Hollywood blockbuster *Independence Day*, directed by Roland Emmerich and released on July 4, 1996, in which the formidable invaders end up being massacred by an earthly computer virus, just as Wells's Martians are exterminated by earthly bacteria. Once again, we are confronted with the homeopathic imperative "Don't act until a virus is slaughtered by another virus." This time the American unconsciousness, in the wake of the Gulf War, clearly reinvented the other as the Middle Eastern. This is why, despite a number of scathing reviews of the film, its xenophobic narrative was appreciated by many and refreshed conservative discourses—probably affecting the course of President Clinton's second administration, which started in January 1997. Of course, I am not sure how seriously Hollywood speculated upon Clinton's presidency, and how much Clinton was aware of the impact of *Independence Day*. And yet it is undeniable that a huge audience in the United States welcomed this politically correct but sexually conservative movie of future war.

The most provocative comment on the movie was made by Arthur C. Clarke, the king of modern science fiction, in the "Sources and Acknowledgments" section of his novel *3001: The Final Odyssey*, published in 1997. Briefly touching on President Clinton's strategy for countering cyberterrorism, the author asserts ironically:

> I have been intrigued to learn that the finale of *Independence Day*, which I have not yet seen, . . . involves the use of computer viruses as Trojan horses! I am also informed that its opening is identical to that of *Childhood's End* (1953), and that it contains every known science-fiction *cliché* since Melies's *Trip to the Moon* (1903). I cannot decide whether to congratulate the scriptwriters on their one stroke of originality—or to accuse them of the *trans-temporal crime of precognitive plagiarism*. In any event, I fear there's nothing I can do to stop John Q. Popcorn thinking that I have ripped off the ending of *ID4*. (Emphasis mine)[13]

Clarke here shows wonderful insight into how much *Independence Day* owes to the future-war novels. But he is being somewhat amnesic himself, for, while playfully asserting his own original ideas and accusing the film's scriptwriters of a "trans-temporal crime of precognitive plagiarism," Clarke manages to conceal his personal literary debt to H. G. Wells and his descendants. It is self-evident that without reading *The War of the Worlds* Clarke could not have updated the image of UFOs and aliens in *Childhood's End*, published in the same year as the film version of *The War of the Worlds*. What is more, without the impact of post-Wellsian future-war narratives Clarke could not have created in his Odyssey series the fabulously virus-like image of the "Monolith," a teaching machine for human evolution. Though the Monolith's rectangular form appears exotic, its virus-like qualities cannot help but conjure up the virus-like aliens recreated time and again in the literary tradition of future-war novels. Hence the representation, in *2010*, of the multiplying monoliths as a kind of virus infecting Jupiter. "So the damn thing's gone down to Jupiter—and multiplied. There was something simultaneously comic and sinister about a plague of black monoliths," says the character Hyam (254).[14] Looking at them, another character, Katerina, states: "Do you know what it reminds me of? A virus attacking a cell. The way a phage injects its DNA into a bacterium, and then multiplies until it takes over" (263). Thus Clarke forbids us to imagine that the Monolith is an intelligent being. In the novel *2061: Odyssey Three* (1987), the sequel to *2010*, the character Bowman, fused with the computer Hal 9000, explains to Dr. Floyd the nature of the Monolith: "It is only a tool: it has vast intelligence—but no consciousness. Despite all its powers, you, Hal, and I are its superior" (263). And finally, *3001* plunges into the future war between the virus-like Monolith and the computer virus: "This tablet contains programs that we hope will prevent the Monolith from carrying out any orders that threaten mankind" (234). Despite Clarke's own strong claim of originality, the logical progress of the Odyssey series invites us to assume that while the mysterious Monolith turns out to have been the high-tech signifier of xenophobia and xenophilia, Clarke now very faithfully recreates the Wellsian catastrophe of *The War of the Worlds*, as well as M. P. Shiel's germ warfare in *The Yellow Danger*, and reconstructs the exemplary future-war imperative, "Don't act until a virus is slaughtered by another virus."

Indeed, postcyberpunk science fiction seems to have updated even the old future-war narratives. What is highly paradoxical, however, is that the more high-tech our society gets, the more atavistic our literature becomes. For us to recognize the extent to which the future-war literary heritage has unwittingly influenced the science fiction of the present, it is important to reconstrue the pre-Wellsian and post-Wellsian narratives that emerged at the turn of the century, in which the signifier of color, whether yellow or black or red—or even white—functioned as the most viable metaphor in the characterization of aliens.

CHAPTER 4 Deep North Gothic: A Postoccidentalist Reading of Hearn, Yanagita, and Akutagawa

Though widely considered a classic of Japanese folklore studies, Kunio Yanagita's *Tono Monogatari* (The Legends of Tono, 1910), has features that seem anachronistic—at first glance. In this work, Yanagita collected tales of the supernatural local to Tono, a town in the Deep North of Japan, which inhabitants of the area believed to be true. According to Kizen Sasaki, the native informant who reported these oral legends to Yanagita, gods who guarded homes (*kami*), ugly goblin-like creatures that impregnated women (*kappa*), and witches or shamans who communicated with the dead (*itako*) could all be encountered in Tono. If Yanagita had presented *Legends* simply as a collection of outlandish fairy tales, the text would have been consumed as popular fiction, but Yanagita instead offered the work—which appeared during Japan's early-twentieth-century high-enlightenment period—as a radical interrogation of the modern western distinction between science and literature, thereby complicating the reading of the text.[1]

At no point in *Legends* does Yanagita condescend to his native informant; instead, he simply stylized—with great care—the oral tales reported by Sasaki, a walking database of Tono narratives. In Yanagita's portrayal, the people of Tono have difficulty telling fact from fiction and the actual from the imaginary—much like the inhabitants of Sleepy Hollow in Washington Irving's famous tale, who all walk about in a continual state of reverie and are given to all kinds of marvelous beliefs. The people of Tono thus not only narrate but also live what might be termed the "Deep North gothic." Read in such terms, *Legends* emerges not as anachronistic but rather—as has been widely recognized among Yanagita scholars—as "antidotal" to Japanese modernization and westernization.

Somewhere between "Discover Japan" and "Exotic Japan"

Let us begin our consideration of the Deep North gothic with a brief overview of the life of Yanagita (1875–1962).[2] Kunio Yanagita was born in Hyogo Prefecture, the sixth son of Misao Matsuoka, a scholar, teacher, and Shinto priest. Following his graduation from Tokyo Imperial University with a degree in law, Yanagita married into the influential family of Naohei Yanagita in 1900, adopting his wife's surname. From 1900 to 1919, Yanagita worked as a civil servant, first in the Ministry of Agriculture and Commerce and later in the Legislative Bureau and the Imperial Household Ministry. From 1919 to 1930, he worked as a journalist for the *Asahi Shimbun* newspaper, the Japanese equivalent of the *New York Times*. An avid traveler and prolific writer, Yanagita published over one hundred books and a thousand articles in the latter years of the Meiji era (1868–1912). *Legends* was published in 1910, at a time when Yanagita was personally involved as a government official in the annexation of Korea to Japan. In short, as a scholar and poet who also worked as a journalist and civil servant, Yanagita wrote prolifically and conducted extensive research, thereby establishing the framework for subsequent folklore studies in Japan.

The contemporary reader may find it surprising that *Legends*, as an elegant work of Japanese literature, has not lost relevance even in the wake of the emergence of cyberculture in the 1980s. Yanagita himself lived through a radical transformation of Japanese society between his birth in 1875 and his death in 1962. "Born in the era of the rickshaw," his translator Ronald Morse observes, "Yanagita lived to see jet airplanes. During his youth he witnessed famine and infanticide, yet before he died Japan was the most advanced nation in Asia."[3]

Shigeto Tsuru has characterized this transformation of postwar Japan as "creative defeat," a term that captures the metamorphosis of masochistic Americanization into technocapitalistic triumph on the Japanese side, a process that has left us prone to equating Japan's rapid growth with a hyperurbanization that has encouraged the demystification of premodernist discourses such as the Tono narratives (*Japan's Capitalism*, 67). Yet as evidenced by the rise of urban folklore in the

1980s and 1990s, the mythic spirit of Tono has regained its significance, extending the domain of its setting from the countryside to the cityscape. As weird rumors circulate that a computer virus will sooner or later biologically infect the inhabitants of the postmodern city, one feels increasingly likely to encounter a ghost child (a Zashiki Warashi) in front of a coin locker, or to have unwittingly communicated with dead or lost boys through computer networks (see Card, "Lost Boys"; Kondo et al., *The Bulletin Board of the Witches*). My point here is that the nativist country of Tono has started to invade the high-tech city of Tokyo; far from vanishing, the significance of *The Legends of Tono* has been amplified.

Let us consider this revival of Tono in the high-growth decades more closely. In her provocative critical work *Discourses of the Vanishing*, Marilyn Ivy discusses an alliance between the huge advertising agency Dentsu and a major public transportation company, Japan Railway, to promote domestic tourism. In the 1970s and 1980s, this alliance conducted a series of nationwide campaigns with the slogans "Discover Japan" (conducted in the 1970s) and "Exotic Japan" (conducted in the 1980s). The more Americanized Japan became with postwar development, the more "nonnative" its "vanishing" culture seemed to the Japanese people themselves. To address the nostalgia for this culture, this alliance of Japanese capitalism and the mass media attempted to reshape the desire for travel and self-rediscovery, especially among women of the younger generation. The images the alliance devised for these campaigns both created and promised to fulfill this desire; more precisely, the alliance appropriated the scathing discourse of industrial pollution and urban overpopulation by associating a spatial displacement from city to country with a movement backward in time, as well as with the boom in folklore and folklore studies of the late 1960s and early 1970s.[4] Thus "Tono tourists" were asked to rediscover Japan in the internationalist milieu of the 1970s, and to estrange and reorientalize it in the multinationalist atmosphere of the 1980s. But the old Japan was lost. During the transitional period between the Discover Japan campaign of the 1970s and the Exotic Japan campaign of the 1980s, distinguished director Tetsutaro Murano loosely adapted several episodes from Yanagita's *Legends* into his beautiful film *The Legend of Sayo* (1982). Looking back on his adaptation, Murano wrote: "I made the film just in time, in the early '80s. Before the Shinkansen, the bullet train, was opened. The hills around here have really been logged over, too. The bullet train means the end of Tono—the end as dream, as image. Now it will be more and more of a movement of—'preserving' things—that's no good."[5]

The Narrative of Forbidden Love

Murano's film adaptation *The Legend of Sayo* does not include all of the tales that Yanagita collected in *The Legends of Tono*. The filmmaker decided rather to devise his own highly plausible story line of supernatural romantic love set in Tono, and embroidered this narrative with a number of mythic signs typical of Tono: Oshirasama, the deity of silkworms; Zashiki Warashi, a supernatural being who takes the form of a "parlor child"; and Nanbu horses, the sexual symbols of interspecies love. To follow the story, you have only to be aware of the extra-spatiotemporal romance between the beautiful lady Sayo and the dead soldier Takeshi, a relationship that cannot help but bring to mind the forbidden love between Heathcliff and Catherine in Emily Brontë's *Wuthering Heights* (1847). Murano's *Sayo*, along with director Kiju Yoshida's 1988 Japanesque remake of *Wuthering Heights*, demonstrates the enduring popularity in Japan of "forbidden love" narratives set deep in the countryside.

There are three "forbidden love" narratives in Yanagita's *Legends* that must have inspired Murano, beginning with the romance between a girl and a horse described in Legend 69:

> Once upon a time there was a poor farmer. He had no wife but did have a beautiful daughter. He also had one horse. The daughter loved the horse, and at night she would go to the stable and sleep. Finally, she and the horse became husband and wife. One night the father learned of this, and the next day without saying anything to the daughter, he took the horse out and killed it by hanging it from a mulberry tree. That night the daughter asked her father why the horse was not anywhere around, and she learned of the act. Shocked, filled with grief, she went on to the spot beneath the mulberry tree and cried while clinging to the horse's head. The father, abhorring the sight, took an axe and chopped off the horse's head, which flew off to the heavens. It was from this time on that Oshira-sama became a kami. The image of this kami was made from the mulberry branch on which the horse was hanged. (49–50)

The imagination that conceives of horses in such a way and that gave rise to this tale—which brings to mind both Peter Shaffer's

Broadway play *Equus* (1973) and voodoo horses—has its origins in the geopolitical conditions of Tono itself. Legend 2 sheds light on what these were: "The town of Tono is located at the spot where two rivers running north and south come together. Formerly commodities for sale were gathered from up to forty-five kilometers back into the seven valleys around Tono. On market days as many as *a thousand people and a thousand horses crowded into Tono*" (12, emphasis mine). From its origins as a planned castle town established in the seventeenth century, Tono gained importance in the eighteenth century as a market and post town; in particular, it was an active center of horse trading and breeding well into the Showa period. Thus (as Marilyn Ivy points out in *Discourses of the Vanishing*) both the love affair between a girl and a horse and Tono's characteristic house design—L-shaped to accommodate horse stables—"highlight the importance of horses in Tono's history" (109). The central role of horses in the life of the town explains also the representation of the deity of Oshira-sama throughout northeastern Japan by "enigmatic paired stick figures of a horse and a human being" (124).

From the viewpoint of mythology, an interspecies "marriage" such as that described in Legend 69 would not have been "enigmatic" in hunting cultures such as that of so-called native Japanese, the Ainu, who have many legends of couplings between man and bear, and woman and sea gull. The Ainu, the earliest inhabitants of northeastern Japan, gave Tono many of its placenames. However, the Ainu were gradually driven back from the area by armies dispatched from the distant Japanese cultural centers to the southwest. To the southern Japanese, who had developed an agriculture-based way of life, the Ainu hunters were radical others; they called the Ainu of Tono "Yamabito," literally, mountain dwellers. It is no wonder that Japanese settlers from the southwest linked the Yamabito with the disappearances of women and children, as evinced by Legends 7 and 8, which deal with the story of a young girl who disappears one day, only to reappear thirty years later, "very old and haggard" (*Legends*, 16). In any event, the Ainu people had to content themselves with the ironic fate of being a diaspora in a country that was originally their own. In this regard, the cultural history of the Ainu people, considered by some of their ethnic successors to be one of the lost tribes of Israel, closely resembles that of the native American peoples.

Another legend from Yanagita's text on which Murano drew—

Legend 99—concerns a supernatural romance between the living and the dead:

> Fukuji . . . lost his wife and one of his children in the tidal wave that struck the area last year. For about a year now, he had been with the two children who survived, in a shelter set up on the site of the original house.
>
> On a moonlit night in early summer he got up to go to the privy. It was off at some distance on the path along the beach where the waves broke. This night the fog hovered low and he saw two people, a man and a woman, approaching him out of the fog. The woman was definitely his wife who had died. Without thinking, he trailed after them to a cavern on the promontory in the direction of Funakoshi village. When he called her name, she looked back and smiled. The man he saw was from the same village, and he too had died in the tidal wave disaster. It had been rumored, that this man and Fukuji's wife had been deeply in love before Fukuji had been chosen to marry her.
>
> She said, "I am now married to this man." When Fukuji said, "Don't you love your children?" the woman's expression changed a little, and she cried. Fukuji didn't realize he was talking with the dead. While he was looking down at his feet, sadly and miserably, the man and the woman started on quickly and disappeared around the mountain on the way to Oura. He tried to run after them but suddenly realized they were the dead. (70)

The discourse invoked in Yanagita's *Legends* of impossible intercourse—between the living and the dead, or between human beings and other species—also informs an American narrative tradition that includes American gothic romancers such as Poe, Bierce, and Thomas Disch, and Hollywood movies such as the *Aliens* series, *The Fly*, *Ghost*, and *American Legacy*.[6]

It bears repeating that the people of Tono lived at the interface of hard fact and speculative fiction. The culmination of Murano's *The Legend of Sayo* in extraspatiotemporal sexual reproduction must therefore be taken literally as well as figuratively. Murano must have meditated deeply upon the transgressive nature of the text to have produced such a horrific effect of the catastrophe. Legend 55 from Yanagita's text, a rape narrative involving kappa—repulsive, frog-like humanoids with water-filled depressions in their skull—demonstrates this point: "Many *kappa* (ugly water creatures) live in rivers. There are especially large numbers in the Saru-ga-ishi River. In a household beside the river in Matsuzaki village women have become pregnant with kappas' children for up to two generations. When they are born, these children are hacked into pieces, put into small wine casks, and buried in the ground. They are grotesque" (41).

The figure of the kappa has been subject to varied interpretations, among which two tendencies are particularly relevant here. On one hand, structuralist anthropology has viewed the kappa as a typical manifestation of the trickster, reminiscent of the African American figure of the signifyin' monkey or Mark Twain's satanic mysterious stranger. In this respect, the Japanese folkloric figure of the kappa, with its commission of interspecies sexual assault, can readily be compared to the western mythological figure of Satan himself, the archetypal transgressor of the boundary between good and evil.

On the other hand, nativist ethnology reexamines the kappa as a figure both of the Japanese working-class "untouchables," who generally inhabit the riverside, and of aborted fetuses and unwanted newborn infants disposed of in streams and ponds to control the population.[7] It is undoubtedly this latter vision of kappa that inspired the novelist Ryunosuke Akutagawa, a great contemporary appreciator of Yanagita and his *Legends*, to write his pessimistic, satirical short story "Kappa" (1927), in which the birth of a kappa depends on the willingness of the kappa fetus to be born. Thus the marginal, subaltern, and vanishing character of the kappa unveils a hidden kinship with the elusive, mountain-dwelling Yamabito and to the Zashiki Warashi, childlike beings who haunt old, established households. Tono folklore, moreover, informs us that both kappa and Zashiki Warashi "bring prosperity and fortune with them when they decide to take up residence in a house, but they also take it with them when they leave."[8]

Undoubtedly, both interpretive tendencies discussed here inform the figure of the kappa to some extent, and thus the dual status of the kappa as a representation of both the living dead and the alien rapist offers a redefinition of the forbidden-love narrative of the kappa tale as a semiotic negotiation between the themes of interspecies adultery and extraspatiotemporal intercourse. The kappa's hidden agenda of radical otherness is embedded within the textuality of Murano's film.[9]

In short, whereas the nativist ethnologist Kunio Yanagita's *The Legends of Tono* attempted to recreate the uncanny other of western modernity in the heyday of the Japanese enlightenment of the early twentieth century, filmmaker Tetsutaro Murano, exposed in his early years to the products of Hollywood and the western logic of causality, tried to reorientalize not only the vanishing culture of Japan's Deep North, but also the deep structure of Hollywood cinema itself, and in so doing skillfully deconstructed the boundary between western mythology and Japanese folklore.

Hearn, Yanagita, Akutagawa: A Comparative Cultural Perspective

As one rigorously attempts to deconstruct the distinction between two cultures, one inevitably comes up against the truth that the notion of binary opposition has long been cherished and developed by the western ideology of modernization.

A similar dichotomy is present in the concept behind the campaign Discover Japan, which I discussed above. Certainly, the transition from the Discover Japan campaign of the 1970s to the Exotic Japan campaign of the 1980s coincided with Japan's transition from the period of high growth to that of hypercapitalism, which some have referred to as the Pax Japonica. It thus seems peculiarly Japanese. However, in *Discourses of the Vanishing* Marilyn Ivy reveals the Discover Japan campaign of the 1970s itself to have been an imitation of the Discover America campaign of the 1960s:

> Far from being an original slogan for a quest for origins, Discover Japan directly mirrored that of a national domestic campaign in the United States only three years earlier: Discover America. . . . Discover Japan is a perfect example of transnational flows of marketing techniques and advertising stratagems, signaling from its inception its place within an entirely global, advanced capitalist economy: Discover Japan and its insistence on the natively local presents the strongest evidence possible for the delocalization promoted by an American-led transnational capitalism. (42)

Ivy's argument here lets us see the Tono revival of the 1960s and 1970s as an effect of transnational capitalism rather than as a radical reaction against western modernization. Indeed, the extent to which the entire town of Tono in Iwate Prefecture has contributed to and capitalized upon its *Legends* industry is remarkable: visitors to the town are unavoidably presented with *Legends*-related sightseeing options ranging from one hour to full-day tours.

In any case, the film version of *Legends* can be seen as revolution-

Fig. 8 Lafcadio Hearn, a.k.a. Yakumo Koizumi, who helped establish Japanese nativist ethnology. Photo © Bon Koizumi.

ary, even metacultural, precisely because of its hybridization of the Japanese nostalgia for the vanishing and the American imperative for transnational capitalism, which enables its successful performance of allegories of hybridity. As translator Ronald Morse explains in his introduction to *Legends*, "Japanese folk religion as revealed in the legends" has been a hybridization of "the indigenous primitive religion with elements from Shinto, Buddhism, Taoism, *yin-yang* dualism, Confucianism, and other beliefs" (xxiii) from its beginning. Insofar as we live in a multicultural age, therefore, I would celebrate rather than denigrate this folkloric tradition as an example of cultural hybridization.

Moreover, the concept of Japanese nativist ethnology must be understood not as having arisen naturally, but rather as a product of hybridization, for one of the founding fathers of Japanese folklore studies—and a principle forerunner of Yanagita—was the Greek-Irish American Lafcadio Hearn, a.k.a. Yakumo Koizumi (1850–1904). Born on the Greek island of Lefkas and raised in Ireland, England, and France, Hearn emigrated to the United States in 1869; settled in

Cincinnati, Ohio, where he lived on a small allowance from his family; and came to Japan in 1890, where he became a naturalized citizen in 1896.

As Peter High explains in his canonical literary history *An Outline of American Literature*, Hearn did not simply translate stories: he transformed them into a new kind of literature. The Japanese—who know Hearn best by his Japanese name, Yakumo Koizumi—love him for doing this. Although he is not widely admired in the United States even now, Hearn has long captured the Japanese imagination.[10] Yet within the limited context of American literary history, Hearn must be understood as one of the first to bring the legends and tales of an unknown culture into American literature, along the lines of precursors such as Hans Christian Andersen and successors such as Paul Bowles. Hearn must also be credited with predicting the conflict between Japan and the West. In Japan, every schoolchild knows the ghost stories of Lafcadio Hearn/Yakumo Koizumi. Thus it was not a Japanese nationalist but rather a multinational author who established the Japanese sensibility for folklore, laying the groundwork for Kunio Yanagita.

The very origin of Japanese folklore discourse, therefore—which Yanagita believed to be antithetical and "antidotal" to modernization and westernization—turns out to be an effect of the western orientalism cherished by Lafcadio Hearn. It would be somewhat unfair to deprecate Hearn for his orientalist and colonialist reappropriation of Japanese folklore, for as the hybrid child of an Irish father and Greek mother, Hearn did not strive to westernize, but rather to deconstruct the critical difference between the Japanese Deep North and the American Deep South; that is, Hearn's literary orientation reflected an interest not in imperialist assimilation but rather in multicultural miscegenation, which he pursued in his own life through his pseudo-marriages to an African American woman in Cincinnati, Ohio, and later to a Japanese woman in Matsue, Shimane Prefecture, where he lived.

To consider the literary ramifications of this interest, let us briefly review the circumstances of Hearn's interracial relationship with the beautiful African American woman Alethea "Mattie" Foley. It is well established that while working as a newspaper reporter in Cincinnati, Ohio, in the 1870s, Hearn fell in love with Mattie, who worked as a cook in the cheap boarding house where Hearn lodged. The young lovers faced a serious obstacle in their relationship: mixed marriages were prohibited in Ohio at the time under strict antimiscegenation laws that were in effect between 1861 and 1877. Lafcadio and Mattie therefore had to keep their romance secret. Nonetheless, Hearn had the courage to renarrativize the exciting ghost stories he learned from Mattie, who had visionary powers of "ghost seeing" comparable to those Hearn reportedly possessed as a child.[11] What makes his romance with Mattie more interesting is that, although their de facto marriage came to an early end, Hearn moved to New Orleans in 1877 partly due to an interest in the supernatural discourses of African American voodoo culture that he gained from her. Both fascinated and repelled by voodoo magic and its remixing of elements of Catholic ritual, Hearn was especially impressed by his encounter in New Orleans with voodoo queen Marie (d. 1881), of whom Cott offers the following description: "admired and feared for her powers of healing and hexing as well as for her psychic and fortune-telling abilities, Voodoo Queen Marie became renowned as a kind of combination mambo-witch-shamaness, who was consulted by both blacks and whites," including Queen Victoria of England.[12] Hearn's African American voodoo connection expands our comprehension of his basic concept of ghosts; specifically, his attraction to the syncretic ghost culture of African Americans increased Hearn's sympathy for the premodern ghost culture of the Japanese.

Consider Hearn's most famous ghost story, "Hoichi the Earless" (1904). Hearn based this story on a historical account of the fall of the house of Heike that was transmitted to him orally by his wife, amanuensis, and greatest native informant, Setsu Koizumi; Hearn's renarrativization of this account is so brilliant it convinces the reader that the story was written by a native Japanese writer. In this story, Hoichi the blind *biwahoshi* (lute priest), whose profession is to recite historical narratives while accompanying himself on the four-stringed Japanese lute (*biwa*), is tormented mercilessly by ghosts from the massacred Heike clan. To protect him from these ghosts, another priest inscribes holy texts on Hoichi's skin. This other priest, however, fails to cover Hoichi's ears with the sacred writings, and the ghosts strip his ears away.

In view of Hearn's own physical impairment and subsequent sensory compensation — as a schoolboy, an accident left him permanently blind in the left eye, and as a result his auditory ability grew keener —

one cannot help but compare Hoichi the Earless, whose profession is to play music, to Hearn himself. This perspective allows a reinterpretation of the story as an allegory of the ghostly world beyond the senses, and of the conclusion of the story not as tragic but rather as a form of radical hypersensitivity. As a contemporary of Mark Twain and Thomas Edison, Hearn could well have believed in the magic of telegraphic instruments such as the telephone, invented by Alexander Graham Bell in 1876 as means not only of conquering distance, but also of enhancing the ordinary senses. The development of new technology does not necessarily enlighten people; it more often rationalizes the irrational and the supernatural, erasing the distance not only between countries but also between life and death, thus fusing our reality with cyberspace.

With these possibilities in mind, let us turn to a lecture on ghosts entitled "The Value of the Supernatural in Fiction," which Hearn delivered at Tokyo Imperial University in 1898. He summarizes the central thrust of his argument as follows:

> Everything that religion today calls divine, holy, miraculous, was sufficiently explained for the old Anglo-Saxons by the term ghostly. They spoke of a man's ghost, instead of speaking of his spirit or soul; and everything relating to religious knowledge they called ghostly. In the modern formula of the Catholic confession, which has remained almost unchanged for nearly two thousand years, you will find that the priest is always called a ghostly father—which means that his business is to take care of the ghosts or souls of men as a father does. . . . It [ghost] means everything relating to the supernatural. It means to the Christian even God himself, for the Giver of Life is always called in English Holy Ghost. . . . The terror of all great stories of the supernatural is really the terror of nightmare, projected into waking consciousness. And the beauty or tenderness of other ghost stories or fairy stories, or even of certain famous and delightful religious legends, is the tenderness and beauty of dreams of a happier kind, dreams inspired by love or hope or regret. But in all cases where the supernatural is well treated in literature, dream experience is the source of the treatment. . . . I believe that there can be no exception to these rules even in the literature of the Far East.[13]

In another passage in the same lecture, Lafcadio Hearn illustrates the points he discusses here with almost structuralist analyses of analogies between examples from the ghost stories of Bulwer-Lytton,

Lewis Carroll, and Edgar Allan Poe and examples from Chinese and Japanese literature.

Hence it is no surprise to discover that in most of his retellings of Japanese ghost stories, Hearn—enabled by his understanding of the structural kinship between Western literature and Asian folk tales—drew on his own experiences and visions as a child. In Hearn's short story "Mujina," for example, Hirakawa demonstrates that the woman whom the protagonist encounters—a woman with no eyes, nose, or mouth—is based on a girl named Jane whom Hearn disliked as a child.

In another of Hearn's stories, "Yuki-Onna," a supernatural femme fatale dressed in sheer white blows her freezing, smoke-like breath over human beings, killing them; this figure was apparently inspired by the Scandinavian legend of the night mara (the term "mara" reappears in the English word "nightmare"). Nonetheless, this tale struck to the depths of the Japanese imagination; without Hearn's image of this femme fatale in white, Yanagita could not have created the vivid character of Yama-uba, a mountain-dwelling she-demon who menaces the village folk in *Legends* (115–117).

Examples such as this are indicative of the gothic influence of Lafcadio Hearn on the Deep North gothic of Kunio Yanagita. Although Hearn was more of a literary storyteller than an authority on folklore, recent scholarship in comparative literature has attempted to redefine Hearn as Yanagita's precursor. Such scholarship has focused in particular Hearn's essay on the Japanese smile (included in *Glimpses of Unfamiliar Japan*) as inspiring Yanagita's *Warai-no-Hongan* (1946). In regard to the relationship of the two authors, however, I am more concerned with the similar oral and auditory aspects of Hearn and Yanagita as cultural mediums of the vanishing: just as Hearn listened to his native informant Setsu Koizumi's stories with intense care, Yanagita meticulously recorded the stories related to him by his native informant Kizen Sasaki. In this sense, both Hearn and Yanagita psychologically assumed the traditional role of *itako* (medium or shaman).

Now in the 2000s, of course, it is not difficult to identify colonialistic and imperialistic aspects in appropriations of native cultures such as those of Hearn and Yanagita; as Hearn has long been underestimated by American Japanologists, who have viewed him as an opportunist of the exotic, Yanagita has recently been attacked for his support of Japan's annexation of Korea at the time he was writing *Legends* (see Murai, *Nanto Ideorogii no Tanjo*). From a theoretical standpoint,

Hearn can be understood to have westernized Japanese folk tales from a Christian perspective, and Yanagita similarly to have renarrativized the folklore of Tono from a colonialist perspective. At the same time, however, Hearn's interest in Japanese polytheism must be understood as a result of his radical critique of Christianity and modernity, as well as perhaps his nostalgia for Greco-Roman mythology, and Yanagita's invention of a new form of polytheistic literature as the product of his antagonism toward Japanese modernization, as well as his antidote for it. Yanagita's Legends 84 and 85, in particular, effectively deconstruct the difference between western and Japanese culture by viewing even western Christians as a kind of other, or the Christian god as one of the many types of gods: "during the 1850s . . . there were many Westerners coming to live at places on the coast. . . . Christianity was practiced secretly, and in the Tono district there were believers who were crucified. . . . At Kashiwazaki in Tsuchibuchi village there is a household in which both parents are definitely Japanese, and yet there are two albino children" (*Legends*, 58–59).

Thus, working from opposite directions as cultural mediums of the minor, the marginal, the subaltern, the invisible, and the vanishing, Hearn and Yanagita strove to surpass the limits of western Christian modernity with their brilliant reconstructions of Japanese folklore. Their purpose, in short, was to foreground the ghostly as a representation of the other, and in my view, the aesthetics of their resulting renderings of the intersection of two world cultures are far more attractive as subjects of critical inquiry than the imperialist or colonialist politics of their reappropriations.

Let me conclude with a glance at the Japanese film *Kappa* (1994), which presents a perfect allegory of multicultural negotiation. Directed by Tatsuya Ishii—better known as rock-and-roller Karl Smoky Ishii—the film appears to be closely modeled on sources of traditional Japanese folklore including *Legends* and Akutagawa's short story "Kappa." However, Ishii tactically remixes the Japanese character of the kappa as a water monster with Spielbergian images of extraterrestrials. Whereas Hearn and Yanagita renarrativized Japanese folk tales of the other, Ishii successfully contrives an interface between already renarrativized traditional Japanese folklore and contemporary American urban legend, particularly that of sprawling suburbia. It is ironic that whereas a typical American entertainment like *Ghost* (1990) brings to mind *The Legend of Sayo*—a movie with a Japanesque look—Tatsuya

Ishii's *Kappa* conjures typical postmodern fairy tales such as *Close Encounters* or *E.T.*, which are themselves closely related to the Japanese fairy tale about Kaguyahime, the Moon Princess, who emerged from a bamboo stalk. Yet lacking this kind of representational irony, these movies would not ignite our multicultural, postcolonialist, and creatively anachronistic imagination.[14]

CHAPTER 5 Which Way to Coincidence? A Queer Reading of J. G. Ballard's *Crash*

I started reading science fiction in the late 1960s, when *Hayakawa's Science Fiction Magazine*, the one and only science fiction prozine in Japan, began featuring the Anglo-American New Wave regularly.[1] With the help of the distinguished translator-critic Norio Itoh, whose skillful translations include works of Arthur C. Clarke, J. G. Ballard, Brian Aldiss, Kurt Vonnegut Jr., Samuel R. Delany, James Tiptree Jr., Cordwainer Smith, and others, the Japanese SF community took New Wave so much to heart that writers such as Koichi Yamano and Yoshio Aramaki began to experiment seriously with Japanese speculative fiction, leading to a heated controversy around 1970 over the literary significance of science fiction. Later, in 1970 Yamano launched the heavily theoretical quarterly NW-SF (edited by Ms. Kazuko Yamada), which led to his becoming better known as a New Wave critic; his provocative essay "Nippon SF Sono Genten to Shiko" (Japanese SF, Its Originality and Orientation; 1969), a scathing attack on contemporary Japanese science fiction, was edited by Darko Suvin and reprinted in the March 1994 issue of *Science-Fiction Studies*. In the same period Aramaki incorporated Ballardian influences in early short stories such as "Yawarakai Tokei" (Soft Clocks; 1968–1971), his hard-scientific reinterpretation of Salvador Dali's surrealistic paintings, which was translated by Kazuko Behrens and stylized by one of the original cyberpunks Lewis Shiner and reprinted in the January–February 1989 issue of *Interzone*.

The greatest reappropriation in Japan of New Wave, however, can be seen in Yasutaka Tsutsui, the winner of numerous awards in both science fiction and the mainstream, whose masterpieces include a Ballardian surrealistic short story "Tatazumu Hito" (The Standing Woman), in which mammals morph into vegetables literally and figuratively. Tsutsui started his career as a science fiction writer in the mid-sixties, and gradually in the seventies came to transgress the generic boundaries between serious and popular literature by establishing his own theory of "hyperfictionality," which reflects back the nature of literary genres and foregrounds the fictionality they tried to repress; of these explorations he writes: "I do not find it accidental that in the 60s and the 70s, just as the postsurrealist mode nurtured British New Wave, North-American Metafiction, and Latin American Magic Realism, I was making every effort to develop my own theory of hyperfictionality though I had no knowledge of those western literary innovations" ("On My Fictional Theory").

Of course, I'm not sure if what was going on in the early seventies in the Japanese New Wave movement (or phenomenon?) made sense to junior-high SF fans, including me. The formation of a Japanese science fiction market in the sixties, ignited by the monthly publication of Hayakawa's *SFM* in December 1959, owes much to the golden age of Anglo-American hardcore science fiction; major Japanese science fiction writers constructed their careers by studying extrapolation and following the examples of Clarke, Asimov, Heinlein, Sheckley, Bester, Bradbury, and others. It meant that what the Anglo-American science fiction market experienced between the 1920s and the 1950s had to be studied and simulated by Japan only in the 1960s, too quickly and in too condensed a fashion. As is the case with all movements in the high-growth period, the Japanese writers also attempted to rapidly assimilate and catch up with the fruits of their Anglo-American precursors, skillfully appropriating them. Around 1970, thus, we did not feel it contradictory to be attracted by both the moon landing of Apollo 11 and the Ballardian renunciation of outer space: insofar as "outer space" signifies some aspect of Americanism, we Japanese shared with J. G. Ballard some ambivalent feeling toward the American frontier spirit in the space age. It is ironic that while we became fascinated with America by reading science fiction, it was through science fiction that we later found it necessary to criticize and defamiliarize the country. But, at that point, around 1970, younger SF addicts in Japan (including me) could not comprehend such a complex logic, but kept reading hardcore and New Wave simultaneously.

Either way, both the cult and the anticult of outer space constituted an Anglo-American cultural literacy that our own postwar occidentalism wanted to acquire. The early seventies did not allow us yet to anticipate the ascendancy of the Pax Japonica in the eighties, following the Pax Americana of the previous decades, when our postwar occidentalism comes to be replaced by cyberorientalism on the part of America.

Therefore, when the Tokyo-oriented publisher Atelier Peyotl asked me in 1990 to write an introduction to the Japanese edition of Ballard's *Crash*, it seemed impossible for me to complete the task without rethinking the relationship between the original publication of *Crash* in 1973 and what followed later. Indeed, when *Crash* appeared as the first of the Technoscape trilogy, it struck us as the deepest insight into the advent of technoerotics, which begins to encroach on the inner space Ballard had consistently explored. And yet, rereading the text from the nineties perspective invited me to recognize an otherwise unnoticed literary historical coincidence in 1973 between *Crash* and Thomas Pynchon's *Gravity's Rainbow*.

The year 1973 saw the end of the Vietnam War, soon followed by President Nixon's Watergate scandal. Disbelief, disillusionment, and disorientation dominated the political atmosphere of the early seventies, at the same time that we gradually became unable to live without the spectacles, pseudo-events, and even sexual effects produced by media technology, as theoreticians such as Daniel Boorstin and Guy Debord have explained lucidly. From this viewpoint, then, the coincidental literary "crash" mentioned above is highly symptomatic: Ballard—the British champion of New Wave—describes an idiosyncratic hero, Dr. Robert Vaughn, obsessed with committing double suicide with Elizabeth Taylor in a car crash, while Pynchon—the American representative of postmodern metafiction—describes an innocent protagonist, Tyron Slothrop, technosexually involved with the mechanics of the V2 rocket. The more we look into these texts, the more apparent their commonalties become, that is, their technosexual politics. In order to investigate the collision of technology and sexuality in the seventies, Ballard reorganized his initial nonlinear, condensed form of novel (*Atrocity Exhibition*; 1970) into the linear or crypto-nonlinear narrative *Crash*, while Pynchon completed the encyclopedic *Gravity's Rainbow*. It seems very natural that the technosexual zeitgeist of the seventies gave both writers deeper insight into innovative literary forms. Literary-historically speaking, it is this coincidence between Ballard and Pynchon in 1973 that later gave rise to the cyberpunk movement in the eighties.

In retrospect, however, it seems that not only cyberpunks but also Ballard himself felt it necessary to reconstruct the central topic of *Crash* in the eighties. Read twice his mainstream bestseller, *Empire of the Sun* (1984), which was published in the same year as William Gibson's canonical cyberpunk *Neuromancer*, and you will notice that this Booker prize nominee shares something with *Crash*.

First, consider some characteristics of Ballard's novels: both *Crash* and *Empire of the Sun* are distinctly autobiographical, for they share a main character called "James," modeled after the image of the author, James Graham Ballard.

Second, *Crash* deals with a scientist obsessed with heterosexual double suicide in a car crash, and *Empire of the Sun* depicts a boy obsessed with binational double suicide in a kamikaze crash: "The fliers fascinated Jim, far more than Private Kimura and his Kendo armor. . . . Above all, Jim admired the kamikaze pilots. . . . Neither Private Kimura nor the other guards in the camp paid the least attention to the suicide pilots, and Basie and the American seamen in E Block referred to them as 'hashi-crashies' or 'screw-siders.' . . . But Jim identified himself with these kamikaze pilots and was always moved by the threadbare ceremonies that took place beside the runway" (198–199). Furthermore, Jim's deep admiration for the bravery of kamikaze pilots makes him feel like "joining the Japanese Air Force" (216).

This episode carries us to my third point: that the analogy between car crash and kamikaze crash was already predicated in the text of *Crash*. The narrator, after relating his car crash experience, speculates on the disjunction between his "own body, the assumptions of skin, and the engineering structure which supported it," and recollects staring at the cockpit of a World War II Japanese Zero fighter airplane at the Imperial War Museum: "The blurring perspex of the cockpit canopy contained a small segment of the Pacific sky, the roar of aircraft warming up on a carrier deck thirty years before" (58).

Whenever we come across dead or incompetent pilots and astronauts in Ballard's fiction, we are tempted to take them as representing Ballard's anti-outer-space and anti-American sensibility. But, rereading *Crash* with *Empire of the Sun* will give us a chance to reconsider the status of dead pilots as not only ideological, in that sense, but also deeply erotic.

In Ballard's writings, we cannot distinguish between eros and thanatos very easily. What is more, Ballard's technosexual rhetoric is closely intertwined with his international politics. While the technosexual novel *Crash* already conceals a binational romance in the analogy it draws between car and kamikaze Zero fighter airplane, the quasi autobiography *Empire of the Sun* contains an imagined technosexual implication in the binational friendship between the British boy and the Japanese kamikaze he admires so much. This is why the boy Jim simulates double suicide, looking at the corpse of the kamikaze in question: "For so long he had invested all his hopes in this young pilot, in that futile dream that they would fly away together, leaving Langhua, Shanghai and the war forever behind him. He had needed the pilot to help him survive the war, this imaginary twin he had invented, a replica of himself whom he watched through the barbed wire. *If the Japanese was dead, part of himself had died*" (363, emphasis mine).

We have long been familiar with the postwar analogy between the United States as the "husband" and Japan as the "wife." The Pax Americana has long feminized Japan. Ballard gives the familiar analogy a new twist by setting up the hyperqueer viewpoint of a British boy who feels homosexual sympathy with a Japanese kamikaze, literally murdered or figuratively ravished by the American army. Thus, when Jim realizes that "if the Japanese was dead, part of himself had died," he must have felt that he had himself been ravished by Americans, who had already dropped the atomic bombs on Hiroshima and Nagasaki.

What complicates this catastrophe, however, is that this novel also implies that Jim will recover from the sense of loss sooner or later and start his life over. Certainly, Jim appreciates Japanese bravery, but he also enjoys being ravished by the stronger high-technology represented by the B-29: "the sight of this immense bomber with its high, curving tail convinced Jim that the Japanese had lost the war. . . . Jim thought intently about B-29s. He wanted to embrace their silver fuselages, caress the nacelles of their engines" (236). Jim's homosexually binational romance with brave Japanese kamikazes turns out to be intricately tangled with man's cybersexually fetishistic romance with sophisticated machines. Thus, if *Crash* is as international as *Empire of the Sun*, the latter is as technosexual as the former. They constitute a hidden diptych delineating our age, in which deeper investigation into multinational politics must involve a deeper speculation into technosexual rhetoric—or vice versa. This assumption will be further endorsed not only by cyberpunk (Gibson, Sterling, Cadigan) and technogothic (Calder, Park, Constantine) but also by Pynchon's fourth novel, *Vineland* (1990), which features contemporary cybersexual and multinational conflicts closely intermingled with supernatural martial arts and brainwashing technologies.

I have compared *Crash* with *Empire of the Sun* in detail, primarily because I have long cherished these texts, among others, and also because I vividly remember Ballard's message for the twenty-first Japanese National SF Convention (1982), in which he encouraged us to do "Pearl Harbor" in our imagination. This message was very complex, for it suggested both technosexual kamikaze and anti-American counterravishing at once—or self-effacement and imaginative creation at once.

Of course, given that Ballard's texts are full of American signs, ranging from Elizabeth Taylor, Ronald Reagan, and Elvis Presley to Ernest Hemingway, we have to be careful in characterizing Ballard's ambivalence toward the United States. For the time being, nonetheless, we may safely say that it is through a looking glass called Japan that Ballard feels more comfortable effacing himself and creating an interzone where his British body melds with his American fantasy technosexually and multinationally. This is where Ballard's own queer version of Americanism came into being, and where we Japanese readers feel greater sympathy for his fiction, though probably for other, ambivalent reasons: Ballard's Americanism makes us keenly aware that we Japanese have also ended up, unwittingly, with an imaginary hyperqueer version of Americanism, however hard we seem to have studied American culture.

In conclusion, let me also note that the year 1973 saw not only the coincidental publication of Ballard's *Crash* and Pynchon's *Gravity's Rainbow* but also the appearance of Kobo Abe's mainstream novel *Hako-Otoko* (The Box Man) and Sakyo Komatsu's hardcore science fiction *Japan Sinks*. In 1973, Ballard and Pynchon tried to speculate on the conflict between the United Kingdom/Europe and the United States, or between Americanism on the British-European side and occidentalism on the American side, while the Japanese authors, Abe and Komatsu, focused on the effacement of identity—individual in Abe's case and national in Komatsu's—promoting the then popular analogy between the Japanese and the Jew. For Japan to catch up with advanced countries and become more international, it seemed desirable in the early seventies to accept and redefine self-effacement and "diaspora" in the more positive sense. Looking backward, then, 1973 turns out to be the year when Anglo-American writers' discursive ravishing of Americanism coincided with Japanese writers' creative reappropriation of Jewishness, and ended up accelerating imaginary internationalism and protoglobalism. At this point, however, an eighteen-year-old high-school kid like me could not discern the technosexual and hyperqueer rhetoric deeply buried within international and proto-multinational politics in general.[2]

CHAPTER 6 A Manifesto for Gynoids: A Cyborg Feminist Reading of Richard Calder

From Androids to Gynoids

When I first encountered a certain young British author sometime during the first half of the 1990s, he was neither particularly well known nor firmly established. Nor was he uniformly accomplished, judging by the four tales he had published in *Interzone*. Yet I cannot forget the deeply moving experience of first reading "Mosquito"—the second story in his Automaton trilogy—informed as it was by the unique nanotech aesthetic that characterizes this writer's world.[1]

Indeed, the impression that I formed of this new talent, Richard Calder—whom *Interzone* subscribers, *Locus* reviewers, and notably, Bruce Sterling immediately recognized as one of the most promising new young British writers—was sufficiently powerful that I was moved to feature a detailed review of his works in my column in *Hayakawa's SFM* (May 1990), in which I also reviewed two other new writers, Susan Beetlestone and Matthew Dickens. Fortunately, the publisher, Treville—a member of the Seibu Zaibatsuary—also became interested enough in Calder to publish the entire Automaton trilogy in book form in November 1991. The publication of the trilogy—which preceded Calder's first novel, *Dead Girls* (1992), and which would expand upon the underlying concept of "Mosquito," as discussed below—thus represents the author's first published book. Various artists, including PVC fashion designers, Tokyo's best drag queens, and house music DJs, quickly embraced Calder, and Treville subsequently published *The Gynoids*, a collection of hyperreal illustrations by Hajime Sorayama based upon Calder's world.

Fig. 9 A hyper-realistic gynoid from Mamoru Oshii's movie *Innocence*. © 2004 Shirow Masamune/KODANSHA·IG, ITNDDTD.

Richard Calder thus came to prominence with great rapidity in Japan. Speculating on this phenomenon, I have to assume that a certain eagerness had been latent in the Japanese political unconscious, a longing for a breakthrough in cyberpunk, which had been avidly consumed as a representative sign of the times. This yearning for a breakthrough focused on Calder, and although he is undeniably an inspiring and inventive writer, it is intriguing to ask why.

The Automaton Trilogy: "Toxine," "Mosquito," and "The Lilim"

The basic concepts of nanotech fantasy that inform the Automaton trilogy are straightforward, though Calder casts them in idiosyncratic form in each of the stories, from "Toxine" to "The Lilim." One might also consider a subsequent Calder story, "The Allure," along with the trilogy—although it is not part of it—since it offers a similar artificial-life-style take on Thomas Carlyle's *Sartor Resartus*, or even Barrington Bayley's *The Garments of Caean*.

It is true that in "Toxine" Calder appears to be engaged in little more than a rereading of gothic romance in terms of postmodern technology; the motifs of high-tech robots, men in love with androids, and the eventual crisis of human identity deployed in "Toxine" are not uncommon in science fiction. This is not to argue that "Toxine" lacks originality, but rather that as far as this first work is concerned, Calder is comparable to "slipstream" writers such as Peter Ackroyd and Steven Millhauser, who are distinguished by their dark romanticism and—to borrow Bruce Sterling's term—"this-is-not-SF,-but-it-sure-ain't-mainstream-and-I-think-you-might-like-it,-okay?" stylistics ("Slipstream," 78). But Calder's particular fusion of science fiction and surrealism in "Toxine" is most indebted to Angela Carter.

In the second tale of the trilogy, "Mosquito," Calder however does something that only he can do—though most readers will at first misread the text as typically cyberpunkish. That is, if you are a reader of John Varley, James Tiptree Jr., William Gibson, or Octavia Butler, the story's intercultural conspiracy ethos, hyperorientalist setting, and transsexual narratology may seem familiar to you—may even strike you as postmodern clichés. Yet a warning against approaching this story as a typical cyberpunk fiction is in order, as a closer look at the story's opening will reveal.

Let us consider the first scene of the story, which is set in Thailand at the Café Gung-Ho, where the native she-male heroine/hero Mosquito is introduced by his/her American colleague Harry to a British man, Mr. James, who is to be called "Milord." Though Mosquito is in male guise when she/he meets Milord, she/he is to fall in love with him *too passionately*. However, Milord is in Thailand—Calder is himself a resident of Nongkhai, a border town between Thailand and Laos—for the specific purposes of acquiring a "doll," a high-quality, sex-specific android, which he plans to smuggle to London, capital of a declining empire.

The scene is strangely reminiscent of the opening of *Neuromancer*, and may sound typically cyberpunkish, but if I understood the textuality correctly, Calder doubly perverts the cyberpunk gimmickry he employs, intentionally disfiguring the idiom in order to open up a new approach for the science fiction avant-garde. A word about the context here: the rise of slipstream literature in the 1980s put science fiction in danger of having its avant-garde status appropriated. Framing this double perversion by defining its unique setting is Calder's ambitious style, which is informed by the mysterious but definitely science-fictional status of the narrator. "Isn't 'he' simply gay?" the reader wonders. Most will, in fact, suppose upon reading the opening of the story that Mosquito is gay; yet the sexual indeterminacy of this narrator will nonetheless leave many readers uncomfortable to a certain extent. Nevertheless, as the story progresses, it is gradually disclosed that the cyborg operation that produced Mosquito's sexual ambiguity is informed by what might be termed a "counter-orientalist" politics that contrasts sharply with the orientalism expressed by the stereotypical Asian caricatures of canonical cyberpunk literature. Indeed, Calder's world might best be described by the term "cyborg feminism," to borrow Donna Haraway's term.

To understand how this term applies to Calder, consider how the cult drama *M. Butterfly*, by the Chinese-American playwright Henry David Hwang, contrasts with the cult movie *Blade Runner*: whereas the appearance of the film coincided with the rise of the cyberpunk movement, the play—first shown on Broadway in 1986—seems more consistent with the theoretical development of cyborg feminism, given its plot of a female-impersonating Chinese spy deceiving a male French diplomat by posing over an extended period as his heterosexual lover.

Haraway's cyborg feminism is also related to such terms as "biofeminism" and "primatological feminism," but note that Haraway's conception of orientalism encompasses not only western discourses that dominate the East, but *any* form of discourse employed for the domination of others—other races, other species, other classes, and in particular other *gender(s)*.

Haraway deconstructs such discourse through a consideration of the development of advanced miniaturization technology. If nanotech becomes universally available, she seems to suggest, all binary-hierarchical oppositions between the organic and the mechanical—in particular, between man and machine—will disappear. That is to say, the greatest potentiality of nanotech, or descending to the next level, picotech, is its power to undermine the myriad ideologies of domination.

Returning to *M. Butterfly*, there is no doubt that the play—though not necessarily science fiction (as may be said of any work of slipstream literature)—is rendered possible by Hwang's attunement to the hypertech/postmodern/deconstructive state of contemporary reality. Hence, his apparently gay appropriation of Puccini's classic opera *Madama Butterfly* reflects not simply sexual decomposition, but in fact a general situation in which everything becomes disfigured. From this perspective, Calder's story "Mosquito" emerges as a kind of "Nanotech Butterfly."

Such a reading leads us to consider an assumption we make when confronting the man/machine relationship, which is that we tend to metaphoricize it in terms of familiar stereotypes of the relations of gender (e.g., male domination of women), class (e.g., elite domination of workers), and race (e.g., European domination of Asians). In its extreme exaggeration of *Madama Butterfly*, Hwang's *M. Butterfly* offers a related metaphorics, that as the ideal woman resides only in the mind of man, so the discourse of the dominator, in the Foucauldian sense, produces the ideal image of the dominated.

Yet "Mosquito," in contrast, depicts a significantly perverted situation, in which the roles of the dominator and the dominated are interchangeable, articulating a limitless chain of displacement: the relationship between man and machine (doll) is displaced by the relationship between master (Milord) and slave (handmaid); by the relationship between Asian and European; and most obviously, by the relationship between male and female. It is the mind of Milord that produces the ideal slave in the form of a nanotech robot, but it is Mosquito who decides to retain "a flow of testosterone" in his veins after his transsexual surgery, reasoning that "only a man could imitate a doll. Women, it was said, were too real. For dolls are not women; they are man's dream of women" (6). Ideal women are the product of men's dreams, and dolls are imitations not of women but of that product; Mosquito is thus eager to imitate not woman but rather her imitation.

At this point, it bears noting the "dolls" in the story are also called "gynoids"—an ingenious coinage originally deployed by Gwyneth Jones, which probably alludes to the rise of gynocriticism and/or "gynesis," discourses developed by Elaine Showalter and Alice Jardine to promote the rewriting of male-dominated history. It parallels the etymology of "android": the term is essentially a catachresis for (hu)man-thing.[2]

Thus Calder's dolls are doubly imitative: they are imitative primarily of men's dreams, and secondarily of androids. Moreover, Mosquito in particular can be read as triply imitative, that is, triply disfigurative. Yet what matters most here is that the gynoids signify the essence of representation. In terms of gender, class, and race, every discourse must be produced as an imitation of an imitation (of an imitation?); thus most of the images presented in media coverage of the Gulf War, for example, were imitations of images of the Vietnam War, which were themselves imitations of images from Hollywood war movies. It is no accident that the 1960s songs used in the soundtrack of the imitation Vietnam movie *Apocalypse Now* constituted much of the music that U.S. soldiers listened to in the Gulf. Calder's recognition of our postsimulation culture is evident in his counter-orientalism, particularly in his representation of counter-domination, in Haraway's sense.

In short, Calder's metaphorics inaugurate a radical departure into the postcyberpunk fiction of cyborg feminism. While cyberpunk coincided with the rise of Derridean–de Manian hypersemiotics/deconstructive criticism, Calder's counter-orientalism corresponds with Foucauldian-Harawayan cyborg feminism/new historicism.

This correspondence deepens in the third story of the Automaton trilogy, "The Lilim." Much as Mosquito outwits and finally murders Milord, the nanotech robot heroine Titania of "The Lilim"—who seems to have jumped into the story straight from the pages of Lewis Carroll's *Alice* books, or perhaps from George MacDonald's *Lilith*—is so jealous of the reproductive ability of human females that she effectively counterrapes the boy narrator: "Titania was robbing me of my human future. But she gave, too. In her saliva, ten billion microrobots—her software clones—coursed into my blood and lymph like a school of mermaids. Ten billion little Titanias swam through me, passing through my urethra, seminal ducts, and into my chromosomes with blueprints for dead girls—my Titania, queen of the fay; my children would be her children."

This counterrape, enacting Calder's counter-orientalism, thus disfigures the very humanity of human history. Much as macroscale robots afford a rethinking of human identity, and as Calder's gynoids in general decanonize the history of androids, Titania—foregrounding the potentiality of man-machine intercourse—reconstitutes the history of the man/machine interface. Thus the tribe of the heroine, the "Lilim" of the story's title, are named after the daughter of Lilith, Adam's first wife in the apocryphal narrative of Creation. And thus do the effects of nanotech vampirism, in an amplification of post-AIDS fear, play the role in Calder's fiction of an ethnic weapon that infects the blood of the gynoids. Bear in mind, however, that history itself has always been produced as an imitation of an imitation, an archaeology of virtual realities.

Dead Girls: Toward the Poetics of Nanospace

On encountering the term "nanofash" for the first time in the title of an essay by David Borcherding in the magazine *bOING-bOING*, now a Web site, I initially mistook the article for a review of Calder's first novel, *Dead Girls*. Borcherding begins his article with a description of nanotech couture: "Tomorrow we will get out of bed and instead of staring at a closet full of clothes, we'll sit down at a terminal and bring up our selection of outfits on the screen. . . . While we shower and eat breakfast, the microscopic robots in our CyberCloset will be creating our selected outfit. . . . No need for undershirts or deodorants; the Drexites (named for their creator, K. Eric Drexler) will keep us dry and odor-free" (8).

Unfortunately, Borcherding's short essay does not address the cutting edge of nanotech paraliterature, but his coinages, including "CyberCloset," "the Drexites," and "nanofash" itself, nonetheless strike one as a veritable user's guide to Calderian gadgetry, as well as a humorous pastiche of his texts.

For Calder is in essence a post-cyberpunk Pygmalion, and "nanofash" captures well the collision between nanotech and the artifices of desire effected in his pathbreaking science fiction. To summarize the progression of Calder's Automaton trilogy discussed above, "Toxine," set in the late twentieth century, can be understood as a typical gynoid story; "Mosquito," set in 2030, comprises a narrative of high-tech transsexual thievery; and "The Lilim," set in 2055, amounts to a report on the doll plague to come. As I have mentioned, I had the pleasure of helping facilitate the emergence of these stories in Japan—along with Calder's story "The Allure," also mentioned above in brief—which culminated in their publication as a collection that was received with enthusiasm both by science fiction and mainstream audiences, including one of the most acclaimed feminist slipstreamers Yoriko Shono. It was thus with great interest that I opened an advance copy of Calder's first novel, *Dead Girls*, in the spring of 1991. I devoured the novel in a couple of days; it completely knocked me out.

Essentially an expanded version of "The Lilim," *Dead Girls* is set in the post-Pax Sovietica world of 2071. The story centers around a pair of Romeo-and-Juliet-like young lovers: Ignatz Zwakh, a human boy of Slovakian descent; and Primavera Bobinski, a Polish nanotech doll who is one of the Lilim, that is, the tribe of self-replicating robots. The story opens in London, where a number of Russian intellectuals have settled as refugees. At the time, Londoners increasingly fear the Lilim, whom they blame for igniting the AIDS-like "doll plague": as in "Toxine," discussed above, the Lilim reproduce through a kind of vampirism, infecting people's blood with the nanotech equivalent of their own genetic material, such that those infected thereafter bear only cyborgian children, literal chimeras of human beings and robots.

Under the leadership of a Russian ultra-eugenicist, Vladimir Constantinescu, the Nazi-like Human Front party is coming increasingly to power in England, and to escape this party's increasingly violent efforts to repress the plague-carrying dolls, Ignatz and Primavera flee to Bangkok.

In Bangkok, Ignatz and Primavera seek help from one Madame Kito, a matriarchal pornocrat (Mama-san) who runs a brothel of gynoids with names like Cartier, Seiko, Gucci, and Swatch. These names suggest the aptness of the term "nanofash" as a description of Calder's gadgets; the dolls—who "step from their vacuum sealed boxes promising to fulfill the most baroque desires" (12)—are consumed by "doll junkies" not simply as a sort of drug or AIDS-like virus, but also as a kind of luxury accessory.

What complicates the story, however, is that the femme fatale Primavera has been infected by the Human Front with another disease, another high-tech nanobot weapon called Magic Dust. This weapon disorganizes the fractal programming of the nanotech dolls by insinuating radically incompatible Euclidean programming into their inner matrices.

How can she get repaired? The nanoengineer Spalanzani unveils a possible means. According to Spalanzani, only Dr. Toxicophorous, the inventor of the Lilim-type dolls, is capable of healing Primavera. The only means of consulting Toxicophorous, however, is to conjure him up from deep within the unconscious of the robots he has invented, where his personality is imprinted. Moreover, Primavera's disease advances to the point of causing a small monsoon that swallows up everyone around her, drawing them into her belly, that is, the inner space of the doll.

From this point in the story onward, Calder offers fantastic prose detailing the dream matrix of the machine unconscious, as in the following passage: "Rising from Lumpini Park, and floodlit, St. Paul's cathedral shone majestically above the rooftops of Bangkok. Big Ben leaned over us from the next street, surrounded by *chedi* and *prang*, and the searchlights of the interdiction described their familiar arcs from across the Chao Phaya river. The Big Weird had suddenly got bigger. Weirder" (132–133).

The characters inside Primavera, now "oneironauts," thus travel an uncanny dreamscape in search of the doll's "event horizon" (153). In contrast to Gibsonian cyberspace, which was constructed between outer space and inner space, the Calderian nanospace is situated in a magic loop between quantum robotics and gynoidal cosmology.

Here note that the logic of this magic permeates the plot of *Dead Girls*. In creating the nanotech dolls, Dr. Toxicophorous imprinted their machine consciousness not only with his ideal of femininity but also—in an act of radical self-fashioning—with himself, a self deeply informed by the bizarre Slavic folklores that Russian intellectual immigrants brought with them to London. However, it is the matriarchal nanotech robots that recreate, multiply, and reappropriate the patriarchal figure of the doctor, with the tribal aim of achieving cosmic triumph for the gynoids. Hence, behind the magic loop of avant-garde robotics and postfeminist cosmology, one discovers a greater magic loop in the very relationship of Toxicophorous and the tribe of the Lilim. The thrilling, never ending, and at times even comical multiplications of magic loop structures in Calder's narrative are ultimately the chief attractions of *Dead Girls*.

From Calder's earlier tales, one might well conclude that Calder is at heart a typically dead serious and highly intensive aesthetician, and accordingly one might wonder in approaching *Dead Girls* if Calder would be able to sustain his intensity for an entire novel-length fiction. The splendid narrative of *Dead Girls* lays such concerns to rest, and moreover frequently reflects a brilliant sense of humor that one does not encounter in his short stories. It is a vein of black humor that runs through this dark romance, and though it is beyond my purposes here to illuminate the comic aspect of *Dead Girls* in detail, let me cite one of the funniest, most ironic, and most philosophical passages of the novel, from the penultimate chapter "Desperadoes" (chapter 12), in which Mosquito addresses Ignatz, Primavera, and Madame Kito: "We measured our self-worth against the consumerism of the West. Our gods were brand names. Our ideology I-shop-therefore-I-am" (186–187). This passage immediately brings to mind Thomas Pynchon's refiguration of God as Hacker in *Vineland* (1990), as well as Bret Easton Ellis's brat pack ideology of "I-shop-therefore-I-murder" in *American Psycho* (1991), and indeed Calder is comparable to these American contemporaries.

Yet in sharp contrast to most Anglo-American writers, Calder has carefully retained a critical distance from western postindustrial capitalism by expatriating himself to Thailand; a consideration of this distance affords insight into the discursive status of "gynoid" (etymologically, a female variant of "android," as noted above), as Calder employs the term. Specifically, the author first encountered the notion of the gynoid in Gwyneth Jones's novel *Divine Endurance* (1984), and was sufficiently inspired by her version of the gadgets to reappropriate them for the representation of his own counter-orientalistic and counter-anthropomorphic take on postmodernity.

In conventional western mainstream science fiction discourses, nanotechnology promises to bring marvelous economic and ecological benefits; for insight into Calder's stance on this promise, let us return for a final look at Borcherding's essay "Nanofash," in which he writes, "Our nanofashions will be better for the environment. . . . Nanotechnology requires only nanoenergy. . . . Never again will we have to face a closet full of outdated styles. . . . Our closets will be our disk drives, full of outfits that will fit us perfectly, every time" (9).

In view of the general tenor of *bOING-bOING* (the issue in which "Nanofash" appears also contains a nasty attack on orthodox ecology entitled "New Facts on Saving Our Environment" by LMNOP [33]), Borcherding's apparent admiration for "nanofash" can be read as a highly ironic comment on nanotech culture per se. Borcherding concludes the essay with the statement that "the future of Nanofash is as varied as our imagination" (9), which echoes the stereotypical discourse of mainstream environmental activism so strongly that one supposes Borcherding wrote his article with a keen awareness of this rhetoric. And as Borcherding employs the term "nanofash" to discuss nanotechnology ironically, so too may Calder characterize his nanotech dolls as mocking nanotechnology: ultimately, the gynoids will at once aestheticize and devastate human society, reconstructing it into a *luxurious dystopia*, the most contradictory but romantic empire that humanity has ever seen. The oxymoronic character of such a society, finally, is profoundly true to the nature of Calder's novel, for in the end, *Dead Girls* is a brilliantly written nanofash comedy with an attraction as fatal as that of the gynoids it describes.

PART 3 Aesthetics

CHAPTER 7 Semiotic Ghost Stories: The Japanese Reflection of Mirrorshades

Coincidence

Bruce Sterling seemed to be teasing me when he concluded his ArmadilloCon introduction of William Gibson with the following remark: "Today, while Tokyo fandom speculates feverishly over his blood type, we Texans can brag, without fear of contradiction, that we know our Guest of Honor well."[1] Indeed, chatting with Bill after interviewing him at Disclave 86,[2] I happened to ask him about his blood type, not so much out of my own curiosity but because it's a postmodern Japanese convention to ask this sort of question as a part of a formal exchange in greeting new acquaintances. I expected that Bill's familiarity with Japanese culture had made him aware already of the many blood-type books that were long-term bestsellers in our country, just like Tarot cards, astrology books, or the Bible. Bill, however, was deeply astonished, almost shocked, at my question and subsequent explanation—an astonishment that astonished me as well as others. At any rate, this is how Bruce came to mention Tokyo fandom's interests in Bill's blood type. Let me, then, apologize to Tokyo fandom, my good old village, for representing it by myself—or, more accurately, being forced to represent it—although I do not doubt that in my high-tech hometown people have actually asked the question more often than not: "What is William Gibson's blood type?" (Tokyo is high-tech, since it is semiotic—or, better, semiotech.)

We arrive at the starting point, dear Bruce. If Japan is now taken for the sign of high-tech, and if most Japanese now take for granted blood-type interpretation as semiotic pleasure (remember Sigmund Freud's *The Interpretation of Dreams*), why should we not enjoy reading Bill Gibson's blood type as his "semiotic ghost" (to use a Gibsonian term) without having seen him in person, just as Bill himself enjoys the signifier of the Japanese-language "Chiba City" or "Gomi no Sensei," for example—as its semiotic ghost (remember Roland Barthes's *The Empire of Signs*) without ever having visited Japan itself? My intent here is not to defend my country's recent trend, nor to compare the Japanese sense of high-tech with the American sense of it, but merely to point out the coincidence just noted between Bill Gibson's reading of the "Japanesque" and our reading of the Gibsonian. It is difficult to decide if Bill's way of reading has always already been Japanesque, or if our way of reading has always already been Gibsonian. All we can say is that in this very coincidence resides the secret of imagination that has long characterized science fiction: something is going on somewhere, at the same time that a similar thing is going on in other places. And it is a historical imperative that makes possible such a coincidence.

NASFiC Shock

To be honest, I had not read *Neuromancer* (1984), though I was familiar with *Schismatrix* (1985), when I attended NASFiC (North American SF Convention) in Austin, Texas, in the summer of 1985, and the first cyberpunk panel, which perhaps appropriately ended in punkish violence. It was coincidental that I selected that panel to attend rather than any of the others, since I was totally ignorant of the term "cyberpunk." I merely wanted to see Bruce Sterling, on whatever panel; Sterling was already one of my favorite writers, and three of his short stories ("Swarm" [1982], "Spider Rose" [1982], and "Spook" [1983] collected in *Crystal Express*) had at that point been translated into Japanese to great popular acclaim. What I discovered about cyberpunk as a movement, then, introduced me to William Gibson, whose style drove me crazy; and the excitement then ignited by John Shirley reminded me of an old essay by Gene van Troyer (1978), in which the author described a controversial (and violent) confrontation between Shirley and Harlan Ellison. Something was already going on in the late 1970s: the Shirley-Ellison controversy told us that John was destined to be the father of punk SF or the John the Baptist of cyberpunk, not the youngest son of the last New Wave.

Reading *Neuromancer* just after NASFiC helped me make sense of all these fragments and encouraged me to write an article about that panel and the movement in *Hayakawa's SFM* (1986). My essay was immediately followed by Yoshio Kobayashi's detailed overview of cyberpunk writers (1986). Since then, we two have promoted cyberpunk in our respective columns in that magazine ("SF Graffiti in the U.S.A" and "Overseas Science Fiction").

Neuromancer Translated: Otherwise

It may be equally revealing and significant, however, that the Japanese translation of William Gibson, whether deliberately or accidentally, came to repeat the structure of multicultural coincidence. The Japanese translation of *Neuromancer* by Hisashi Kuroma appeared in July 1985. Despite the almost two-year time lag, this novel has been more fortunate than Samuel Delany's cult novel *The Einstein Intersection* (1967), which was translated in Japan in 1997. *Neuromancer* was translated more quickly than most Anglo-American novels. And the more influential cyberpunk becomes, the shorter the translation time: thus *Mona Lisa Overdrive*, which Gibson published in October 1988, appeared in Japanese in February 1989. This is the primary point. The Japanese acceleration of translation was itself made possible by the effect of the cyberpunklike development of a global communication system—a system that endorses the synchronic nature of cyberpunk.

Next, let me point out that Kuroma's translations are aptly distinguished by his frequent and adventurous juxtapositions of Chinese characters and the Japanese alphabet for cyberspatial terms. Frequently, Japanese readers are required to read two kinds of representations of one word simultaneously. Such a technique is employed according to a Japanese typographical convention called "ruby," which enables us to print smaller "kana" (in *Neuromancer*'s case, mainly "katakana," characters devised to represent loan words) alongside Chinese characters. The Japanese character set gives phonogramic representations of words, while Chinese characters are ideogramic. For instance, "cyberspace" written in Chinese characters is pronounced "denno-kukan," whereas if written in the Japanese alphabet it is pronounced "cyberspace" (saibaa-supeesu). The convention of "ruby" forces us to read both Chinese characters and the Japanese alphabet at the same time. Thus, Kuroma's stylistics foregrounded the coincidence between the Anglo-American within the oriental (the Japanese alphabet) and the oriental within the Anglo-American (Chinese characters)—a process that is consistent with *Neuromancer* thematics.

Of course, Kuroma's translation gave rise to great disputes, dividing its audience into extremes. Some reviewers denounced his methods, complaining about its "too frequent use of ruby" (Kurei) or its "unreadability, which might seem fashionable to other readers" (Nakajima). Others praised the translation, commenting on the linguistic advantage of Japanese (Hamamoto). According to Norio Itoh (1986), the one-time Karel Award–winning translator and critic: "If you are under the age of 25, you may easily visualize the world translated in this style" (*Asahi Shinbun* [Asahi newspaper] September 7, 1986). Therefore, just as the original *Neuromancer* induced Gardner Dozois to call its innovative style "cyberpunk," so the Japanese version gave birth to the controversy about its innovative style, inciting the editor of the Japanese edition to call it an "A-bomb translation." If Rudy Rucker's definition in 1985 of cyberpunk's style as being "harder, faster, greater, and louder" still hits the point, Kuroma's translation successfully repeated the effect of the style by challenging the limits of the Japanese language.

"Cyberspace" = 電脳空間 (サイバースペース)

Chinese characters (= Dennou-kuukan) alongside Japanese alphabets/ruby (= Saibaa-supeesu)

The topic of translation style is, of course, only part of the Japanese reception of *Neuromancer*. With regard to its narrative structure, Japanese reviewers have given mostly the same range of comments as Anglo-American reviewers did: "The first half is exciting, while the latter half gets boring" (Fukumoto); "This work lacks the conceptual games that have marked science fiction" (Suikyoshi); "Seemingly up-to-date, actually old-fashioned" (Kagami). One of the best ways to read *Neuromancer* might be as "a novel of the very 'present' " with regard to its thematics (Takahashi), and as the pioneer work of cyberpunk.

Semiotic Ghostwriters

The Japanese translation of *Neuromancer* not only imported the idea of cyberpunk, but also helped publicize various simultaneous happenings that had remained unnoticed in Japan. For instance, audiovisual creators such as junk artist Seiko Mikami and playwright Norimizu Ameya began asserting that they had always been doing the same thing as Gibson, as did film director Sogo Ishii, who in the late 1980s had a collaboration in progress with William Gibson. From 1987 through 1988, cyberpunk reached the peak of its popularity in Japan, attracting numerous articles and discussions in magazines and journals outside the "proper" field of SF, exactly as it was doing in the United States. In the spring of 1988 Gibson's and Sterling's respective visits to Japan further promoted the excitement, nicely coinciding with the publication of the Japanese versions of *Schismatrix* and *Mirrorshades*, translated by Takashi Ogawa, "the Tokyo liaison of cyberpunk." A variety of conventions and seminars were devoted to this brand-new subgenre. The imported term "cyberpunk" caught the eye of so many people that it rapidly transgressed the boundaries of any generic categories and came to refer to anything having to do with dead-tech environment, hypermedia activity, and outlaw technologists. It was, like cyberpunk itself, a semiotic ghost.

In the field of science fiction in Japan, cyberpunk coincided with the activities of a younger generation of writers. The first half of the 1980s saw the rise of the third generation of native Japanese SF writers, mainly people in their mid-twenties, and the major Japanese SF magazines began devoting more and more pages to their new works. It is this generation that produced certain talents analogous to cyberpunks, best represented by Mariko Ohara, who developed her own style, modeled chiefly on one of cyberpunk's precursors, Cordwainer Smith. I remember talking to Bruce Sterling in 1986 about O'Hara's unwittingly cyberpunklike short story "Mental Female" (1986), in which a Tokyo mother computer and north Siberian father computer appear on TV as a girl and a boy, Ms. Kipple and Mr. Techie, who fall in love with each other and, as foreplay, begin playing catch—a foreplay that launches missiles from both sides. The important thing to note is that the author had written this before Kuroma's translation of *Neuromancer* was published.

Furthermore, the year 1987 saw the debut of Goro Masaki, a young writer who deserves the title of the first hardcore Japanese cyberpunk writer. He claims to have read one of the major precyberpunk stories—James Tiptree Jr.'s "The Girl Who Was Plugged In" (1973)—more than thirty times, both in English and in translation. Masaki's contest-winning "Evil Eyes" vividly describes the conflict between a mind software company and a new religious organization, culminating in the revelation that Maria, a fully armored woman working for the company, and Mugen, the charismatic head of the religious organization, were both products of a multiple personality, who had been born a disfigured baby. Although Masaki denies the Gibsonian influence, pointing out the difference between his emphasis upon humanity and Gibson's lack of morality, it is also true that his best readers are probably deeply sympathetic to cyberpunk poetics. This new talent should thus be construed not as a child but as a brother of cyberpunk, because he shares so many things with Gibson and others. Masaki's works, then, help to prove another coincidence between our two countries.

What, then, is transpiring in the exportation of Japanese works? If the above discussion suggests the coincidences between American cyberpunk, Japanese translation, and Japanese cyberpunk, the question immediately arises about the problem of English translations of Japanese science fiction. Indeed, great effort has been made with regard to Japanese-English translation. American residents in Japan, including David Lewis (a.k.a. Dana Lewis), Edward Lipsett, and Gene Van Troyer, have translated Yasutaka Tsutsui, Kazumasa Hirai, Taku Mayumura, and Tetsu Yano respectively. But what matters most in terms of cyberpunk is that in recent years there has been an increasing number of American writers and editors who have noticed cultural coincidences between the two countries and have become more interested in translating Japanese fiction. For instance, my friend Kazuko Behrens, now living in San Francisco, has translated Yoshio Aramaki's protocyberpunk tale "Soft Clocks" (1968–1971), which was stylized and finally sold to the British science fiction periodical *Interzone* by Lewis Shiner, one of the original cyberpunks.

In the wake of cyberpunk, the acceleration of translation, like the effect of the postsimulation society, takes place on both sides of the Pacific. To be more precise, it is not that the acceleration of translation effaces the time lag, but that the act of translation, insofar as it usually retrofits the past as synchronic with the present, has always been synonymous with the effacement of time lag. In other words, the logic of coincidence assumes that the text precedes translation, at the same time that translation precedes the text. In the case of *Neuromancer*, it is safe to say that the translator Kuroma did a word-by-word *transplantation* of the text, while rediscovering what had already been as cyberpunk as any thing in the semiotics of a Japanese frame of reference. If "translation" is another name for "misperception," the post-cyberpunk age can be seen to have realized that perception and misperception take place at the same time. Gibson's Chiba City may have sprung from his misperception of Japan, but it was this misperception that encouraged Japanese readers to correctly perceive the nature of postmodernist Japan. In short, the moment we perceive cyberpunk stories that misperceive Japan, we are already perceived correctly by cyberpunk.[3]

Coda

Thus, near the conclusion of this chapter, we may be reminded, once again, of the postmodernist paradox that the perceiver literally becomes the perceived, just as the junk artist immediately becomes the raw material of junk art. What cyberpunks seem to consume is not merely Japan, but their own science fiction projected in the future called Japan, while what the Japanese audience seems to consume is not merely American SF of the 1980s, but their own image synchronic with cyberpunk. As soon as we feel like metaphorizing something, we are literally identified with that object. As I suggested earlier, cyberpunk prohibits us from metaphorizing AIDS (or Chernobyl), because we live in the times when these panics may be rapidly followed by a literal coincidence of biological and high-tech territories. This is precisely why cyberpunk is sometimes called postmetafiction. Whereas metafictionists are involved with metaphorization of fiction as such, cyberpunks are so conscious of the totally computerized reality around themselves that they take for granted the decomposition of boundaries between the literal and the metaphorical, trying to repress any easy act of metaphorization. Cyberpunks perceive the "semiotic ghosts" of the present-day Far East; meanwhile, they are misperceived as the "ghost-writers" of our future.[4]

CHAPTER 8 Junk Art City, or How Gibson Meets Thomasson in *Virtual Light*

No city can exist without bridges. Now in the twenty-first century we feel more and more attracted by the meditations on bridges nurtured by Anglo-American literary history; Thornton Wilder's *The Bridge of San Luis Rey* (1927), Hart Crane's "The Bridge" (1930), Iain Banks's *The Bridge* (1986), Terry Bisson's *Talking Man* (1986), and even Robert James Waller's megahit *The Bridges of Madison County* (1992). But I have never seen a more brilliant construction of a bridge than William Gibson's fourth solo novel, *Virtual Light*, which beautifully envisions the near-future, hyperrealistic, and junk-artistic atmosphere on the postearthquake San Francisco Bay Bridge in a fictional 2005, around when California itself has split into two states—SoCal and NoCal. A huge earthquake, "the Little Grande," has closed the Bay Bridge linking San Francisco and Oakland to traffic, letting ex-hippies and former homeless storm the bridge and build themselves a new self-governing community in that space. This new tribe—called "bridge people"—radically redesigns the whole bridge, whose Dadaistic archaeology is named "Thomasson" by Yamazaki, the Japanese sociologist from Osaka University doing research on the formation of the bridge culture.

As is usually the case with Gibson, it must have been through his own private transactions with Japanese subcultures that he picked up the otherwise incomprehensible term "Thomasson," promoted by Genpei Akasegawa to signify a phase of the Japanese neo-Dadaistic movement that he championed from the 1960s through the 1990s. Whereas Gibson once appropriated the American Dada-surrealist Joseph Cornell's enclosed, box-like structures (in his second novel *Count*

Zero [1986]), in *Virtual Light*, he attempts to bridge the distance not only between city and suburb, city and islands, but also between reality and unreality, occidentalism and orientalism, San Francisco and Tokyo.

The bridge culture depicted in the novel represented its informational traffic as well as its informational distortion, fusing the real with the unreal. We should therefore interpret high-tech and dead-tech cultures in *Virtual Light* from the hyper-civil-aesthetic perspective, with multicultural semiotic ghosts in mind.

Catcher in the City

Gibson describes the near-future Bay Bridge as the ultimate utopia of the homeless, partly reminiscent of the actual history of the Golden Gate Bridge in the mid-1980s, when a number of homeless moved in as squatters while a heated controversy was going on over the closing of the nearby U.S. army base. And yet, unlike actual history, Gibson's Bay Bridge takeover abruptly becomes well known all over the world and attracts many international sightseers eager to see its junk-artistic atmosphere. It is especially lyrical and humorous that the members of this idiosyncratic community lead their life in containers and trailer houses hanging from the cables of the bridge, supported financially by multinational corporations, which provide them with not only food and medicines but also advanced adhesives.

The plot itself is a variation of the Holy Grail quest. The main protagonists are all in search of the virtual light "sunglass" (VL) that the courier Bricks has brought with him to San Francisco. VL is unique, since it does not make use of photons but connects directly to the optic nerve. Even if you don't have eyes—as long as your optic nerve is intact—when you wear glasses made of VL sunglass you can see virtually not just the scene around you but also vivid, simulated scenes from the past, including top secrets of civil engineering—all of which VL makes available thanks to its extraordinary capacity for data sampling. VL was anticipated by Bob Shaw's masterpiece "Light of Other Days" (1966) and its expanded version *Other Days, Other Eyes* (1972), in which the author invents an exhilarating high-tech device, "slow glass," through which light takes years to travel, thus making it possible for us to view scenes from the past. Gibson's "virtual light sunglass," therefore, is undoubtedly the updated version of Shaw's "slow glass."

One night at a party, Bricks's VL sunglasses are stolen from him by

Chevette, a bike messenger and an inhabitant of the bridge. She has committed the theft out of pique, quite ignorant of the information that the sunglasses contain; she was just annoyed by something Bricks had told her. And yet, when the theft is followed by the mysterious murder of Bricks himself, we have to suspect Chevette is a murderer as well as a thief: she is in fact chased by unofficial associates of the big corporations, in particular by Berry Rydell, a rent-a-cop hired by the American Vietnamese Lucius Warbaby of IntenSecure. We are then introduced to the true criminal, Loverace, who is responsible for the murder of Bricks, and the true identity of Lucius is revealed: he is a double agent, who wants to repudiate the civil engineering plan detailed and concealed within VL.

Gibson's basic concept has survived the passage of time: the greatest currency is information, and the greatest information is the medium through which information is conveyed. We must also admit, however, that this novel gives priority to junkyard over cyberspace, bike messenger over cyber-cowboy. Despite the high-tech title, what *Virtual Light* achieves in the long run is not so much an admiration of VL technology as a deeply ironical attitude toward the relationship between streamline technophilia symbolized by cityscape and junk-artistic Ludditism represented by bridgescape.

From Cyber-Cowboy to Bike Messenger

For us to speculate upon the contemporary significance of bridge culture it is helpful to start by examining the textual history of *Virtual Light*.

The outline of the novel first took shape when William Gibson accepted Paolo Polledri's offer to participate in the exhibition Visionary San Francisco held in 1989 at San Francisco Museum of Modern Art, to which he contributed a short story, "Skinner's Room," based on the idea of bridge culture that he had devised with Ming Fung and Craig Hodgetts. It hardly matters that the author had not been born in San Francisco or grown up there. For San Francisco has not just a physical geography on the west coast of the United States; it also has a psychogeography applicable to the American sixties in general.

Historically speaking, the city of San Francisco started developing in the mid-nineteenth century, around the year of the gold rush (1849), in defiance of its topography and distance from other cities. Since then it has come to represent a twentieth-century capital, a "Paris of

Fig. 10 San Francisco Bay Bridge taken over and deconstructed by the homeless. Illustration of scene from William Gibson's "Skinner's Room" (Paolo Polledri, *Visionary San Francisco*), now incorporated into his novel *Virtual Light*. Drawing © Craig Hodgetts and Ming Fung, photograph by Ben Blackwell.

the West,"[1] and, especially during the sixties, the capital of all flower children. As Kevin Starr has said, while Boston signifies Puritanism, New York finance and taste, Atlanta and Omaha railroads, and Los Angeles show business, San Francisco represents urbanism as such. "San Francisco has always been dreaming of itself and calling these dreams into being."[2] Put another way, San Francisco is at work as the self-referential metaphor of city itself. This explains how Gibson came to be attracted by the civil-aesthetic potentialities of San Francisco, and to write the short story in question, in which Skinner, the leader of the first generation of bridge people, became the first man to climb the towers of the fallen bridge, singing endlessly in the rain and building his "room" finally atop one of the cable towers.

It took Gibson three years to expand the short story into a novel. He seems to have taken much time reorganizing the role of the girl taking care of Skinner in the short-story version, calling her Chevette in the novel and featuring her as the heroine. To clarify the alluring contrast between high-tech and low-tech cultures in the text, the author must have felt it necessary to foreground Chevette and the San Francisco subculture of bike messengers to which she belongs.

Of course, the job of bike messenger is not itself new; it has developed rapidly in recent decades. Especially in a steep-hilled city such as San Francisco, bike messengers are preferred to car couriers or fax machines, since the heaviest traffic jam won't prevent them from carrying a spot commodity or top secret papers from one point to another. San Francisco requires bike messengers to flourish, so you can always meet bike messengers in a bar called Zeitgeist on Friday near Haight-Ashbury. Gibson himself comments on the significance of bike messenger culture: "I'm inclined to believe what somebody says in the book about why there are still bicycle-messengers. I think there'll always be people needed to physically carry information around, mainly for security reasons."[3]

Since 1981 when he published one of his first stories, "Johnny Mnemonic," Gibson has been obsessed with the role of the courier who carries information around without knowing what it is; all Johnny does is not to know but carry. As Poe's detective skillfully resolves the mystery just by understanding the signifier of the purloined letter, not what it signified, so Gibson's courier brilliantly achieves his or her purpose merely by safeguarding the container of secret information, not the content. Gibson's signifier mania, thus, makes the low-tech job of bike messenger perfectly match the junk-artistic culture of bridgescape. What is more, from its beginning cyberpunk literature has consistently been involved with the paradoxical relationship between high-tech and lo-tech cultures, as we find in Gibson's Cyberspace trilogy as well as in his early short story "The Winter Market" (1985). Without the ultrafunctionalism of the cyberspace cowboy, the hyperaesthetics of lo-tech junk-artistic Luddites would not have been possible, and vice versa. We cannot separate these two paradigms so easily, but must find their logics very closely intertwined. This is why bike messengers such as Chevette hold the same status as cyber-cowboys or computer hackers in general, who are not marginal but crucial to the high-tech cityscape.

Gibson, Süskind, Akasegawa

Gibson's phantasmagoric description of bridge culture seems essentially nostalgic, recalling not only a psychedelic bridge in Brighton, England, but also a classy arcade on a bridge in eighteenth-century Paris, as detailed in the novel *Perfume* (1985) by the German writer Patrick Süskind. Let us compare two passages, the first by Süskind and the second by Gibson:

> The bridge was so crammed with four-story buildings that you could not glimpse the river when crossing it and instead imagined yourself on a perfectly normal street—-and a very elegant one at that. Indeed, the Pont-au-Change was considered *one of the finest business addresses* in the city. The

> most renowned shops were to be found here; here were the goldsmiths, the cabinetmakers, the best wigmakers and pursemakers, the manufacturers of the finest lingerie and stockings, the picture framers, the merchants for riding boots, the embroiderers of epaulets, the molders of golden buttons, and the bankers. And here as well stood the business and residence of the perfumer and glover Giuseppe Baldini. (53, emphasis mine)

> Its steel bones, its stranded tendons, were lost within an accretion of dreams: tattoo parlors, gaming arcades, dimly lit stalls stacked with decaying magazines, sellers of fireworks, of cut bait, betting shops, sushi bars, unlicensed pawnbrokers, herbalists, barbers, bars. *Dreams of commerce*, their locations generally corresponding with the decks that had once carried vehicular traffic; while above them, rising to the very peaks of the cable towers, lifted the intricately suspended barrio, with its unnumbered population and its zones of more private fantasy. (62–63, emphasis mine)

While Süskind rediscovers "one of the finest business addresses" of Paris on the eighteenth-century Pont-au-Change (see Isherwood, *Farce and Fantasy*), Gibson reimagines "dreams of commerce" on the defunct twenty-first-century San Francisco Bay Bridge.[4] What intrigues me here is not the possible influence of one writer on another, but the literary coincidence between the two postmodern writers, Süskind and Gibson, both of whom seem to have experimented with the recuperation of the medieval function of bridges. As the history of London Bridge shows, the medieval bridge was constructed not so much as a means of transportation, but as an invisible city where a variety of information gets transacted very rapidly. According to William Zuk, writing on the old London Bridge constructed between 1176 and 1209: "Numerous shops and dwellings were superimposed in makeshift fashion on the bridge and piers, making the bridge almost a city in itself" (*Encyclopedia Americana* 1:525). The discourse of bridge as a means of transportation was established after the Industrial Revolution, that is, only two centuries ago. Gibson's text further emphasizes the medievalistic character of the bridge by making bridge people as well as virtual reality people the victims of witch hunts, and by having the Elvis-like martyr Shapely, AIDS saint, assassinated by fundamentalists. This medievalization of the near future is another perfect example of Gibsonian junk-artistic decontextualization.

Since his sensational debut, Gibson has continued to develop and reorganize the portrait of a junk artist in our cyberpunk age, from Gomi no Sensei (Master of Junk) in "The Winter Market," the Joseph

Cornellian AI in *Count Zero*, and the Mark Paulinian machine art factory in *Mona Lisa Overdrive*, to the steam-driven computer collaging textual and historical fragments of *The Difference Engine*. To Gibson, junk art uncovers the invisible unconscious of the cyber-cityscape. But what seems most intriguing about the junk art bridge in *Virtual Light* is that here the author seems to decontextualize the very notion of western junk art. Indeed, a close examination of the Gibsonian bridge culture, with the self-multiplying dwellings out there, will remind us primarily of the post sixties and hippie tradition of the tree house. Skinner's room, especially—located atop one of the cable towers, a "caulked box of ten-ply fir, perched and humming in the wind" ("Skinner's Room," 155)—is undoubtedly a descendent of that domed wooden tree house constructed by Ian Christoph and Matt Darrieu and inspired by Buckminster Fuller's geodesic dome; supported by cables, "their tree house seems to float in the air like some unearthly cocoon or spaceship."[5] But, simultaneously the junk art bridge absorbed not only the heritage of the post–flower power renaissance culture but also the impact of the Japanese neo-Dadaist art form "Thomasson," as its guru Genpei Akasegawa called it. Let us take a glance again at *Virtual Light*, at what is recorded in the notebook of Yamazaki, the young researcher from Osaka University who is interviewing Skinner:

> Thomasson was an American baseball player, very handsome, very powerful. He went to the Yomiuri Giants in 1982, for a large sum of money. Then it was discovered that he could not hit the ball. The writer Gempei [*sic*] Akasegawa appropriated his name to describe certain useless and inexplicable monuments, pointless yet curiously artlike features of the urban landscape. But the term has subsequently taken on other shades of meaning. If you wish, I can access and translate today's definitions in our *Gendai Yogo no Kisochishiki*, that is, *The Basic Knowledge of Modern Times*. (64–65)

The Genpei Akasegawa mentioned in the story is not an imaginary figure created by the author, but a real person, born in 1937 in Yokohama, and well known in Japan as a neo-Dadaist and mainstream writer. What matters here is that while Euro-American Dadaism, however avant-garde it was, presupposed a work of art designed by an individual genius in the conventional sense, Japanese neo-Dadaism radically displaces the conventional notion of "work of art," completed teleologically by an individual artist, with the revolutionary idea of a "hyperart Thomasson," that is, the mostly junk-art-like junk objects scattered all over a cityscape, which become an alternative "art" by being discovered and authorized as "art" by ordinary passersby, not necessarily artists. Thomasson, then, transgresses not only the boundary between junk and junk art, but also the difference between self-claimed Dada artists and potentially Dadaistic but generally anonymous city dwellers. It is interesting that Akasegawa radically reevaluated or, most comically, "Japanized," from the eighties perspective, Marcel Duchamp as the near-precursor of Thomasson who "could not attain Thomassonian perfection, unluckily," but whose sense of "non-art" brilliantly "corresponded with the Japanese heritage of tea ceremony represented by Sen-no-Rikyu," in which the very natural world has consistently been considered full of "ready-made" objects.[6]

Gibson gets easy access to a database of postmodern Japanese vocabulary through his wife, Deborah, who has long taught English to Japanese business people in Vancouver, so it is no surprise that he was able to pick up information about the great Japanese neo-Dadaist somehow and somewhere. Gibson shifted his focus of junk art from Joseph Cornell and Mark Pauline to Genpei Akasegawa, in the process disclosing an aspect of the paradigm shift that took place between the heyday of the bubble economy in the 1980s and the peak of restructuring/reengineering in the 1990s. Most recently, Gibson seems to have appropriated the avant-pop aesthetics of Japanese art, as well as the ultrapragmatic ethics of Japanese high-tech industry.

How San Francisco Meets Tokyo

Such a background gives the hardboiled plot of *Virtual Light* a new twist. For instance, take a look at Yamazaki, who had made up his mind to conduct research on the post–Little Grande San Francisco, hoping to get good information for rebuilding Tokyo, which had been destroyed by another massive earthquake, called Godzilla. Yamazaki seems thoughtful, especially when he speculates in his notebook on the semiotic difference between Little Grande and Godzilla:

> When the Little Grande came, it was not Godzilla. Indeed, there is no precisely equivalent myth in this place and culture (though this is perhaps not equally true of Los Angeles). The Bomb, so long awaited, is gone. In its place came these plagues, the slowest of cataclysms. But when Godzilla came at last to Tokyo, we were foundering in denial and profound despair. In all truth, we welcomed the most appalling destruction. Sens-

ing, even as we mourned our dead, that we were again presented with the most astonishing of opportunities. (126)

What Gibson unveils here is not so much a racist perspective as a deeper insight into the mental history of the postwar Japanese, characterized by concepts such as creative defeat and creative masochism,[7] which powerfully and ironically promoted Japanese hypercapitalism. It is ironic that the harder Yamazaki studies the art in the reengineering of San Francisco, the more aware he becomes of the traditional "art" structured by the Japanese "Thomassonian" mentality.

The self-reflexive aesthetic of Yamazaki coincides beautifully with the self-recycling ethics of West Coast ecologists. For it is not only Yamazaki's socioanthropological gaze but also the top secret conspiracy available for view with VL that wants to Japanize and "Thomassonize" San Francisco, following the example of the post-Godzilla Tokyo. "They'll start by layering a grid of seventeen complexes into the existing infrastructure. . . . Completely self-sufficient. Variable-pitch parabolic reflectors, steam-generators. New buildings, man; they'll eat their own sewage" (251). Thus the novel ends up envisioning a Tokyoized San Francisco, a self-sufficient and self-recycling city.

At this point, let us take a closer look at the narrative structure of *Virtual Light*. On the surface, the author seems to have juxtaposed the Holy Grail quest and the bridge culture narrative at random. A close reading of the text, however, reveals the interactive and interdeconstructive relationship between the technological principle of city and the junk-artistic principle of bridge. The self-recycling logic of Thomassonianism naturally jeopardizes the distinctions between technopolis and junkyard, city and bridge, the homeless and the Thomassonians. The Gibsonian vision of the postinformation city features a self-sufficient society, in which Japanese neo-Dadaistic art and American hypertechnology do not contradict but recycle each other.

In his *Hyper-Art Thomasson*, Genpei Akasegawa stated: "Insofar as we inhabit cities, inflicted with our own consciousness, we could witness the 'Hyper-Art Thomasson' looming between cityscape and innerscape every now and then" (11). The entity of city and the ghost of city cannot be distinguished semantically, only recycled semiotically. This logic will be endorsed by Kevin Lynch's book *Wasting Away*, in which junk and information are not incompatible but intertwined very closely; the act of wasting away and reengineering has been and

Fig. 11 Once opened, Agrippa self-effaces its text. Cover of William Gibson's *Agrippa*. © William Gibson and Dennis Ashbaugh.

will remain essential to the growth of the information city. This is why Gibson dreams of reconstruction in the Thomassonian utopia.

Ready-made Book, Self-Reflexive City

Back in the 1960s John Barth started recycling the literary heritage in his self-reflexive metafiction, promoting his theory of "the literature of exhaustion." Now, in the post-eighties, William Gibson, a representative flower child, wants to sketch a self-reflexive and self-recycling cyberscape in which even self-reflexive metafiction is always already involved.

This is why I am particularly impressed by the final sequence of *Virtual Light*, where Yamazaki descends "in the yellow lift to do business with the dealers in artifacts," tries to sell in vain "a damp-swollen copy of *The Columbia Literary History of the United States*, and ends up leaving it "atop a mound of trash" (321). Since *The Columbia Literary History* (published in 1988) features Gibson's *Neuromancer* and the advent of cyberpunk in a chapter called "The Fictions of the Present," written by Larry McCaffery, the final chapter of Gibson's book seems to work, in the primary sense, as a self-referential device typical of metafiction, by which the author criticizes ironically even the literary historical discourse of cyberpunk.[8] By the same token, however, we should also note that the scene of Yamazaki's failed bid to sell the history highlights the copy of *The Columbia Literary History* as another ready-made and Thomassonian object. Unlike what preceded *Virtual Light*, the self-effacing art book *Agrippa* that he created with Dennis Ashbaugh in 1992, Gibson's self-reflexive text illuminates back the Thomassonian self-reflexive city aesthetics, part of which the very text constitutes.[9] While Kevin Starr once defined San Francisco as a self-reflexive metaphor of city, now William Gibson redefines it as a self-reflexive metaphor of the self-reflexive city itself. No other postmodern novel describes the self-recycling and self-reviving magic of cityscape more vividly.

CHAPTER 9 Pax Exotica: A New Exoticist Perspective on Audrey, Anna-chan, and *Idoru*

Enter Eurudice: Toward the Poetics of Avant-Pornocracy

There is no doubt that literary texts have represented the most critical negotiations between sexuality and nationality.[1] For instance, Bill Clinton was the first president in history who "openly campaigned for the civil rights of gay men and lesbians."[2] Clinton won the 1992 presidential election, strongly supported by the homosexual community, 95 percent of which voted for him—providing more than his margin of victory. If an American president is the greatest fictionist, and if it is not so much his politics as his poetics that helps structure the American popular unconscious, it is logical that up until the 1980s Clinton appealed to neither traditional macho patriarchy nor radical feminist matriarchy, but by the 1990s he was appealing to the "pornocracy" of that period. Clinton's presidency undoubtedly foregrounded the theoretical industry of queer theory, which has revolutionized existing approaches to literary texts, reappropriating deconstruction, new historicism, and postcolonialism. Something that I have found most amusing, however, is a new exoticist "queer" reading of the Clinton presidency, performed by a brilliantly talented multicultural writer, rather than any avant-garde literary critics.

Enter Eurudice, a postfeminist Greek American writer. I will illustrate what is the most innovative politicosexual poetics of the nineties with her reading of Clinton's presidency as avant-porn, that is, as avant-garde pornography. In her 1995 article "Why Clinton's Foreign Policy Shows He Is Good in Bed," Eurudice's basic point is that although President Clinton's insecure and uninspired foreign policy had gradually damaged his reputation as a "World Leader," it is just such a lack of patriarchal leadership that powerfully demonstrates that "Clinton is a better lover than any President in recent U.S. history." To Eurudice it seems that if the world were the bed, few past presidents has ever "cared about their partner's orgasm." But, Clinton is exceptional, for he is the one and only president who "delays his own climax to coincide with his mates." In short, Eurudice regards Clinton's foreign policy not as an opportunistic political failure but as a sexually promising experiment.

> Clinton is in no danger of creating future genocides, because he doesn't force the will of an elitist antiseptic Washington masculinity, via army or money or seduction, on to the objects of his desire. He doesn't like to choose, knowing that in our world the criteria shifts too fast to freeze it down to a prefab staid policy. Instead, he gets chosen. And we chose him because he looked sweet, sensual and lovable in the world of power hungry self-controlled politicians whom none of us could trust. . . . Like a tantric monk, he desires the very moment he is desired, the very thing that desires him. . . . What is most interesting about the tantric religion, of course, is that its prevalent form of worship is sex. (15)

Eurudice's analysis is quite unique, since this Greek-American Japanophilic postfeminist avant-pornographer not only feminizes Clinton as compared with past macho presidents, but also orientalizes him as a tantric monk, for whom sex is the most religious prayer. Now the United States is neither an innocent girl nor a macho husband nor a lustful slave master—just a queer, transvestite world lover. In the wake of queer theory, which is perfectly coincident with Clinton's nonpolitical politics, it became necessary for all of us to reconstrue nationality as deeply intertwined with sexuality, thereby reinterpreting the discourse of sexuality as shedding light on the multiethnic unconscious of the United States. In the wake of the Clinton–Monica Lewinski scandal in 1998, and in the heyday of President George W. Bush's ultramacho politics—a politics whose recuperation came in response to the 9/11 terrorist attack—Eurudice's critical insight is gaining more and more significance.

Indeed, we have already developed a number of literary critical approaches to this topic. But, if we want to further investigate the possibility of American literary history in the twenty-first century, it will be more convenient to single out the one particular literary tendency that has become increasingly conspicuous lately. While the 1980s saw the international expansion of the magic realist literary mode in the wake of postcolonialist literary criticism, the mid-1990s began to see the explosive negotiation between orientalism and occidentalism, in which it became more difficult to distinguish between one's ethnic gaze and one's sexual gaze.

Now we feel obliged to reconsider the significance of exoticism once again. Something exotic seems fascinating and disgusting at once. Someone exotic arouses one's desire to colonize and the desire to be disciplined simultaneously. Without this ironic discourse of exoticism, however, the United States could have developed neither its own literature nor its own literary history. As we have already seen, racist and colonialist discourses have been nurtured by the double logic of exoticism, that is, the fascination and hatred of the other. And very recently, as if repeating the fin-de-siècle scenario of Japonism and the yellow peril which I discussed in chapter 1, the Pax Japonica very naturally gave birth to the discursive chimera of Japanophobia and Japanophilia, in the context of what I would like to designate "new exoticism." I'm not sure if this will be part of the mainstream literature of the coming century. But, unlike the pseudoorientalist fiction very pervasive in the 1980s, which was full of such stereotypes as Fujiyama-geisha-sushi-harakiri, new exoticist fiction seems to plunge precisely into the semiotic intersection between cultural understanding and misunderstanding, which I believe will constitute part of American literary history to come. Let me illustrate this point with three texts published in the last decade of the century in the United States: Michael Keezing's "Anna-chan of Green Gables," Alan Brown's *Audrey Hepburn's Neck*, and William Gibson's *Idoru*.

New Exoticism Case A: Michael Keezing, "Anna-chan of Green Gables"

In his thirties (he was born in 1964), Michael Keezing was studying with Robert Coover in the Graduate Creative Writing Program at Brown University. When I read the manuscript of this short story, an avant-porn take on Lucy Maud Montgomery's famous novel *Anne of Green Gables* (1908), I found its subversiveness was sufficient to deconstruct the existing canon of American literary history from the new exoticist perspective.[3]

Basically, this is a family romance about a Japanese salaryman, Masao, his wife, Mariko, and their daughter, Anna-chan. The underlying concept is easy to spot in the daughter's nickname "Anna-chan": in Japanese, the suffix "chan" can be added to a name as a term of endearment. Like many postwar Japanese women, Mariko is deeply attracted by Anne of Green Gables as an aesthetic and moral ideal—so deeply attached that she has attempted to imitate Anne Shirley's lifestyle and style the interior of her house in the fashion of Green Gables, dreaming of studying one day at Holland College on Prince Edward Island, like Anne. Masao, who feels the deepest affection for Mariko, wants to let her achieve her goal. So, when their daughter Anna-chan turns eleven years old—the same age that the orphan Anne Shirley gets adopted by the Kusparts—Masao and his family make their pilgrimage to Avonlea on Prince Edward Island and stay there for a short while. When they return to Japan, however, Mariko's fanatic obsession with Anne Shirley grows to such a point that the family moves to Prince Edward Island permanently. Masao becomes a shameless money-grubber, who does not hesitate to make a profit, with the help of his Yakuza cousin, on producing and selling porn videos loosely modeled on *Anne of Green Gables*.

The project proves successful, making his family very wealthy. And yet, the more money he makes, the more ambitious Mariko becomes to replicate the entire house of Green Gables, perfectly furnished in the original Victorian fashion. That is to say, Masao's income cannot accommodate Mariko's expenditures forever. To resolve this dilemma Masao has to make the content of his videos more sensational, more subversive, and more marketable. One day, Masao decides to hire his daughter Anna-chan, who has turned sixteen years old at that point, as the heroine for one of the forthcoming videos, *Anne's Humiliation*. It becomes a hit, immediately outstripping even *Anne of Pink Gables*, his previous bestseller. Masao's cousin's associates will forgive his debt and advance funds for the next Anne production. And yet, life is always ironic. Now that Anna-chan has become a star, capable of producing a huge amount of money, she takes on this job as her own calling, just as Anne Shirley eventually finds her own way of life. Anna-chan therefore refuses to stay on Prince Edward Island and goes back home to Japan, moving into the hardcore adult video mainstream. The final paragraph of the short story reads as follows: "In the end I could not refuse her. Indeed, what other prospects did either of us have? Anna-chan was a young woman now, full of her own dreams, eager to follow her own path, just as Mariko and I had followed the tortuous path which led us to Green Gables. If Anna-chan's path followed back in the direction from which ours had come, who was I to stand in her way? It was, at last, just another bend in the road" (128).

Of course, this short story could well offend a number of avid readers of *Anne of Green Gables*, leading them to accuse the author of blasphemy. But, by the same token, we should not ignore the fact that "Anna-chan of Green Gables" is designed as the most serious tribute to *Anne of Green Gables*, and that the protagonist Masao simply wanted to satisfy his wife Mariko's deepest desire for the world that Lucy Maud Montgomery created in her novel. Therefore, however blasphemous the ending of Keezing's story seems, it is none other than the most serious outcome of the author's speculation on *Anne of Green Gables* from the hypercapitalist perspective.

What is more, this Japanese family's pilgrimage to Prince Edward Island reminds us of pilgrimages made to the very fictional grave of Charlotte Temple, the heroine of Susanna Rowson's 1794 novel *Charlotte Temple*. Just as readers in the republican era flocked to the place designated as the site of Charlotte's grave and signaled their cultural participation in the novel by leaving there tokens of themselves—bouquets of flowers, locks of hair, and the ashes of love letters[4]—Japanese women readers of Lucy Maud Montgomery's novel are conditioned to visit Prince Edward Island and simulate Anne's narrative completely. While the development of republican print culture promoted revolutionary heroines such as Charlotte Temple and thus helped constitute a particular kind of American femininity, the expansion of postwar multimedia dispersed such human pseudo-events as Anne Shirley all over the world and ended up reconstructing Japanese femininity.

Why, however, is Anne Shirley so popular in Japan? Finding the analogy between Japan and Avonlea, especially in terms of islander mentality, patriarchal society, and the ordeal of the entrance examination, scholars have assumed that it is the figure of Anne Shirley surviving in an ultratraditional society and establishing her own identity that must have enchanted postwar Japanese women.[5] Since Michael

Keezing lived in Japan for three years in the early nineties and married a Japanese woman who provided him with the details of the cult of Anne Shirley in Japan, he seems to have understood this aspect of Japanese sensibility very correctly. What makes "Anna-chan of Green Gables" highly exotic is not only its avant-porn slapstick style but also its multinationalist reconstruction of femininity in the age of hyperspectacle.

New Exoticism Case B: Alan Brown's *Audrey Hepburn's Neck*

It is coincidental that the year 1996 saw the publication of another Japanophilic fiction, *Audrey Hepburn's Neck*, written by a New Yorker, Alan Brown, who was born in 1950 and who lived in Japan almost for seven years, between the late eighties and the early nineties, teaching English and doing research on Japanese culture. While Michael Keezing's story took up as its central topic the cult of Anne of Green Gables among postwar Japanese women, Alan Brown starts with the cult of Audrey Hepburn among postwar Japanese men.

The protagonist is a twenty-two-year-old comic book illustrator, Toshiyuki (Toshi) Okamoto, now working in Tokyo. Growing up in a small town on Hokkaido, the northernmost island in Japan, Toshi has been fascinated by all things American, especially western women, ever since his mother took him to see *Roman Holiday* (1953) for his ninth birthday, an experience that left him spellbound by the beautifully exotic neck of Audrey Hepburn. Since then, Toshi has had a few foreign girlfriends, but nothing has prepared him for Jane Borden, the American woman teaching his intermediate English conversation class at the Very Romantic English Academy in Shibuya, who strikes up an acquaintance that ripens alarmingly into sadomasochistic sex. And it will turn out that in a kind of mirror image of Toshi's adoration of Audrey Hepburn, Jane has been attracted by Japanese men, ever since she saw, at the age of fifteen, the beautiful thighs of Toshiro Mifune in Kurosawa's movie *Rashomon* (1950). Toshi's increasing hesitation in the relationship accelerates Jane's neurotic tendencies. She goes as far as saying that she's "going to cut the skin off Toshi's thighs and line her coat with it, so she can feel [him] against her always" (150). Toshi's affair with Jane ends only when she stuffs a burning newspaper into his mail slot; the bizarrely obsessive English teacher has became a pyromaniac. After this debacle, Toshi makes friends with a homosexual American named Paul, who falls in love with Japanese boys because he saw a picture of Yukio Mishima in a loincloth when he was sixteen. But their friendship does not involve sexual relations, and later in the story Toshi finds another American girlfriend, Lucy, who looks exactly like Audrey Hepburn.

What makes the plot more suspenseful is that while Toshi is involved with love affairs in Tokyo, something serious happens to his parents back in Hokkaido. His parents divorce and immediately afterward, his father dies. This tragedy prompts Toshi's mother to confess that she has concealed the secret of her own true identity. Born a Korean, named Kim Chun-Ja, she came to know Toshi's father while working as a military prostitute for the Japanese army. Toshi is therefore half-Korean. "He can't stop shaking, and his lack of control—over his own body and his own life—frightens him" (249). Toshi has been entranced by something exotic, but he cannot live with the idea of his being exotic himself. Simultaneously, however, we can assume that his xenophilia has always already been imprinted and nurtured within his mother's Japanophobia. Thus the climax of the novel dramatically foregrounds Audrey Hepburn's neck as an exotic fetish, which has been radically Japanized by Toshi's multinational imagination:

> Images appear on the white sheets. A silent movie screen, the voices of his mother and father drowned out by the rain as they move through their lives together, unable to speak the truth. . . . The screen turns a lush green, the fields his mother walked through as a girl. Toshi smells the spring air and the young rice plants. He longs to go to Korea to find his mother's family. His family. And to his father's hometown in Kyushu. There are palm trees, his father had told his mother. He drifts in and out of sleep, and his desires spread like the rain-splattered patterns on the rippling sheets. Audrey Hepburn's white-gloved hand rests on his arm. Under blazing chandeliers, they enter a crowded ball-room. Everyone applauds as they dance across a marble floor that reflects their gliding image like melting ice. Her neck, wrapped in diamonds, is luminous, a white birch branch trembling under the weight of new snow. Toshi leaps into the landscape of Audrey Hepburn's neck. (259)

Despite its humor, *Audrey Hepburn's Neck* tries to reconsider the impacts of wartime imperialism, which is not incompatible with the political unconscious of the movie *Roman Holiday*. In the early 1950s, when this movie was made, McCarthyism was at its peak in the United States. Nevertheless, the director William Wyler, the scriptwriter Dalton Trumbo, and the lead actress Audrey Hepburn all shared an antipathy to fascism. In 1954 in Japan, when *Roman Holiday* was first shown there, a notorious shipbuilding company scandal erupted, the Self-Defense Forces were formed, and a Japanese ship stumbled into the American thermonuclear test off the coast of Bikini. On both sides of the Pacific, people were so depressed that they longed for a holiday, the slightest freedom. This is why Audrey Hepburn's character in *Roman Holiday*, enjoying her slight freedom, captured the Japanese imagination in the early fifties. And, this will to freedom is skillfully recreated in Toshi's vision of another world, the snowscape of Hokkaido melted into the whiteness of Audrey Hepburn's neck. In this visionary scene the hero probably indulges in transvestitism, making his own subjectivity more exotic, just as the famous Japanese transvestite artist Yasumasa Morimura dresses himself as Audrey Hepburn. At this point, author Alan Brown's orientalism intermingles beautifully with Toshi's occidentalism. What Brown feels most exotic is Toshi's own subjectivity, desperately seeking for something exotic. While traditional orientalism has flaunted some weirdly misleading cultural stereotypes, Alan Brown's meta-orientalism starts by understanding exoticism within the exoticizing other as correctly as possible.

New Exoticism Case C: William Gibson's *Idoru*

While Anne Shirley and Audrey Hepburn are both human heroines, William Gibson's fifth novel, *Idoru* (1996)—the companion piece to his fourth novel, *Virtual Light* (1993)—features an Asian heroine Rei Toei who is not human but a creature with artificial intelligence, reminding us of typical Japanimation characters: she is an "idol" as well as an "AI-doll." Certainly, there have been many artificial intelligences, if not AI-dolls, in the history of postmodern fiction. Gibson's spin on the concept, is, however, unique. In the title, he did not misspell but simply Japanized the English term "idol," because he uses Tokyo as the main setting for the novel's action, focusing closely on its celebrity and technosubcultural scenes. Once again, Gibson's choice of setting is fortunate: it coincides perfectly with what was going on at the time in postmodern Tokyo, for the year 1996 saw both the publication of *Idoru* in the United States and the almost simultaneous creation of a virtual idol, "Kyoko Date," in Japan. Invented by Hori Production, one of the major theatrical agencies in Japan, this sixteen-year-old idol Kyoko has regaled people's eyes and ears in cyberspace, and is expected to keep growing older therein.[6] In this sense, *Idoru* is an insightful fiction of the present.

In *Idoru*, everything takes place in about 2006, almost one year after the post-earthquake events in San Francisco that are narrated in *Virtual Light*. Around this time, nanotech engineering has enabled the post-earthquake Tokyo to get quickly reconstructed. Elaborate virtual spaces have been constructed as well, replicating even the whole "bad taste" quarter of the Kowloon Walled City (Hak Nam), a place of interest in Hong Kong destroyed in the early 1990s (the text at this point coincides nicely with the creation of the Japanese postcyberpunk computer game *Kowloon's Gate*, marketed in 1996 by Sony Music Entertainment).

The story itself is, once again, a very simple, hardboiled variant of the traditional Holy Grail quest, centering on a couple of protagonists: Colin Laney, a natural-born netrunner capable of discovering nodal points in the cybersea, who gets so exhausted with a celebrity business conspiracy in Hollywood that he finds another job in Tokyo; and Chia McKenzie, a fourteen-year-old media-saturated fan of a Sino-Celtic rock 'n' roll duo Lo/Rez, who is asked by her Mexican friend Zona to fly to Tokyo and discover the truth about a scandal involving the Chinese-Irish singer Rez. Laney's plot and Chia's plot are constructed in a series of cutbacks. To put it simply, once the story gets started, we are quickly led into the "double plot" thematically and structurally, as is usually the case with Gibsonian narrative. Colin's and Chia's unwittingly shared mission is to find out whether it is true that Rez really has decided to marry the completely artificial Japanese idol Rei Toei, the virtual product of some Tokyo information designers. But, when Chia arrives at the Narita airport, someone secretly puts a nanotech assembler—a most dangerous high-tech weapon—in her bag. This act involves her in a political conspiracy. While Chia seeks the rock 'n' roller Rez, she is herself chased by someone else. But, since Chia is able to stay with Mitsuko, the social secretary of the Tokyo chapter of the global Lo/Rez fan association, she is also helped by Mitsuko's "Otaku" brother, Masahiko.

Here let me elaborate on the significance of the Otaku, a personality type that began to appear in Japan in the nineties, who "simply view their PC or television as another animistic object, like a rock or a tree or a kimono, which is of nature and hence of themselves,"[7] and who desperately chase idols or even virtual starlets. With the help of this Otaku boy, Chia discovers that the rock 'n' roller Rez does indeed plan to marry a virtual idol, through use of a nanotech assembler. By the end of the novel, Chia comes to know that even her Mexican friend Zona, who grew so jealous of Rez's impending marriage that she spread faked information about the death of Rez globally, is herself half-virtual. Of course, you can nurture a friendship with someone in cyberspace for a long time, putting on virtual bodies called "iconics" and meeting in virtual chat rooms. And yet it is also possible that your cyberfriend is neither human nor AI but someone hovering forever on the boundary between the organic and the inorganic. If pop stars are virtual, their fans could well be virtual—this is the central theme Gibson pursues in *Idoru.*

Of course, in the wake of Andy Warhol, the topic of celebrities has itself deeply pervaded postmodern fiction. Nevertheless, Gibson draws a sharp distinction between the Warholian kind of celebrity found in the Pax Americana and the cyberpunkish celebrity found in the Pax Japonica. While back in the sixties there used to be genuinely famous people, in the Gibsonian near future, as a character named Kathy Torrance remarks, the media makes celebrities out of assholes. So if a popular rock band like Lo/Rez stays famous for years and years, it could well be considered an exception, as well as "a living fossil, an annoying survival from an earlier, less evolved era" (7). "Kathy thought of celebrity as a subtle fluid, a universal element, like a phlogiston of the ancients, something spread evenly at creation through all the universe, but prone now to accrete, under specific conditions" (7). Now it is time to produce, at least in Hollywood, a radically artificial pop star as "some industrial-strength synthesis of . . . last three dozen top female faces" (175). The Japanese artificial idol, however, is attractive not because she epitomizes human beauty, but because she is part of an iceberg of some unthinkable volume of information" (178). To put it another way, the Japanese idol is loved not as a pseudo-entity or a human pseudo-event (to use the terms of Daniel Boorstin), but as a totally inhuman, imaginary, artificial character. As Greenfeld pointed out in *Speed Tribes*, already in the summer of 1991 the Japanese Otaku sensibility had helped produce an archetype of the virtual idol, if not of AI—a performer called Yui Haga, who was a composite of different bodies and different voices: "At concerts her face remains obscured and her voice is prerecorded. . . . Everybody knows Yui Haga doesn't exist. Therefore she can be all things to all people" (273). Just by being nonexistent, Yui Haga could capture the imagination of the audience and appeal to their sense of reality as vividly as any other "individual" idol.

You may assume that it is impossible to love a nonhuman semiotic ghost. But think twice, and you will also understand that it is our increasing commitment to high-tech media that enables us to find sexuality not only in humans but also in nonhuman agents created from software. And it is this aspect of the "semiotic ghost" that William Gibson, since his debut, has perennially elaborated in several texts before writing *Idoru*: "Fragments of Hologram Rose" (1977), "The Winter Market" (1985), and especially *Mona Lisa Overdrive* (1988).

Sounds queer? But in the wake of Internet revolution, it is not ideology but high technology that has revolutionized the existing concept of sexuality, making it far more exotic. This is why in his novel *Idoru* Gibson devoted an entire chapter to one of the Japanese queer tribes—the Otaku—which Gibson defines as "pathological-techno-fetishist-with-social-deficit" (88). In *Speed Tribes* Greenfeld conjectures that "the Japanese Otaku may be the final stage in the symbiosis of man and machine," since "they dream that some of virtual reality and digital compression technologies will allow them to have cybersex" (282). To Otaku, then, the interspecies marriage of a human pop star with an artificial idol represents the most sophisticated form of man-machine interface. From another perspective, it is the figure of idol that will make all of us members of the Otaku. This is why Stephen P. Brown, the editor of *Science Fiction Eye*, told me on the phone in March 1996 that he felt like making a splendid pun on Gibson's title; yes, "Idoru" invites all of you to confess, "I-adore-you."

With the concept of such cyber-queer sensibility in mind, we can explain why Eurudice's queer reading of President Clinton's foreign policy sounds both charming and persuasive. Indeed, the rise of queer theory is consistent with the technosexual revolution of the 1990s. Whereas in the mid-eighties Donna Haraway pointed out that we were all cyborgs, in the mid-nineties we could say we were all queers. Thus it is not that Audrey Hepburn and Anne of Green Gables paved the way for the Japanesque birth of Idoru, but that the queer marriage of Idoru and Otaku makes us rethink the essence of classical idols like Anne and Audrey.[8] Without this recognition of a cultural paradigm shift, in which Japanese technoculture played a significant role, we cannot fully comprehend the rise of the new exoticist milieu.

PART 4 *Performance*

CHAPTER 10 Magic Realist Tokyo: Poe's "The Man That Was Used Up" as a Subtext for Bartók-Terayama's Magical Musical *The Miraculous Mandarin*

The year 1997 saw the Japanese staging of a dance performance entitled *Poe Project*, the product of a collaboration between choreographer Min Tanaka and the American writer Susan Sontag. This multicultural event had an illuminating precursor. Twenty years earlier, in 1977, the renowned Japanese playwright Shuji Terayama (1935–1983) had staged a phantasmagoric, hyperkitsch musical entitled *The Miraculous Mandarin* in downtown Tokyo, a work he described as incorporating his adaptations of *The Miraculous Mandarin* (1919), by Hungarian composer Béla Bartók, and the short story "The Man That Was Used Up" (1839), by Edgar Allan Poe. In this chapter, I investigate the trilateral artistic negotiations between Bartók, Poe, and Terayama, with special attention to the cultural development of the Shibuya district of Tokyo during Japan's high-growth period.

Bartók's Ballet, Terayama's Magic Musical

Let us begin with a brief biographical introduction to Shuji Terayama, *enfant terrible* of postwar Japanese decadent literature and one of Japan's best known and most influential playwrights, both domestically and internationally. Terayama was born in rural Aomori Prefecture in 1935. At nineteen, he won a major national prize for the composition of tanka poetry, whereupon he dropped out of Waseda University. He published a collection of poems, *Den'en ni shisu* (To Die

Fig. 12 The playwright Shuji Terayama, 1935–1983. Photo © Kyoko Kujyo.

in the Country) in 1965, by which time he had also begun to write and produce plays. In 1967 Terayama founded his own troupe, Tenjo-Sajiki (Upper Balcony). Terayama's most successful plays include *Aomori-ken no Semushi Otoko* (The Hunchback of Aomori, 1967), *Aohige-ko no Shiro* (Blue Beard's Castle, 1968), *Saraba Hakobune* (One Hundred Years of Solitude [Terayama's own theatrical adaptation of García Márquez's novel], 1982), and *Nuhikun* (Instructions to Servants, 1978), the last of which won wide international acclaim. Terayama's tremendous talent extended to the writing of feature film scripts—including a movie version of *Saraba Hakobune*, which he directed—and radio and television plays as well. Terayama also directed other films, including *Sho wo suteyo machi e deyo* (Throw Away the Books, Take to the Streets, 1971) and *Den'en ni shisu* (A Pastoral Death, 1974). He died at the age of forty-eight in 1983 of cirrhosis of the liver and septicemia.

Terayama's was a diverse talent. The *Encyclopedia of Japan* describes him as an "avant-garde playwright, critic, scriptwriter, novelist, filmmaker, essayist, and poet." Yet I would like to refigure him primarily as a playwright whom we must recognize for having revolutionized the Japanese sensibility of the urban in the 1970s. In this regard, Terayama's magic musical *The Miraculous Mandarin*, first performed at the Seibu Zaibatsuary's Parco Theatre in Shibuya, Tokyo, in 1977, particularly merits reconsideration.

Fig. 13 Tenjo-Sajiki Building, Shibuya, the birthplace of Terayama's avant-garde plays. Photo © Kyoko Kujyo.

Béla Bartók (1881–1945) composed the original music for *The Miraculous Mandarin*, the ballet on which Terayama based his play, and thus a brief introduction to this great Hungarian composer and his composition may be useful. Bartók can be considered a nativist ethnologist in the field of music, comparable to—and a contemporary of—the turn-of-the-century writers Lafcadio Hearn (Yakumo Koizumi) and Kunio Yanagita, whom I examined in chapter 4. Like Hearn and Yanagita, who sought to substantiate their exoticist viewpoint, Bartók did not hesitate to exoticize the other, even while it was a typical product of its era. Edward Downes characterized Bartók's *The Miraculous Mandarin* as "a gruesome distortion of the love-death theme which runs through so much nineteenth-century Romantic literature and music, reaching its climax in Wagner's *Tristan und Isolde* (50).

The story of the ballet, which Bartók created in 1919 at the age of thirty-seven in collaboration with the playwright Menyhért Lengyel, centers on a brothel located on an unnamed back street of an unknown country, where a trio of scoundrels conspire with a young

Fig. 14 The composer Béla Bartók, 1881–1945. AP-Photo/Roehnert.

prostitute to rob her customers of their valuables. When the Miraculous Mandarin appears, the prostitute dances for him, shyly at first, then with increasing abandon. During her long dance, the mandarin remains motionless; only his eyes betray his rising passion: the mandarin has discovered in the girl the true love for which he has long been looking. When at last the prostitute throws herself on his knees, the mandarin tries to embrace her, but the girl becomes terrified of his sudden fervor and struggles free. The mandarin catches hold of the girl and they fight. The three scoundrels rescue the girl, rob the mandarin of his jewels and money, and attempt to kill him. However, the intensity of the mandarin's longing keeps him alive despite the best efforts of the thugs, who try smothering him and running a rusty old sword through his body. At last, the scoundrels hang the mandarin from a chandelier. The lights go out and the mandarin's body begins to glow a greenish blue, but his eyes, still filled with longing, continue to follow the girl. When the mandarin is finally cut down to resume his pursuit of the girl, she no longer resists. His longing appeased, the Miraculous Mandarin's wounds begin to bleed, and he passes away in ecstasy.[1]

In short, Bartók's original *The Miraculous Mandarin* is a masterful depiction of the power of human aspiration, unconquerable even by death, as other critics have observed. Downes finds this theme entirely in harmony with Bartók's profound idealism: "Bartók's own tragic life bears witness to his unflinching aspiration in the face of frail health, misunderstanding, neglect, poverty, exile, disease, and the death he faced in a New York hospital, far from his native land which meant so much to him."[2]

Nonetheless, the ballet itself was condemned as immoral in the extreme, and ballet companies everywhere refused to perform it. As late as 1926, a production in Cologne was banned after a single performance. Only after World War II did *The Miraculous Mandarin* come to be performed widely on European stages, and not until 1951 was the work performed in New York as a ballet. How, then, did the Japanese playwright Terayama remix Bartók's ballet with Poe's short story in his magic musical adaptation?

Let us begin by noting some differences between Terayama's musical and Bartók's ballet. First, Terayama replaced Bartók's "unnamed back street in an unknown country" with Shanghai in the 1920s, when rumors of a coup d'état were rampant (at the opening of the play, a number of ruffians in pigtails all light matches almost simultaneously). Terayama's play also departs from the ballet in its plot line, for Terayama—exhibiting striking originality—introduces a family romance between the male protagonist, Baku, and his thirteen-year-old younger sister, Kacho.

The story begins just after Kacho is kidnapped and sold into a brothel, where she is to be trained as a prostitute. Her brother Baku is so anxious to get her back that he accepts a deal offered by a woman police officer: if Baku murders the ageless Miraculous Mandarin, the officer promises to help him find Kacho. However, the Miraculous Mandarin can die only by winning the true love of a truly innocent girl, and thus the narrative proposes a radical paradox: Baku cannot rescue his sister from prostitution without killing the mandarin, but in order to kill the mandarin—who has survived numerous assassination attempts—Baku must deliver to him Kacho's true love, and thus, in essence, her innocence. That is, to rescue his sister from losing her innocence as a prostitute, he must commit a murder that requires the sacrifice of her innocence. The hero Baku is thus trapped in the deepest predicament.

Indeed, when Baku cuts off the mandarin's head, the mandarin

Fig. 15 The climax of Shuji Terayama's "Magic Musical." Scene from Shuji Terayama's *The Miraculous Mandarin*. Photo © Kyoko Kujyo.

picks his head back up; when the mandarin is sawed in two, he says, "Don't worry, I'm safe. With a handsaw you may be able to damage my body, but not my life itself." Such scenes cannot help but bring to mind another of Edgar Allan Poe's tales, namely, "A Predicament" (1842), in which the protagonist, Signora Psyche Zenobia, remains alive after her neck is severed by the huge minute-hand of the clock on the steeple to which she is tied, and watches as her own head rolls down the side of the steeple, lodges for a few moments in the gutter, then plunges into the middle of the street: "With my head I imagined, at one time, that I, the head, was the real Signora Psyche Zenobia—at another I felt convinced that myself, the body, was the proper identity."[3]

However, Terayama's Miraculous Mandarin, who is obsessed with finding his true love, ends up being completely dismembered when at last he hears the heroine, Kacho, confess her love for him. The irony of the story does not end here. By making even "true love" into a commodity, the innocent Kacho transforms herself into a respectably professional prostitute. And whereas Baku is for a couple of days desperate to recover his sister, the Miraculous Mandarin has been afflicted by the absence of true love for two hundred years; it is not that he does not die, but that he cannot die. On his happy demise the woman police officer picks up the parts of his body and offers the following insight: "Everything was fake. He wasn't flesh and blood. From the beginning, the Miraculous Mandarin never existed. He turned out to have been a malicious automaton invented by four hundred million Chinese."

But even as the officer speaks, the Miraculous Mandarin is resurrected once again out of a desire to witness the crucial events of Chinese history that will transpire in the near future. The mandarin concludes, "Thank you for enabling me to die twice. When and where can I die next time—in the second floor of an opium den in Inner Mongolia, in a girls' revue at the border of the province of Konan, or inside a tent during the Nanjing Massacre?" (114). Responding to his call, a number of prostitutes, including Kacho, approach the mandarin. A man selling mirrors starts to read from *The History of China*. Fade out. This hyperexotic magic musical struck audiences as at once incredibly beautiful and extremely weird.

As may be gleaned from this brief overview, Bartók's mandarin is in effect a eunuch, and Terayama's an immortal cyborg. According to the playwright, the actor who played the Miraculous Mandarin—Juzo Itami—suggested that the figure be presented as a literal cyborg, with artificial organs, limbs, eyes, and ears, and even a removable head.[4] This suggestion reflects profound artistic insight, and indeed, such insight led Itami to a career as an internationally renowned film director in the 1980s.

How Did Terayama Read Poe?

Terayama created his Miraculous Mandarin with the cyborg hero of Poe's short story "The Man That Was Used Up" in mind. Let us now consider how the Bartók/Terayama cyborg character relates to that hero, Brevet Brigadier General John A. B. C. Smith. Some have argued that Poe modeled Smith on Vice President Richard M. Johnson, who had been a leader in a war against the Shawnees in which he had been severely injured.[5] The protagonist's name also evokes Captain John Smith, a figure who was taken captive by Powhatan, the father of Pocahontas. Either way, Poe's point lies in the irony that this character—a universally admired hero of the "Bugaboo and Kickapoo War" whom ignorant mobs of Americans nearly deify—turns out to be no more than an automaton invented through antebellum ambivalence toward American Indians.

Thus, when the narrator of the story, pleading urgent business, is shown into General Smith's bedroom while he is "dressing," the narrator looks about for the occupant of the room in vain. However, there is a large and exceedingly odd-looking bundle on the floor which the narrator happens to kick; this turns out to be none other than the general, who is in the process of being "dressed" by the old Negro valet Pompey, a character who is to reappear three years later as a servant of Psyche Zenobia in the short story "The Predicament," mentioned above.

Much as Poe's cyborg general arouses contemporary fears of an international relationship between whites and Indians, Terayama's cyborg—recreated through the Chinese unconscious in a time of upheaval—represents the magic multinational cityscape of Shanghai in the 1920s, insofar as it comprised a free zone that was neither Chinese nor Japanese wherein it was difficult to distinguish between the colonizer and the colonized. Indeed, the cyborg as such is a signifier of a multiethnic and transcultural creole subjectivity.[6]

This begs the question of why Terayama wanted to foreground a creole atmosphere by carefully linking North America of the 1830s and Shanghai of the 1920s with Shibuya of the 1970s. For the image of the cyborg that Terayama pursued was not simply a revival of the American unconscious of the 1830s and the Chinese unconscious in the 1920s, but also a representation of the Japanese unconscious of the 1970s, the heyday of the high-growth period. Terayama has remarked that "whoever is powerful and official becomes frustrated by contradictory desires—the desire to be as common as everyone else and the desire to grow far stronger, like Frankenstein's monster or King Kong."[7] This perspective mirrors the political and economic status of Japan in the late 1970s, for in this decade of high growth, Japan—much like the Miraculous Mandarin—was frustrated by contradictory desires, in the case of the country, both to remain as it had been and to catch up with the United States.

Of course, Terayama was not a conservative politician but rather an ultra-avant-garde artist. By 1977 Terayama was both famous and infamous for such radical experiments as his "street theater," which incorporated ordinary citizens as they passed on the street. In one representative performance, entitled *Knock* (1975), Terayama designated an area of Suginami Ward in Tokyo as a setting for street theater, going so far as to demand that passersby join performers in the *sento* (public bath). Not surprisingly, the performance provoked a number of complaints and was stopped by the police. Terayama's intention with this street theater was not simply to challenge people just for fun, but rather to question the fundamental theatricality of politics. As he explains in his essay "Scandal: The Strategy of Street Theater," "Disturbance and scandal constitute the essence of street theater, which radically challenges the subjectivity of the ordinary citizen, who rejects any intrusion of theatricality into daily life but who is very likely to accept crypto-theatricality disguised as plain reality."[8]

Freak Show as the Origin of Spectacle

Terayama's taste for freaks is reminiscent of that of the great antebellum entrepreneur P. T. Barnum, whose commercialization of the spectacular via his "American Museum" must have inspired Poe, among other writers of the American Renaissance.[9] Much as Barnum reappropriated the handicapped as freaks in the spectacles he presented at the dawn of American museum culture, Poe featured a mutilated General Smith in "The Man That Was Used Up" as a nationalistic spectacle. Vice President Richard Johnson, the supposed model for the hero of Poe's story was viewed by his contemporaries as Poe wished General John A. B. C. Smith to be viewed, that is, as "a man upon crutches; his frame all mutilated; moving with difficulty yet an object of patriotic interest with everybody."[10]

By virtue of his disfigurement, Smith thus served Poe not only as a representative man but also as a magnificent spectacle. Consider, for instance, the excitement of Miss Arabella at the presence of Smith in the Rantipole Theatre: "Smith? . . . why, not General John A. B. C? Horrid affair that, wasn't it?—great wretches, those Bugaboos—savage and so on—but we live in a wonderfully inventive age!—Smith—O yes! Great man! Perfect desperado—*immortal* renown—prodigies of valor! Never heard!"[11] This passage reflects how the advent of spectacle in the history of a country goes hand in hand with the rise of nationalism. In this light, the figure of the cyborg might be reinterpreted as a version of Leviathan, in the sense of Thomas Hobbes, who defined the figure of the absolute ruler (Leviathan) as an artificial man with an artificial soul.

The extent to which Shuji Terayama was familiar with the achievements of P. T. Barnum is uncertain—he mentions Barnum only in passing in his own writings—but Terayama had a deep interest in freak shows, and indeed designed his troupe, Tenjo-Sajiki, as a kind of freak show that featured a number of extraordinary bodies, including an extremely fat woman, a hunchback, and midgets. Terayama also examined the significance of freaks, specifically in reference to Poe's "The Man That Was Used Up," in a lengthy essay, "The Symbolism of Freaks" (1978): "Given that any entity is governed by the logic of its own inherent order, the subjectivity of General A. B. C. Smith is definitely shaped by the logic of freaks. . . . Thus, General Smith allegorizes the substance of modern individuality evacuated, unbinding all freaks from the vicious circle of diachronic history" (23–24). Terayama here reinterprets not only "The Man That Was Used Up" but also his own magic musical, *The Miraculous Mandarin*, which had been staged the year before he published the essay, and into which he had incorporated Poe's tale. Through the fiction of Barnum's contemporary, Poe, Terayama thus imbibed the essence of the Barnum freak show.

Historicizing the Cityscape of Shibuya

It is noteworthy that where the antebellum romantic genius Barnum exploited the freak show to question the idea of the individual in Victorian America, the postwar situationist genius Terayama redeployed the freak show to attack a nationalistic theory of spectacle in hypercapitalist Japan. Faced in 1977 with an offer to stage *The Miraculous Mandarin* at the Parco Theatre in Tokyo—run by the Seibu Zaibatsuary (the postmodern version of the financial conglomerate, and one of the leading conglomerates in Japan) and located inside the Parco department store in Tokyo's Shibuya district—Terayama must have seen an important opportunity to realize and formally expand his idea of street theater in the interior of the postmodern department store.

The Seibu Zaibatsuary began to redevelop Tokyo by reconstructing the entire town of Shibuya in the early 1970s. During the 1960s, Shibuya station had been a typical transfer point: everyone found the station convenient but no one paid much attention to the surrounding urban area. With the opening of their own department store in Shibuya in 1973, the Seibu Zaibatsuary planned to revolutionize this image of Shibuya, transforming the town itself into a kind of spectacle. Aimed at reinventing the cityscape of Shibuya as a festive space in which something is always going on and anything can happen, this plan was doubtless inspired by the concept of street theater. In order to achieve their aims for the district, the Seibu Zaibatsuary produced a variety of pseudo-events on the slopes of Shibuya, appropriating Terayama's experimental street theater for the purposes of their capitalist philosophy of management.

Terayama's acceptance of the offer to stage *The Miraculous Mandarin* at the Parco Theatre therefore aroused great controversy, seemingly signaling the playwright's radical conversion to capitalism. Indeed, numerous fans and critics concluded that Terayama, in a betrayal of underground oppositional culture, had allowed himself to be swallowed whole and totally digested in the growth of Japanese capitalism. Yet on closer consideration, Terayama cannot be viewed as having been seduced by the Seibu Zaibatsuary; on the contrary, the playwright skillfully connected the opposing elements of Seibu's capitalism and his own avant-gardism.

The plot of *The Miraculous Mandarin* submits to an intriguing reinterpretation in terms of this highly poetic strategy. Specifically, Terayama's remixing of capitalism and avant-gardism is reflected within the production itself: the mandarin—a sort of embodied colonialist institution—achieves ephemeral ecstasy and a happy death through the true love of the innocent Kacho, a signifier of the oppositional populace. That is, the story can be understood as an allegory for the postmodern negotiation between Seibu's capitalistic colonization of Shibuya and Terayama's avant-garde decolonization of the city from within.

It was in the context of his resistance to this advanced-capitalist conspiracy, finally, that Terayama drew on Poe's "The Man That Was Used Up" as perhaps the most critical subtext for *The Miraculous Mandarin*. Although department stores are ordinarily expected to sell the commodities of "good taste," Terayama invited the Seibu Zaibatsuary's Parco department store, through its Parco Theatre, to sell not only good taste but also bad taste. In this regard specifically, Terayama is indebted to the antebellum American artists Poe and Barnum, both of whom helped establish the good taste of bad taste, radically questioning the canonical distinction between the normal and the abnormal, Beauty and Deformity, and the sophisticated and the kitsch. In the spirit of Poe, the romantic artist of spectacle, Terayama exposed the conspiracy of spectacle in the postmodern age, informing city dwellers that the whole city could have been controlled as a "reality studio," in the sense of William Burroughs and Larry McCaffery.[12]

Since the performance of *The Miraculous Mandarin* in 1977, Terayama's revolution of taste has exerted a lasting influence on the cityscape of Shibuya. In the 1980s, Shibuya became one of the major nuclei of the city of Tokyo, attracting 500,000 visitors a day on weekdays, and 700,000 visitors a day on weekends and holidays. It has become increasingly difficult to know whether the Miraculous Mandarin–like cyborgian institution is still controlling the strollers who pass daily through the district, or whether these flâneurs have themselves metamorphosed into cyborgs.

Thus, Terayama's spectacular appropriation of Bartók and Poe not only criticizes the high-growth ideology of Japan during an early stage of that era but also reflects back on the nature of modern spectacle made possible by P. T. Barnum's American Museum, which profoundly influenced Terayama's artistic unconscious and his magical musical, *The Miraculous Mandarin*.

PART 5 Representation

CHAPTER 11 Full Metal Apache: Shinya Tsukamoto's *Tetsuo* Diptych, or The Impact of American Narratives on the Japanese Representation of Cyborgian Identity

One day an ordinary Japanese salaryman shaves himself, only to find his face partly metallicized. He cannot prevent this transformation from taking place uncannily in his own body. When he visits his girlfriend's apartment, this syndrome has so thoroughly invaded him that his penis is transformed into a roaring electric drill, with which he ends up gruesomely murdering his girlfriend. What is more, he finds himself being followed by a "metal-psychic" stranger who is able to transport himself anywhere through metallic space, and whose left arm functions as a terrifying rifle. These two men become fused with each other, metamorphosing themselves into a huge and bizarre cyborg monster stalking downtown Tokyo, armed with a number of strafing guns on its gargantuan body. It becomes fixated on destroying the city and making the whole world rusty, junky, and apocalyptic.

Oriental Kitsch: A Double Reading of the *Tetsuo* Diptych

This is the plot of the first film of a Japanese cyberpunk movie series *Tetsuo*, the Grand Prize–winner of the ninth Rome International Fantastic Festival, directed in 1989 by the promising young talent Shinya Tsukamoto, who was born in Tokyo in 1960.[1] Since William Gibson's 1984 novel *Neuromancer* was translated into Japanese in 1986, ignit-

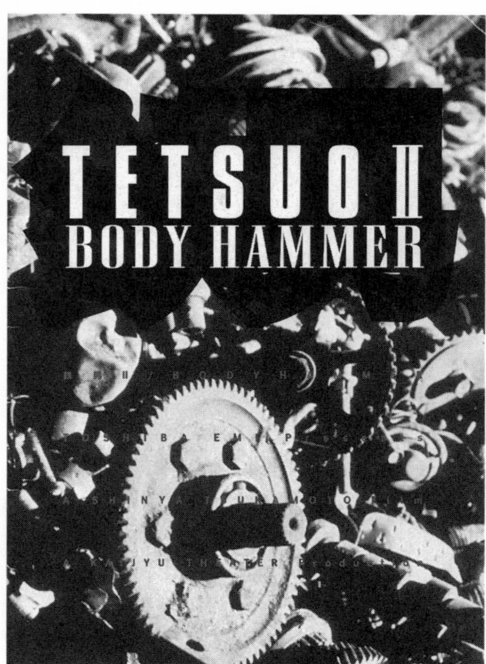

Fig. 16 Program cover for the film *Tetsuo* and *Tetsuo II: Body Hammer*, directed by Shinya Tsukamoto, 1992. © 1992 Toshiba-EMI/Kaijyu Theater.

ing the cyberpunk fever also in Japan, at first glance *Tetsuo* may strike one as a little derivative. For Tsukamoto's visual representation will quickly remind you of Ridley Scott's masterpiece *The Terminator* (1984), Katsuhiro Otomo's anime *Akira* (1988), the TV series *Power Rangers* (1993–), and other cyberpunk films and novels. There is no doubt that the name of the cyborg tribe "Tetsuo," which means "iron man," derives from that of the psychic protagonist of *Akira*. The director Tsukamoto himself confessed that he was so keenly conscious of the rise of cyberculture in the late 1980s, that sometimes he distracted American interviewers on purpose, strategically relating the theme of *Tetsuo* with the ongoing pop cultural movement.[2] But, at the same time, we should not ignore that *Tetsuo* embodies an epistemological avant-gardism that discourages us from determining that metallicization in the story figures an AIDS-like fatal illness, say, or the superevolution of human beings. Tsukamoto's antirational artistic approach must have been very satisfying to highbrow film critics.

From this perspective, the sequel to *Tetsuo*, *Tetsuo II: Body Hammer*, completed in 1992—the winner of special prizes at many international film festivals—may seem less avant-garde and more pop-oriented, possibly even melodramatic, because in it the director attempts to demystify the roots of the tribe of iron men, locating the secret of metallicization in the protagonist's personal history. Its plot leaves nothing in doubt. *Tetsuo II* deals with metallicization not as a symptom of a new type of plague but simply the effect of a new kind of medical experimentation performed on a living person. Thus *Tetsuo II* starts with the conspiracy of a mad scientist, who tries through high-technology to transform a group of skinheads into bioweapons, training their conditional reflexes so that whenever they feel the impulse to murder, they can automatically transform themselves into powerful cyborg soldiers, with hypermetallic rifles growing out of their bodies. But the problem then becomes one of how to make that murder impulse stronger. The solution: kidnap the beloved child of an ordinary-looking petit-bourgeois salaryman, and have him cultivate within himself the revenge impulse, a more sinister intent to kill. This is why the protagonist, Tomoo Taniguchi, is selected as the most appropriate subject for experiment.

At the mad scientist's laboratory-factory, however, the experiment on Tomoo turns out to have been far more successful than expected. The reason is simple. It is not that the mad scientist has helped Tomoo develop the revenge impulse and become a bioweapon, but that as children Tomoo and his elder brother had already been trained by their own father—another mad scientist—to become bioweapons. Tomoo's father began his experiments by fusing a cat with a kettle and later applied his theory to the transformation of his own children. As a result, the hero's elder brother murders the parents while they are making love. Thus the murder impulse in *Tetsuo II* is closely related to the Oedipus complex. On this scene of parenticide, we hear the hero's own voice-over: "After the parenticide, my brother lost his memory. His amnesia was caused by neither the loss of the mother nor the repentance on parenticide itself. My brother felt destruction beautiful. He was so deeply scarred by the aesthetics of destruction that he forgot everything."

To complete our first reading of the *Tetsuo* series, we will consider Tsukamoto's idiosyncratic characterization of the bioweapon brothers, which naturally conjures up the portrait of Tyron Slothrop in Thomas Pynchon's *Gravity's Rainbow* (1973). One of the best known bioweapons in postmodern metafiction, Tyron Slothrop was sexually conditioned as a child to have an erection whenever he smelled the launching of a V2 rocket, and erased—or was forced to erase—the

Fig. 17 The mad scientist's laboratory-factory, from *Tetsuo II: Body Hammer*. © 1992 Toshiba-EMI/Kaijyu Theater.

fact of his being a radar/rocket man from his consciousness. Pynchon argues in his meganovel that our postmodern self is always already constructed by a skillfully controlled network of politics,[3] a view that is undoubtedly applicable to the thematics of the director Tsukamoto. Although he would not have had the chance to read the translation of *Gravity's Rainbow* in the period between 1989 and 1992 (the Japanese edition came out from Kokusho-Kanko-kai Publishers, Tokyo, only in the summer of 1993), Tsukamoto certainly could have absorbed the Pynchonesque atmosphere through a number of cyberpunk texts or contexts composed by post-Pynchon writers and artists. *Tetsuo*'s proximity to Pynchon may be one of the reasons why *Tetsuo* was more highly appreciated in the United States than in Japan.

I would not, however, like to limit our viewpoint to posteighties discursive history. It is time to construct a second reading of the *Tetsuo* series. Certainly, at first glance, the seminude skinheads of *Tetsuo II*, as well as "Yatsu" (the Guy)—always played by the director himself in the series—seem to simply reproduce the post-eighties stereotype of outlaw technologists. But, by the same token, I believe that a large part of Tsukamoto's appeal lay in his representation of "yellow" punks, which must have appealed vividly to the traditional audience of postforties western movies and postseventies Vietnam War movies, both of which powerfully foregrounded the fear of yellow skin and red skin, that is, the orientalist fear of Mongoloids. What is more, the period between the 1970s and the 1980s saw an explosion of popularity among American intellectuals of Japanese avant-garde theater and dance, as represented by Shuji Terayama, Kazuo Ohno, and Tatsumi Hijikata. Aware of the international cultural poetics of "Mongoloid skin" (a color complex that covers the spectrum between yellow and red), Tsukamoto completed *Tetsuo II* by employing a number of skinheads from the famous avant-garde dance company Dai-Rakuda-Kan and an experimental theatrical group, Shinjuku-Ryozanpaku, whose leader and main actor, Kim Sujin, was assigned the role of Tomoo's father, the primary mad scientist. We can therefore witness the paradox that while the director Tsukamoto demystified the making of bioweapons in *Tetsuo II*, the ordinary American audience of the *Tetsuo* series did not demystify but "remystified" the Mongoloid skin, which recalled the sense of defeat created and amplified by the loss of the Vietnam War and the threat of the Pax Japonica. This is how the *Tetsuo* diptych came to accelerate the orientalist fear and allure of Mongoloid cyborgs as posthuman, ending up with a reorganization of postmodern kitsch aesthetics, with Mongoloids as the ideal brides of celibate machines.

Of course, we have available the shared assumption that, as David Mogen has aptly pointed out, cyberpunks have tried to reconstruct frontier narrative, thereby reappropriating traditional western novels and movies.[4] And yet, for now, before speculating upon the immediate relationship between the Gibsonian technoscape and Tsukamoto's metallic space, I would like to review some postwar Japanese cultural history, focusing on how American western idioms became so widely naturalized and domesticated that in the period between the 1950s and the 1960s the scrap metal thieves of the junkyard of Osaka came to be nicknamed "Japanese Apaches."

The Literary History of the Japanese Apache

Iron has been a feature of human civilization since 3000 B.C., when the Sumerian city of Ur found traces of iron within a meteorite. The making of the Orient owes much to the Hittite technology of iron manufacture, which would be largely appropriated by the Assyrians for the development of weaponry. The introduction of iron helped Greek people to replace archaic communities with the archetypal city "polis"—a more productive, rationalistic, and technodefensive body politic. The same can be said of China (first unified by the Ch'in dynasty in 600–500 B.C., thanks to various iron products and weaponry), and also of Korea (first unified in 700 B.C. by the kingdom of Silla, which was endowed with ironworks as well as many gold mines). Immigrant iron manufacturers from Silla encouraged the rise of the Japanese iron industry between the late fourth century and early fifth century, making the Yamato dynasty powerful enough to unify Japan for the first time. And, there is no doubt that the Pax Britannica of the nineteenth century would not have been possible without the British industrial revolution, which opened the age of iron and coal.[5]

Since the opening of the country in the mid-nineteenth century, Japan has fully digested the fruits of industrial revolution, importing raw materials at cheap rates and imitating imported iron products. The Sino-Japanese War (1894–1895) induced Japan to promote the importation of ships and the construction of railroads, igniting the national spirit of enterprise. Following soon after, the Russo-Japanese War (1904–1905) radically expanded the munitions and railroad industries in Japan.[6] In other words, the industries generated by war and capitalism on a national scale cultivated one another, disseminating the benefits of iron manufacturing all through the body politic. As the ex-Nazi engineer Wernher von Braun developed German V2 rocket technology in wartime and American space flight technology in the postwar years, so Japanese air space engineers committed themselves to developing sophisticated fighter planes in wartime and cars and ships in the postwar period. The advanced technology of the war industry made it easier to design the high-speed railroad Tokaido Shinkansen, as well as high-tech light vehicles such as the Subaru. Many U.S.-made tanks used in the Korean War (1950–1953) were transported into Japan in 1954, scrapped, and transformed into high-quality steel, which was reappropriated as building material for the Tokyo Tower in 1958.[7] The destruction of war and the construction of the city go hand in hand, establishing an ironic logic of recycling and the perverse aesthetics of bad taste, that is to say, metataste metamorphosing the most junky and the most disgusting into the most kitsch and the most camp. As soon as the existing standard of aesthetics collapses, the hypercapitalist imperative incorporates the weirdest into the most marketable, the most avant-garde, and the most beautiful. This is the radical paradigm shift in accordance with which we should redefine the industrial effects of war industry as the metaesthetic cause of the postwar processing industry, with iron as its very useful currency.

In retrospect, all developing communities have been motivated by a certain kind of "gold rush" ethos.[8] We can replace "gold" with whatever we consider commercially most attractive, such as oil, oranges, dinosaurs, Hollywood, Silicon Valley, or the Amazon. From this viewpoint, postwar Japan can be considered to have started reconstruction by refiguring iron as another target of the gold rush ethos. But, unlike the Gilded Age of the American fin de siècle, when real gold was clearly distinguished from fake, the Japanese gold rush toward iron did not set up very clearly the difference between iron and scrap, but accelerated a relation of recycling between them. While the postwar Japanese steel industry contributed much to the modernist aesthetics of the good taste of "streamlined" buildings, our scrap factories ironically made more sophisticated the good taste of the bad-taste junkyard. This is the point in time where the postwar aesthetics of kitsch gives rise to a new trend in Japanese literature, in which a new tribe of scrap thieves, the so-called Japanese Apache, is vividly featured.

The literary history of Japanese Apache fiction starts with Ken Kaiko's mainstream novel *Nippon Sanmon Opera* (The Japanese Three Penny Opera) in 1959, named after Bertolt Brecht's *Die Dreigroschenoper* (1928). It was followed by Sakyo Komatsu's science fiction *Nippon Apacchi-Zoku* (The Japanese Apache) in 1964, written in homage to Karel Căpek's *War with the Newts* (1937), and then by the semiautobiographical novel *Yoru wo Kakete* (Through the Night, 1994) by the former Apache, Korean immigrant writer Yang Sok Il (Yan Sogiru).[9]

Chronologically speaking, the novels of Kaiko and Komatsu, both written around 1960, can be grouped together, while Yang's fiction was written more than thirty years later. And yet, taking a look at their birth years, you notice that these three writers belong to the same generation: Kaiko was born in 1930, Komatsu in 1931, and Yang in 1936. The contrast between them is very sharp, since while Kaiko's *Nippon Sanmon Opera* deals with the explosive energy of lower-class people, Komatsu's *Nippon Apacchi-Zoku* concentrates on not so much the fate of human beings now as a new type of mutant in the future, who live by eating iron. Yang's *Yoru wo Kakete*, meanwhile, foregrounds the Koreans among the Japanese Apache—the majority of whom are in fact Korean, including him. Despite the difference between Kaiko's humanism, Komatsu's posthumanism, and Yang's multiculturalism, however, it is remarkable that these writers of the generation of the 1930s all meditated on the course of a nation, regarding the Japanese Apache as a distorted reflection of the Japanese people themselves.

The origin of the scrap thieves called the Japanese Apache can be traced back to the day before the end of World War II: August 14, 1945. On that day, the Osaka army factory—in those days the largest munition plant in Asia, located in Sugiyama-cho between the Osaka Castle and the Nekoma River—was destroyed by American B-29 bombers. Since this factory had three large plants, a munition institute, and a school for engineers, its destruction meant the total evacuation of the Japanese munition industry. In the postwar years the American army removed most of the usable weaponry and materials from the Osaka site, and the Japanese government designated the ruins a national property in 1952. But at that point, more than 30,000 machine relics still remained there, intact, and partially embedded in the ground. Some of the mostly Korean people living in the shabby shelters on the other side of the Nekoma River noticed that this junk machinery was highly marketable. The community consisted not only of Koreans but also of Japanese and Okinawans, many of them outlaws ranging from bank robbers and bicycle thieves to get-rich-quick schemers. So it was very natural that the junkyard of the Osaka army factory stimulated their dream of digging out precious scrap from the ruins and exchanging it for huge amounts of money, more than 10,000 million yen, probably (equivalent to at least $1,000 million). Unless Japanese Apaches were caught in the act of stealing scrap, they were not arrested. The ruin of Sugiyama-cho was such a perfect site for this Japanese gold rush that it was nicknamed the Sugiyama gold mine. Kaiko sums up its significance in a very philosophical sentence: "The Japanese Apache made every effort to recycle scrap and junk, at the same time that they speculated deeply on how to give the last and greatest role to the junky dregs of society" (43).[10]

The Korean War enabled Japan to revive its economy very rapidly, since our factories supplied the U.S. army with weaponry. This is how Japan finally entered boom times, scrap per ton being bought at rates between 30,000 yen ($300) and 10,000 yen ($100). Thus the year 1957 saw the appearance of the first scrap thief in Sugiyama-cho, as both Kaiko and Yang narrate in their respective stories. After that point, almost all the community members on the opposite side of the Nekoma River became scrap thieves, starting an eight-month struggle with the police.

Let me comment briefly on the etymology of the term "Japanese Apache." It is not that the scrap thieves themselves chose the term "Apache" for their tribal name, but that contemporary journalists saw

Fig. 18 Cover of the DVD edition of Yang Sok Il's *Yoru wo Kakete*. © 2004 Artone Co. Ltd.

an analogy between the scrap thieves of Osaka and the American Apache tribe that the film director John Ford had represented in westerns such as *Fort Apache* in 1948 and *Rio Grande* in 1950. John Ford impressed his audience by dramatically depicting the war between white settlers and the Apache Indians, who fought against leaving their land by making small, surprise raids on the settlers. By the early 1950s Geronimo, the chief of the Apaches, became one of the superstars in Hollywood. It cannot be doubted, then, that by 1958 Ken Kaiko had become so familiar with John Ford's films that he would have developed a deep insight into the journalists' analogy between the Hollywood Apache and the Japanese Apache: the Japanese Apache, with their metal scrap, speaking in Korean or Okinawan, would flee from the police who came in pursuit of them, just as the American Apache fought with whites, uttering the strange sounds of their language. Yang Sok Il's main character, Kim, a big fan of westerns himself, tells his companions: "Don't mind if you're looked down on. We've been despised in plenty of ways. But I feel great sympathy with the Apache Indians. They waged a war just to get their lands back, because their land had been stolen from them by the whites. It's true of us too. Our fathers came down to Japan, because they had had their lands stolen by

Fig. 19 A conflict in the village of the Japanese Apache. Scene from the DVD *Yoru wo Kakete*. © 2004 Artone Co. Ltd.

the colonialists. Whether they're Indians or Koreans, repressed people share many things" (*Yoru wo Kakete*, 152).[11]

What makes Yang Sok Il's story more intriguing is that in 1958, when he was an active Apache, he was interviewed by Ken Kaiko, who had just received the Akutagawa Award for *Hadaka no Osama* (The Emperor's New Clothes) and was planning his next novel, *Nippon Sanmon Opera* (The Japanese Three Penny Opera).[12] Kaiko's interest in and research on the Apache that year also coincided with the growing popularity of Robert Aldrich's film *Apache* (1954), featuring Burt Lancaster as the last of the Apaches. It is this beautiful coincidence that helped popularize the signifier "Apache" also in Japan, disseminating its meaning in different ways. As French people had already called the outlaw Parisian youths "Apache," so the Japanese came quite naturally to accept scrap thieves as the Japanese version of "Apache."

Although the term "Apache" originally referred to all southwestern Athapascan Indians with the exception of the Navajos, the Spanish sometimes applied the term to non-Athapascan Indians, particularly to those who were effective in resisting the European invasion of their lands.[13] Since the term, from the colonial period on, has been open to a variety of interpretations, it is no wonder that whoever resists government or institutions became liable to be called "Apache." Yang was so keenly aware of this signifying history that he complicated the romantic plot of *Yoru wo Kakete* ethnopolitically by depicting the tragedy of Korean communists exiled to the Omura concentration camp in Nagasaki, the Japanese equivalent of Auschwitz. *Yoru wo Kakete*, then, can be appreciated not only as a critical homage to Kaiko's *Nippon Sanmon Opera*, written thirty-five years before, but also as a radically experimental recreation of the Indian captivity narrative,[14] set not in the postcolonialist United States but in postbubble Japan, where the serious demands of restructuring and reengineering society transformed many unfortunate salarymen into a new type of Apache, inhabiting cardboard boxes.

In contrast to Yang Sok Il's multiculturalist interpretation of the figure of the Apache, Sakyo Komatsu's *Nippon Apacchi-Zoku* (written in 1964, five years after Ken Kaiko's *Nippon Sanmon Opera*) offers mainly a techno-primatological reading. While Yang tried to investigate the ethnic problems of Korean Japanese inherent in the figure of the Apache, Komatsu had devised a new ecology, ending up with a highly cyborgian new species called the Japanese Apache, with a man called Niké Jiro, whose name consists of Chinese characters liable to be mispronounced as "Geronimo" (Jiro Nimou), as their chief. Since their mutant and extraordinary organisms enabled them to eat and digest and even recycle iron and metallic scrap literally and biologically, this new Apache could survive postwar Japan very easily. Thus Komatsu—who, unlike Kaiko, had lived through the campaign against the Japan–U.S. security treaty in the late sixties—succeeded in displacing the ethnopolitical problems of the Korean Japanese with the superevolutionary potentiality of the Japanese Apache.[15] When the novel *Nippon Apacchi-Zoku* came out in 1964, Komatsu succeeded in attracting a larger audience than expected; as Ken Kaiko pointed out in his dialogue with the author, Komatsu's narratological playfulness exhibited in the text fascinated more than sixty thousand readers.[16]

Let me at this point investigate further the "narratological playfulness" of Sakyo Komatsu. To begin with. Komatsu started by radically disfiguring the existing idioms of the Japanese Apache. Consider their slang, already depicted in Kaiko's *Nippon Sanmon Opera*. In those days in Osaka, by the idiomatic expressions like "eating iron scrap" ("Tetsu wo taberu") or "laughing at iron scrap" ("Tetsu wo warau") the Japanese Apache actually meant stealing scrap and making money out of it.

The reason why such strange expressions were invented is very simple. For the Apache to survive in postwar Japan it was necessary to transport scrap secretly by boat down a polluted river. If detected by the police, they escaped quickly, capsizing their boats and the scrap with them. Later, specially trained Apache divers would return to retrieve the scrap, often swallowing the scummy, contaminated water. Their job was critical, for in diving so deep to retrieve their "treasure," some divers drowned, choking on the green, weird slime; others survived and contributed much to the whole community, thanks to their extraordinary lung capacity. These Apache divers are impressively described in Yang Sok Il's *Yoru wo Kakete*, in which a diver called Kim so skillfully survives the conditions of the grotesque river that he is applauded by his fellows as a hero (117). If he did not "eat scrap" in this way, the diver could not have enriched his own community. To put it another way, whoever is able to "eat scrap" and literally become one with metallics deserves the name of hero or (figuratively) of "superhuman."

With this history in mind, we can understand why Ken Kaiko, from the seventies, began foregrounding the Rabelaisian aesthetics of eating bizarre foods,[17] while Sakyo Komatsu, in the early sixties, had come up with the idea of disfiguring the idiom "eating scrap" and creating a "metallivorous" species. In retrospect, both Kaiko and Komatsu seem to have promoted the new aesthetics of postwar "bad taste," by radically questioning the significance of seemingly depressing ruins and junkyards. Such a metallocentric revolution of sensibility can be reaffirmed by a glance at the history of postwar Japanese comic strips, in which Japanese children have fervently welcomed metallic superheroes such as Tetsuwan Atomu (*Astro Boy*, 1952–), Tetsujin Nijuhachi-Go (*Iron Man*, no. 28, 1956–), Eito-Man (*Android*, no. 8, 1963–), and Saibogu 009 (*Cyborg 009*, 1964–).

Of course, as a literary critic Kiichi Sasaki astutely points out in his introduction to the Shincho Pocketbook edition of Kaiko's *Nippon Sanmon Opera*, what Kaiko does in the novel is not to represent the beauty of the ugly Apache community mimetically, but to discover in it his own genius for kitsch aesthetics, which the writer had long cherished and nurtured within himself (291–292). If this is the way Kaiko was to develop his original theory about "the beauty of deformity," and if this new aesthetics of Kaiko's inspired Komatsu to invent a science-fictional possible world in which the act of eating bizarre scrap is totally rationalized, we should reappraise both of the writers as the originators of the postwar Japanese epicureanism of kitsch.

What is especially noteworthy is that Komatsu illustrates the relativism of bad taste with creatures eating inorganic things: the Chinese mythic monkey Sun Wu Kong eating an iron ball while imprisoned within rock, and the French symbolist Arthur Rimbaud, who encouraged the audience to eat minerals (*Nippon Apacchi-Zoku*, 92–93). In Komatsu's novel scrapped cars also undergo some kind of biotechnological operation by which they are genetically combined with the metallivorous Apache and reproduce themselves; scrapped cars are raised, just like dairy cattle—by "carboys," not cowboys. In this way, Komatsu parodies formulas of the classic western novel.

What makes *Nippon Apacchi-Zoku* most remarkable, however, is that Komatsu even sets up the econoindustrial body politic as a subject that eats bizarre foods, namely, the excretions of the Japanese Apache. Since the superdigestive systems of the Japanese Apache parallel an actual ironworks where one can make high-quality steel out of raw minerals, the establishment of more lavatories for the Apache will help the whole steel industry flourish. While Shozo Numa metamorphosed Japanese people into coprophagous animals in *Yapoo the Human Cattle* (1970 and 1991),[18] Komatsu has metaphoricized the whole Japanese body politic as coprophagous, incorporating the metallivorous biology of the Apache into its econoindustrial system. Thus the narrator of *Nippon Apacchi-Zoku* states: "Think twice, and you won't find abnormal taste very abnormal. What used to be bizarre food is now considered very normal, as is the case with the taste for cigarettes and chewing gum that American Indians taught us about. And right now, it is the Japanese Apache who will revolutionize our existing taste, by popularizing the good taste of iron scrap" (219–220).

Given this statement, we should hesitate to read into the act of scrap eating an ontological renunciation of the status quo, as was proposed by Masami Fukushima, the founder of *Hayakawa's SF Magazine* and the first editor of Komatsu.[19] What Komatsu emphasizes here is not the limit of human existence symbolized by the bad taste of scrap, but a revolution in our very conservative taste, which is indicative of the superevolution of human beings. This reading is confirmed by a most impressive scene in the opening of *Nippon Apacchi-Zoku*, in which simple iron scraps gradually arouse the appetite of the protagonist (12).

Even now, we have not lost the spirit of the Japanese Apache. The tribal chief Jiro Nimo speaks to the radio: "Let's see if men will win, or if we Apache will win—go ahead, and eat as much as you like!" (341). We cannot help but hear in that cry a dramatic echo of the decision of one of the Tetsuo tribe—very possibly a descendent of the

Japanese Apache—to destroy the metropolis in Tsukamoto's *Tetsuo*. As Komatsu's Apache tribe attempted to retake Japan, so Tsukamoto's Tetsuo tribe wants to demolish the whole city of Tokyo. This vision is further elaborated in *Tetsuo II*. Listen to the hero of the film talk to his brother as follows: "Don't be afraid anymore. If you find it beautiful, keep destroying whatever you like. Overthrow the greatest." At this point, we become convinced that the cyborgian tribe of Tetsuo is a distant variation of the "Japanese Apache."

The Genealogy of the Metallocentric Imagination

A literary-historical perspective has helped us locate the archetype of Tetsuo in the texts of writers ranging from Ken Kaiko and Sakyo Komatsu down to Yang Sok Il. Even so, we should raise a serious question. Why have the postwar Japanese people been so intrigued by the metallocentric imagination? Let me construct a more complete theory concerning this topic.

In the first place, we should not forget that it is not merely literary-historical discourse but also the intellectual-historical genealogy of the Kyoto school that must have inspired Komatsu to reconsider the identity of the Japanese Apache as essentially cyborgian. Recent Japanologist and critical feminist observations on the cyborg make us aware that the pre-deconstructive theory of "zettai mujunteki jiko doitsu" (absolute contradictory self-identity) proposed by the Kyoto philosopher Kitaro Nishida, had, as Mark Driscoll has pointed out, always already been concerned with the making of the cyborgian body,[20] and that the primatology of the Kyoto biologist Kinji Imanishi had, as Donna Haraway has suggested, been systematized as a socioanthropological pseudocolonialist theory.[21] Insofar as the cyborgian identity is fashioned at the intersection of deconstructive body politics and imperialist primatology, it seems very natural that Komatsu, a devotee of the Kyoto school, came to mock the discursive history of evolutionism by envisioning the metallivorous Apache basically as "more than human" (*Nippon Apacchi-Zoku*, 317). For evolutionism has sharply distinguished between the human and the nonhuman, or between Caucasian and Asian and African. But it is also true that Komatsu designed the metallivorous Apache in the image of the future Japanese. And he conceived this idea by indulging himself in the texts of another Kyoto intellectual, the literary-critical, charismatic Kiyoteru Hanada. A brief glance at the importance of Hanada as a representative theoretician of postwar metallocentric avant-gardism will clarify why postwar Japanese romancers have persistently been fascinated with cyborgian or coprophagous or metallivorous subjectivities such as the Japanese Apache, Yapoo the Human Cattle, or Tetsuo.

The only neat way to comprehend Hanada's perspective on the metallocentric imagination is to reread "A Note on Don Juan," one of his best known essays of 1949.[22] In this essay Hanada locates Don Juan's greatest pleasure not in his romantic love of voluptuous women but in his acceptance of an invitation to dinner by the stone statue of the Commander in the denouement of Molière's play *Don Juan* (1665). Thus, Hanada considers Don Juan's romantic love not ephemeral, like fireworks, but enduring, like crystals. Hanada does not attempt to recuperate Molière's real intention, but to positively misread and radically deconstruct *Don Juan*. What makes such a misreading remarkable is that Hanada wants to illustrate the superevolutionary possibility of Don Juan by closely rereading the characterization of this prodigal son.

Since the Renaissance, Europeans have tended to give priority to the organic over the inorganic, that is, to vegetation over minerals, animals over vegetation, and especially human beings over other animals. What a humanistic, too humanistic perspective! For us to trespass the limit of modernity, it is indispensable to displace such a hard-core anthropocentricism with metallocentricism, to get more interested in the inanimate. Here, let us recall that, as Hanada pointed out, T. E. Hulme once noticed that the focus of twentieth-century art was moving from the vital and the organic to the geometrical and the inorganic. Hulme seems to have found it significant that the new talents of art had come to prefer the inanimate to the animate, and minerals to animals and vegetation. Certainly, many people now are more attracted by the geometric outlines of mineral crystals than the vaguely curved outlines of animals and vegetables (Hanada, "A Note on Don Juan," 51). I would redefine Don Juan as one of the metallocentric precursors of Tetsuo and the Apache.

Hanada's representation of Don Juan convinces us that it is not minerals but "ideas and bodies that seem such impure and weak and unstable raw materials as to be dismembered radically and reorganized more systematically" (55). And yet, why did Hanada feel obliged to recharacterize Don Juan as an idol of metallocentricism?

The answer is not very difficult. Inasmuch as Hanada has long speculated on the significance not just of the Renaissance but of the "transition period" per se, Don Juan seemed to him the perfect representation of a transition period, for "his society was facing a radical turning point between the stage of organic evolution and that of revolution, destroying and reconstructing the society mentally and physically" (64).

Historically speaking, it is true that Molière's Don Juan appealed to the spirit of Restoration in England. But let me note that Hanada started his discussion of the European Renaissance by reading that period as the ideal model that the postwar Japanese people should follow in our own age of transition and "reconstruction."[23] In other words, Hanada created the metallocentric Don Juan in the ideal image of the postwar Japanese. And, it is the metallocentric imagination that Hanada had delineated as a perfect crystal of his kitsch aesthetics and his superevolutionism, which resulted in the amazingly powerful image of the metallivorous Japanese Apache in the science-fictional imagination of Sakyo Komatsu.

At the end of Komatsu's *Nippon Apacchi-Zoku*, the whole nation is dominated by the metallivorous and metallicized freaks, and a refugee government is established by other, unmetallicized Japanese. This novel thus splendidly envisions a multinational and multicultural future Japan in which even the pure Japanese have to go through struggles, as one of the minorities, with other minority groups. While Ken Kaiko, writing *Nippon Sanmon Opera*,[24] had in mind only existing minority groups represented by the Koreans, Komatsu in his novel does not model the Japanese Apache necessarily on Korean scrap thieves, but extrapolates the future Japanese themselves as the radical other. This is how Komatsu comes up with his own enduring literary topic of the "diaspora of the Japanese," based on the possible disjunction between nation as a geopolitical entity and nation as an ethnopolitical majority. It is no accident, therefore, that in the early seventies, Shozo Numa's far-future speculative fiction *Kachikujin Yapoo* (Yapoo the Human Cattle [1970])—in which the Japanese people are reconsidered not as *Homo sapiens* but as *Simias sapiens*[25]—and Isaiah Ben-Dasan's *Nihonjin (Nipponjin) to Yudayajin* (The Japanese and the Jew [1970])—which attempts a highly inventive comparison between Judaism and "Nihonism"[26]—were followed by Sakyo Komatsu's four-million-copy bestseller *Nippon Chinbotsu* (Japan Sinks) in 1973, in which an apocalyptic earthquake causes the whole of Japan to sink literally and dramatically, with the Japanese people being forced to follow the example of the Jewish diaspora. While the ancient Jews experienced its original diasporic dispersion (597–598 B.C.) as an ontological predicament, Komatsu radically reconfigures the notion of diaspora as a powerful engine of Japanese capitalism in the high growth period in the 1970s. Although this novel is being revalued now as an extraordinarily accurate prediction of what happened in the wake of the devastating Kobe earthquake, which shook western Japan on January 17, 1995, *Nippon Chinbotsu*, back in the seventies, had helped popularize diaspora as the most ideal form of internationalism, not depressing but encouraging contemporary Japanese businessmen to go abroad as volunteer exiles, and to develop Japanese economic hegemony.[27] That is why the blurb for the first Kobunsha edition of the novel described Sakyo Komatsu as an "international literary figure," and *Nippon Chinbotsu* as a work "awaited internationally." While *Nippon Apacchi-Zoku* represented the metallocentric spirit of postwar reconstruction, *Nippon Chinbotsu* symbolized the econo-internationalist spirit of the high growth period.

In retrospect, the genealogy of the metallocentric imagination is essentially compatible with the history of the postwar Japanese mental condition, of what I have called "creative masochism" in this book. The year 1946, one year after the end of the war, saw the coincidental publications of Ango Sakaguchi's sensational essay "Daraku-Ron" (An Invitation to Total Depravity) and Kiyoteru Hanada's literary-historical book *Fukkouki no Seishin* (The Spirit of Renaissance), both of which brilliantly reflected their contemporary zeitgeist and helped establish the econopolitical principle of total destruction and radical reconstruction in postwar Japan. Without Sakaguchi and Hanada as the postwar ideologues, we could not have seen, between the mid-fifties and the early sixties, the appearance of the metallocentric Japanese Apache, the far-future Japanese (Yapoo) as human cattle, and the representative Japanese monster Godzilla (1954–2004). It is the postwar discourse of creative masochism that prepared the way for the popularity of the megahit *Nippon Chinbotsu*. We should not forget that the concept of postmodern diaspora is further developed by recent "virtual reality" narratives, especially Goro Masaki's *Venus City* (1992) and Alexander Besher's *RIM* (1994), in both of which the erasure of Japan or Tokyo takes place not in geospace but in cyberspace. Furthermore, the emergence of the postbubble economy in the mid-nineties makes it easier for us to accept other creative masochistic concepts such as "creative defeat" (Shigeto Tsuru), the "mental history of failure and defeat" (Masao Yamaguchi), and "the strategy of being radically fragile" (Seigo Matsuoka).[28]

In short, Japanese intellectual history has gradually systematized the metallocentric philosophy of creative masochism by radically transforming the humiliating experience of the diaspora into the techno-utopian principle of construction. This enables us to explain the reason why we Japanese are more tempted to naturalize and "digest" the digital electronic information network of virtual reality, feeling as we do that we are essentially metallivorous. Accordingly, for the time being, we can safely characterize Shinya Tsukamoto's *Tetsuo* diptych as the most experimental junction of the postwar literary history of the Japanese Apache and the postwar intellectual history of creative masochism.

Conclusion

I would like to close by revisiting my theory about why the film of *Tetsuo* has been more appealing to the American audience than to the Japanese. I have already considered post-Vietnam America's fear of and fascination with Mongoloid skin, and explained the philosophical background of *Tetsuo* in the postwar Japanese context. But let me here investigate how the story of *Tetsuo* might strike the American audience as a dazzling re-Japanization of the Indian captivity narrative and the Jewish diaspora narrative.

As I noted above, Sakyo Komatsu's *Nippon Apacchi-Zoku* skillfully reinvents the conventions of the Indian captivity narrative, in which an ethnic majority tries to capture minorities within its own discourses by narrativizing the threat of the latter, as shown in the Puritan theocratic writings of America. On the other hand, *Nippon Chinbotsu* vividly recreates the convention of the diaspora narrative, in which the most stable and most dominant become exiled, as we see not only in Jewish history but also in the legend that American Indians may be one of the lost tribes of Israel.[29]

The publication of *Nippon Chinbotsu* in 1973 coincided not only with the explosive popularity of Jewish discourse in Japan, but also with the end of the Vietnam War. These events were followed, from the seventies through the eighties, by a number of Vietnam War novels and movies, and these narratives ended up as another version of the Indian captivity narrative, in which the Vietnamese were another colonialist and orientalist target. An example is Stanley Kubrick's 1987 film *Full Metal Jacket*, in which American soldiers in Vietnam compare themselves to western cowboys, and the Vietnamese are featured as a new version of "vanishing Americans."[30] Given that most Vietnam War movies cannot help but arouse the fear of high-tech Mongoloid soldiers as a type of cyborg, the western discourse of orientalism in these films turns out to be closely intertwined with the western construction of cyborgian subjectivity.[31]

To untie such a complex entanglement of postmodern discourses, it will be more convenient to reconstrue the figure of Arnold Schwarzenegger, who made his major debut with *Conan the Barbarian* in 1982 (a typical slave narrative recalling the tradition of the captivity narrative) and became famous for the *Terminator* series (1984 and 2003)—a masterpiece of cyborg narrative with the future diaspora as its narratological drive.[32] The decade between the 1980s and the 1990s made it possible for Schwarzenegger to prove the colonial subjectivity of the near-Mongoloid barbarian as basically cyborgian, and the transtemporal subjectivity of T-1000 as essentially colonialist. It is through this representational complex that the Vietnam War movie as a postcolonial Indian captivity narrative encounters the cyborg movie as a high-tech diaspora narrative. In consequence, to the ordinary American audience familiar with the discourse both of the Vietnam War movie and the cyborg movie, *Tetsuo* must seem to radically reproduce the most uncanny fear of and fascination with the techno-Mongoloid, just by conjuring up the American love-hate ambivalence toward the cyborgian subjectivity. And, if the cyborg, as Jonathan Goldberg has suggested, can be reinterpreted as the ultimate form of a celibate machine menacing the modern hegemony of heterosexual reproduction,[33] *Tetsuo*'s world as the paradise of Mongoloid cyborg bachelors will also refresh the hyperorientalist discourse of the Mongoloid gay, as developed in gay films such as *Kitchen* (1989), *Kirakira Hikaru* (1992), *Okoge* (1992), *M. Butterfly* (1993), and *Wedding Banquet* (1993).[34] It means that someday in the United States, *Tetsuo* will also enjoy the privilege of being analyzed or misread from a postcolonialist, hyperorientalist, and queer-theoretical perspective, which has remained a blind spot back in Japan.

Thus what the *Tetsuo* series constitutes is a very interesting revolving door of reading, for it has been skillfully circulating between the postwar Japanese discourse of creative masochism and the post-Vietnam American discourse of postcolonialism. If you choose the one, you will miss the other, and vice versa. To say the least, we should not doubt that the *Tetsuo* diptych is one of the best wrought avant-pop western movies,[35] in which traditional Japanese Apaches metamorphose into postmodern Luddites, now domesticated as "cyber-cowboys." However, whether this figure of cyber-cowboy has always already been that of drugstore cowboy or not is still open to numerous interpretations.

CONCLUSION Waiting for Godzilla: Toward a Globalist Theme Park

The Late Capitalist Synchronicity between Different Cultures

This conclusion starts by beaming you back to the first chapter and letting you find what has happened to "the three stages in the development of mimicry," especially the latter two stages that I promised to spell out in more detail: the late capitalist synchronicity between different cultures, and the multicultural and transgeneric poetics of chaotic negotiation.[1]

As far as "literature" is concerned, Japan has been a country of excessive importation, not excessive exportation. This kingdom of translation is very good at translating and popularizing foreign cultures, however invisible Japan itself is to other nations, because it does not translate and export many of its own national literary products. As a result, Japanese literature is nearly invisible abroad, where it constitutes a minor culture, or what Samuel Delany would call "paraliterature." Like women's fiction, black fiction, gay fiction, experimental fiction, and the commercial genres, Japanese literature abroad is undoubtedly marginal.[2] However, situated on the margin, paraliterature has recently become the model for literature itself. At the same time, in Japanese postmodern literature, the logic of imitation has been replaced by "synchronicity"—a synchronicity between American and Japanese works.

This paradigm shift from the logic of imitation to the logic of synchronicity is especially evident in the artistic development of Haruki

Fig. 20 Final view of Godzilla, from *Godzilla: Final Wars*, 2004. © 2004 Toho Pictures, Inc., trademark and © 2004 Toho Co. Ltd.

Murakami, one of the best known postmodern Japanese writers in English-speaking countries. Murakami started writing in the late seventies by imitating the literary styles of H. P. Lovecraft, Scott Fitzgerald, and Kurt Vonnegut. More recently, we see a deeper sense of the past, characteristic of his *Nejimakidori Kuronikuru* (The Wind-Up Bird Chronicle), beautifully coinciding with the historical consciousness apparent in the young American video artist David Blair, who stormed our late-postmodern reality studio with his avant-pop masterpiece video *WAX, or the Discovery of Television among the Bees* in 1991, and who is now completing a hyperhistorical romance called *Jews in Space*, featuring Israel in Manchuria. These examples suggest that the more cultural transactions and translations occur between any two cultures, the more synchronic these cultures and their national narratives become.

Indeed, it has become increasingly difficult for us to identify who is the precursor and who is the follower. Thus *Moon Palace* (1989) by the American writer Paul Auster and *Higan-Sensei* (Master and Discipline, 1992) by the Japanese writer Masahiko Shimada are two typically "avant-pop" novels: both skillfully displace the boundary between literature and paraliterature, and both use a Chinese restaurant, Moon Palace in New York, as their central setting. Their plot structures are likewise similar, as they weave their exemplary "orphan" narratives. Shimada, who wrote *Higan-Sensei* without reading Auster, narrates the story of an orphan-seeking father, who mirrors strikingly the father-seeking orphan in Auster's *Moon Palace*.

In another example of synchronicity, *F/32* (1990) by the Greek-American writer Eurudice and *Oyayubi-P no Shugyo-jidai* (Apprenticeship of Bigtoe-P) (1993) by the Japanese writer Rieko Matsuura are both typically "cyborg-feminist" novels that radically mock the boundary between patriarchal and feminist literature. Presumably influenced by Kathy Acker's *The Empire of the Senseless* (1988)—which itself was deeply inspired by Nagisa Oshima's 1976 film *In the Realm of the Senses* (*Ai no korrida* [Bullfight of Love]; *L'Empire Des Sens* in French)—both novels characterize genitals as independent protagonists, either male or female. While Eurudice describes a woman's cunt running away from her body in a Gogolian way, Matsuura tells us about a woman's big toe that metamorphoses into a penis in a Kafkaesque fashion.

If you find yourself fascinated by Jesse Detwiler—the weird garbage guerilla in Don DeLillo's meganovel *Underworld* (1997), who stole and analyzed "the household trash of a number of famous people" and whose activities had "a crisp climax when he was arrested for snatching the garbage of J. Edgar Hoover from the rear of the Director's house in northwest Washington" (286–287)—you should take a look at the hypercult nonfiction *Kichiku no Susume* (How to Enjoy the Life of a Garbage Guerilla), by Hyakuro Murasaki. It was published in 1996, a year before *Underworld*, and its author, one of the most dangerous Japanese journalists writing today, tactfully invites you to poke around garbage of neighbors; this work will deepen your insight into the other, making visible the invisible in our everyday life.

In addition to such an intercultural synchronicity, the 1980s saw another revolutionary paradigm shift. For the first time since John Luther Long's novel *Madame Butterfly* (1898), Anglo-American writers, through their own logic of mimicry, imitated and appropriated Japanesque images, that is images that at once draw on and distort Japanese culture. At the same time their Japanese counterparts came to realize that writing subversive fiction in the wake of cyberpunk meant gaining an insight into a radically science-fictional "Japan." Thus, the significance of Japonism in the fin-de-siècle period is carefully repeated and radically modified by the rise of what I would like to call neo-Japonism around the turn of the millennium. Of course, while American representations of Japan become attractive precisely because of their distortions of Japanese culture, they often give rise to

Fig. 21 Gojiro, a.k.a. Godzilla, as a stand-up comedian. Cover of the Penguin edition of *Gojiro*, by Mark Jacobson, 1991. © Peter Garriock.

heated controversy on the part of the Japanese audience. I remember one of my friends from Chiba City reacting angrily when he read the first chapter of William Gibson's *Neuromancer*, "Chiba City Blues"; which seemed to him to represent the Chiba people very pejoratively.

In another appropriation of Japanese images, the American avant-pop writer Mark Jacobson became so fascinated by the most famous Japanese villain, Godzilla, that, in his first novel, *Gojiro*, in 1991, he "reorientalized" Japan by making the Huck-and-Jim-like friendship between Godzilla and a Japanese boy, Komodo, its central topic. Indeed, in the history of Japanese cinema, by the 1980s Godzilla had undergone a transformation in Japan. The image of Godzilla the gigantic public enemy of the fifties was displaced by Godzilla the all-Japanese superhero in the economic boom period. While Godzilla the radioactive green monster of the 1950s revived the fear of Moby-Dick, the great white whale, Jacobson now encourages not only Japanese screenwriters but also American novelists to recreate the postnuclear romance between Japan and the United States. The more synchronic the two cultures get, the more accepting the Japanese become even to the rise of postmodern orientalism.

Of course, you could well have mixed feelings toward such a conversion narrative involving Godzilla. Did Godzilla attempt to adjust to the contemporary condition of political correctness? Indeed, the year of 1995 saw the abrupt cancellation of the Smithsonian Museum's exhibit of the atomic bomb, for various "politically correct" reasons. While Japan has continually emphasized the threat of the atomic bomb, the United States has never forgotten the indignity of Pearl Harbor. It is the then prevalent discourse of political correctness that helped cancel this exhibit. Responding to the contemporary imperative, Godzilla himself could not help but become neutral, only to lose thus his cinematographic appeal.

And yet, a postcolonialist rereading of Godzilla by Yasuo Nagayama, highly critical of this conservative trend of political correctness, provides us with a religious-historical background that promotes a nationalistic image of the monster.[3] Linguistically speaking, despite the Japanese etymology, in which "gorira" (gorilla) and "kujira" (whale) get combined, the English etymology of "Godzilla" naturally conjures up the image of the "god" of all "lizards." I am not sure how the name came to be spelled this way. But, historically speaking, this English etymology comes beautifully to the point. For, as Nagayama has pointed out, one of the origins of Godzilla can be discovered in a pseudoscientific and pseudoreligious theory championed by a nineteenth-century new Shintoist, Masumi Ohishigori. Now that Godzilla has become the all-Japanese superhero, his former role of global enemy is assigned to King Ghidorah, whose golden scales represent Caucasian blondness). From the end of the Edo era up through the Meiji era, Ohishigori was so aware of the limits of Shintoism that he modernized it so it could catch up with Christianity or Buddhism. Thus, deeply influenced by the rise of Darwinism and paleontology, Ohishigori the Shintoist, a practitioner of ancestor worship, came to invent an amazing theory that located the origins of man in dinosaurs born of Japanese gods. This theory of dinosaurs as the origin of the Japanese had a tremendous impact on one of the mystic cults, Oomoto-kyo, which was very active in the Taisho era. The members of this cult further expanded Ohishigori's theory by asserting that some dinosaurs are still alive deep within the sea as dragon gods, and that Japanese myths and legends, as we can read in *Kojiki* and *Nihon-Nihongi*, all narrate incidents occurring in Jurassic Japan. Just as Thomas Hobbes's political theory in *Leviathan* (1651) promoted the western idea of the nation-state, and just as Herman Melville's encyclopedic fiction *Moby-Dick* (1851) not only revived the image of Leviathan but also that of dragons and whales "strangely jumbled together," so, in the heyday of manifest destiny and the dinosaur gold rush, Masumi Ohishigori's theory of dinosaurs as the origin of the Japanese doubtlessly helped Meiji Japan modernize itself, and even survive the postwar junkyard, all in the form of Godzilla. With this new Shintoist background in mind, we are encouraged to radically reinterpret Godzilla as the Japanese God, who would threaten western countries as the fearful other. A typical example of this was the appearance, at the peak of the American Japan-bashing period, of a cartoon satirizing Japan as Godzilla storming American real estate in the April 5, 1990 issue of the *San Francisco Chronicle*.

Perhaps this image inspired William Gibson to reconsider—in his fourth novel, *Virtual Light* (1993), and the sixth novel, *All Tomorrow's Parties* (1999)—the significance of the San Francisco earthquake of 1989 and the one he predicted for Japan in the near future, which he nicknamed "Godzilla." Tim Burton included Godzilla in his slapstick film *Mars Attacks!* (1997). And Roland Emmerich, in 1998, radically transformed and redesigned the monster in his film *Godzilla* (1998), trying to comically remix the Japanese monster with the Hollywoodian dinosaur. The more popular the figure of Godzilla gets in global culture, the more immune contemporary people become to any threat of foreign power and any possibility of cultural miscegenation. In this way, Godzilla encourages us to survive the age of total apocalypse.

The Multicultural and Transgeneric Poetics of Chaotic Negotiation

In the late 1990s, American and Japanese cultures entered a new phase of interaction: from then onward, essentially chaotic and transculturally infectious negotiations occur between orientalism and occidentalism; between the western belief in eternity and the Japanese aesthetics of the moment; between a western productionist and idealist sensibility and a Japanese high-tech-consumerist and posthistorical mentality; or even between the science-fictional Japan of the American imagination and Japanese science fiction itself. The creative clash between cultures has made it easier for us to envision a new kind of

Fig. 22 Ms. Downer as a rocket girl (left). From Erika Kobayashi's anime "Bombastic Melancholy." © Erika Kobayashi.

theme park beautifully constructed within global space. Its features can be found in Philip K. Dick's alternate postwar America, controlled through yin-yang in *The Man in the High Castle* (1962); Sakyo Komatsu's postwar junkyard in *The Japanese Apache* (1964); William Gibson's "Walled City," simulated in cyberspace in his fifth novel. *Idoru* (1997); Toshihiko Yahagi's "Mount Fuji," reconstructed by nuclear acupuncture in *A-Ja-Pan!* (1997); Kyoji Kobayashi's phantasmagoric kabuki production, *Sekai-za* (The World Theater), featured in *The Day of Kabuki* (1998), which won a Yukio Mishima Award; Neal Stephenson's post-Tolkienian and postorientalist version of Manila in *Cryptonomicon* (1999); and Mark Danielewski's globally labyrinthine haunted house, constructed in his first meganovel, *House of Leaves* (2000).

In order to detail what I would like to call a globalist theme park built by the nuclear imagination, it will be useful here to talk about some narratives by Erika Kobayashi, the self-proclaimed avant-pop girl, born in 1978 in Tokyo, whose post-Pynchonesque comic strip video narrative *Bakudan-Musume no Yuutsu* (Bombastic Melancholy: A Story of Ms. Downer, the Human Bomb) (1999) has received numerous national and international awards and is highly admired in the

United States and Russia. I have called it post-Pynchonesque, simply because her characterization has much in common with the rocket man Tyron Slothrop, one of the central figures in Pynchon's *Gravity's Rainbow*, who serves as a human radar, hypersensitive to and hypersexually connected with the destination of V2 rockets. What is more, Kobayashi confesses to have been directly influenced by David Blair's nonlinear video narrative *WAX, or The Discovery of Television among the Bees*, which we can interpret as a post-cyberpunkish take on *Gravity's Rainbow*. Theoretically speaking, while the nuclear imagination that expanded through the Godzilla series could well have inspired Komatsu and Pynchon to write their major novels, it is the post-Pynchonesque narratology made possible through Gibson and Blair that very naturally led Kobayashi to create her own avant-pop work, which deals with the impossible romantic love affair between Ms. Downer, a humanoid atomic bomb, and her boyfriend. Note that the rise of the Godzilla series, which featured a mutant dinosaur revived by a nuclear explosion, took place in the mid-1950s; around the turn of the millennium Kobayashi's "Bombastic Melancholy" is foregrounding Ms. Downer as a nuclear weapon herself. While nuclear disaster began as an essential tragedy in the mid-twentieth century, it has gradually transformed itself into a kind of literary motivation for black comedy. In this respect, I cannot help but appreciate Erika Kobayashi as an avant-pop black humorist endowed with a postnuclear imagination, capable of blurring the cultural distinctions between the All-American Disneyland and the All-Japanese Godzillaland.

Thus I cannot resist the temptation to discuss her first novella "Neversoapland," printed in the autumn 2000 issue of Kawade Publishers' quarterly *Bungei* and published in book form by the same publisher in March 2001. Take a look first at the strange title, and you will be disturbed by its extraordinary combination of concepts, for the title consists of our familiar term "Neverland" in the sense of J. M. Barrie and the Japanese-English coinage "Soapland," signifying a contemporary brothel—what used to be called a Turkish bath in Japan until the mid-1980s. Thus you are also invited to interpret "Neversoapland" primarily as a pornographic version of *Peter Pan*.

The story opens quite shockingly: "I have played the role of Wendy for fifteen years" (3). Sounding like an orthodox fairy tale, the story then abruptly introduces an extremely bizarre murder, shamelessly copying the scenario of *Ai no Koriida* (In the Realm of the Senses) directed by Nagisa Oshima. You may understand the extent of its impact simply by looking at Kathy Acker's homage to the film, *The Empire of the Senseless*, which inspired her young followers, like Eurudice, to weave new avant-porn texts, as I briefly explained above. Oshima's film itself is an adaptation of the famous true story of Ms. Sada Abe, the maid who in 1936 killed and castrated her lover, Kichizo, as an act of love; the two had shut themselves in for what turned out to be six nights of sexual indulgence culminating in Kichizo's death and mutilation. A similar scandal occurs in Kobayashi's "Neversoapland" with Wendy's neighbors, a notoriously lustful couple, when the wife, Haruneko, suddenly bites off her husband's genitals. Journalists, all curious to know what in fact happened, storm the narrator Wendy, "How do you think of the accident, old woman?" (12).

Yes, this novella starts with a tremendously blasphemous mélange of the canonical fairytale *Peter Pan* and the hardcore pornography of *In the Realm of the Senses*. The narrator, Wendy, however, is not an adolescent girl, as in the original J. M. Barrie tale, but an old woman imitating the life style of Samantha, the beautiful young witch in the famous TV soap opera *Bewitched* (ABC, 1964–1972)—an old woman, that is, who decides not to become mature. Thus, "Neversoapland" centers on an old-fashioned romantic love affair between Wendy and her husband Peter, an old man affected with Alzheimer's disease who is always wetting his pants. On one hand, Peter murmurs: "Wendy, I find it more and more difficult to remember things. . . . But Wendy, probably it means that I'm now approaching childhood. Recently I have felt strongly that I'll end up by becoming the real Peter Pan" (25). On the other hand, Wendy is so anxious to visit a "Neverland" designed for children that her fear of sexuality increases day by day, and she becomes more and more particular about cleanliness. Then, whenever she is having a bath together with him, Wendy becomes afraid of Peter's erection. "Anyhow," she says, "I've never had sexual intercourse with anyone. This means I can't be mature forever. I will definitely become a child sooner or later" (33).

Despite this asceticist and puritanist way of life, however, the narrator and her spouse get involved in an extremely pornographic narrative. Wendy's elder brother meditates so deeply upon the relationship between the quantity of sperm he has produced and his longevity that he becomes a woman. Wendy herself is afflicted with the horrific fantasy of being raped by a swan. She sees a number of penises start jumping in the air just like a school of flying fish. In her fantasy, Wendy's beloved "Asian" husband transfigures himself into Peter Pan.

Through her postmodern and postcolonialist logic of mimicry, Erika Kobayashi's concept could well enrage Oshima fans as well as Disney freaks. For her mostly avant-porn imagination is as subversive as the atomic bomb and Godzilla. Nevertheless, think twice, and you will undoubtedly remember J. M. Barrie's original characterization of Peter Pan as an amnesiac, just like a person with Alzheimer's: "Every child is affected thus the first time he is treated unfairly. All he thinks he has a right to when he comes to you to be yours is fairness. After you have been unfair to him he will love you again, but he will never afterwards be quite the same boy. No one ever gets over the first unfairness; no one except Peter. He often met it, but he always forgot it" (128). Indeed, whenever Peter Pan gets fascinated with a new adventure, he is most likely to forget his most important friends and enemies. "Who is Captain Hook? . . . Who is Tinker Bell?" (232).

Peter Pan is permitted to remain in Neverland, precisely because he is amnesic, exempted from any kind of trauma, without which you cannot become mature. Accordingly, the All-American Disneyland, in which Neverland plays the central role, gives people the best chance to forget traumas and recuperate innocence. Without such a hyperreal theme park the American people could not have recovered from the trauma of the Vietnam War. Thus the multiplication of Disneylands all over the world will implant within all of us the seed of amnesia. Disneyland's amnesia is nonetheless complicated: the prototype Disneyland in Anaheim—built in 1955, one year after the debut of Godzilla in 1954—embraced in its center, especially with its attraction the "Swiss Family Treehouse" in Adventureland, the apparently racist discourse of hardcore orientalism, through which the visitors are trained to see "Japan" as an exotic Far Eastern country providing them with a number of marvelous adventures. Yes, Disneyland, from the beginning, has been not only All-American but also radically orientalist.

As if faithfully repeating this exoticist scenario of Disneyland, William Gibson once suggested to me in 1988 that the Japanese are all living in the future, and Larry McCaffery, in his 1994 essay, affirms the essential similarity between Disneyland's postwar hyperreality and Japan's traditional "floating world." If you take into account these neo-Japonistic statements, made at the peak of Japan bashing, it becomes easier to assume that what we call the age of Pax Japonica in the 1980s must have given the United States the worst trauma since the Vietnam War, and that North American writers and intellectuals have attempted to invent the best discursive strategy for resolving and neutralizing this nightmare. Thus the ideology of the best theme park in the world strongly requires us to always "exoticize," so you will enjoy the highest stage of amnesia, which will erase every trace of national trauma. The multiplication of Disneylands since the 1980s promotes not only globalization as a form of Americanization, but also exoticization as a prescription for conquering national trauma and enjoying global amnesia. But, as Hubert Selby Jr. and Darren Aronofsky beautifully depict in their film *Requiem for a Dream* (written by Selby in 1978 and filmed by Aronofsky in 2000), in which the classic theme park Coney Island is transformed from utopia to dystopia, the American Dream could well become not simply a globalist dream but also a globalist nightmare.

From this perspective, Kobayashi's avant-pornographic ambition gives us an opportunity to criticize, deconstruct, and reexoticize the American standard represented by Disneyland, which has globally naturalized the avant-pop reality studio, spectacle-centered society. Her heroine Wendy makes up her mind to retain her innocence until her death, dreaming of living life in peace in Neverland together with the amnesic Peter. Now we have to read carefully Wendy's response to the Haruneko couple's erotic scandal simulating *In the Realm of the Senses*. Wendy declares that if Peter has an erection, she will respond by "cutting off [his] penis with a kitchen knife." She continues: "Then, I will be taken to court, surrounded by TV cameras. . . . Next, I will definitely be raped . . . not only by swan but also by the whole TV crew" (29). And, ironically, Peter has a "silent erection" in the final sequence of the novella.

We are therefore automatically invited to the unwritten climax in which Wendy, acting the role of Abe Sada, castrates Peter, transforming the pornographic version of *Peter Pan* into the fairy tale version of *In the Realm of the Senses*. Thus Kobayashi's "Neversoapland" convinces us that the most amnesic theme park may contain within itself the most traumatic labyrinth. However hyperreal it seems on the surface, Disneyland has ironically kept growing into both the most innocent playground and the most bureaucratic panopticon. Is this novella a blasphemous appropriation of Disneyland by an ignorant Japanese writer? No, I do not think so. For it was Walt Disney who both entertained American children and committed himself so deeply into the FBI's investigation of suspected communists that he betrayed his left-wing colleagues in Hollywood.[4] Despite its ironic commentary upon the American Dream, Neversoapland turns out to have been so faithful to the contradictory spirit of Walt Disney that it succeeds in disclosing the power of blackness hidden within the political unconscious of Disneyland, that is, of the United States itself. This is why I argue that Kobayashi is one of the contemporary artists whose post-nuclear imagination in the wake of Godzilla brilliantly reveals an aspect of the chaotic negotiation between the discourse of Japan's hyper-occidentalism and that of North America's postorientalism.

Always Exoticize!

While ultraconservative western essentialists might dismiss these kinds of chaotic and transcultural negotiations as being nothing but "trash," this "trash" in fact has complex meanings. As Donald Kuspit points out, "capitalism joins forces with trash culture to destroy human dignity, indeed, to eliminate the very idea and possibility of it."[5] From the perspective of conservatives, Kuspit's "human dignity" seems to mean western white phallocentric dignity. An Australian journalist praised the prophetic nature of Sakyo Komatsu's *Nippon Chinbotsu* (Japan Sinks) after the Osaka-Kobe Earthquake, saying: "At a time when government white papers are laughable, perhaps it should not be surprising that trash can make sense."[6] If one redefines the term "trash" to apply to invisible culture and paraliterature, it becomes applicable not only to popular fiction in the United States but also to all nonwestern literary discourses, including Japanese literature. While nonwestern artists have started their careers by imitating western works of art, their art of "mimicry" has domesticated and even outgrown the other. They paved the way not only for the late capitalist synchronicity between different cultures but also for the highly chaotic and splendidly creative negotiations between western and nonwestern cultures that have recently occurred.

We can reconfirm this creative potential of "mimicry" by tasting the multicultural artistic fruit of miscegenation and metamorphic cross-fertilization between western and nonwestern cultures. Examples include Kiju Yoshida's reorientalization (1988) of Emily Brontë's novel *Wuthering Heights*; David Henry Hwang and Philip Glass's collaborative opera *The Voyage* (1992), on the life of Christopher Colum-

Fig. 23 *Japan Sinks* (a.k.a. "Submersion of Japan"), based on Sakyo Komatsu's novel *Japan Sinks*. © 1973 Toho Pictures, Inc., Toho Eizo Co. Ltd.

bus; Wayne Wang's film *Smoke* (1995), a visual adaptation of Paul Auster's tale; Roland Emmerich's remake of *Godzilla* (1998), and the Japanese unit t.o.L's post-cyberpunkish post-anime *Tamala 2010* (2002). These contemporary films and performances reveal the ways Asian and/or Asian-American directors adopt and adapt Euro-American texts but also the ways Euro-American directors reappropriate Asian narratives.

This trend leads me to reconsider the history of Godzilla as emblematic of the history of these unpredictable and mostly chaotic interchanges. In the 1950s the film *Godzilla* started its career as a typically occidentalist adaptation of Hollywood's dinosaur-like creature movies. In the late 1990s, after a multimillion-dollar deal between Toho Studios and America's Tri-Star Films, the monster Godzilla achieved its present status of the international superhero. I believe this superhero will keep entertaining us, around the new turn of the century, as a multicultural, transgeneric, and postorientalist monster of postmodern representation.

One could therefore agree with Mark Jacobson that "the green of Gojiro (Godzilla)" is not the color that God splashed upon the spectrum, but that of men, "the green we have created" (110) in the globalist age. This vision beautifully coincides with the superb metaphor that Don DeLillo, in *Underworld* (1997), uses for one of the New York skyscrapers: "They were on the roof of a new building, forty stories, it loomed over the reservoir in the park and they stood a while watching runners in the night. . . . Miles thought they resembled fleeing crowds in a Japanese horror film . . . and he came up with a name for the forty-story building . . . *Godzilla Towers*, he thought they ought to call it" (388, emphasis mine). It is noteworthy that DeLillo's character skillfully avoids an orthodox nickname such as "The Tower of Babel." On reading this passage, I felt the imperialistic godhead peculiar to Japan had been dramatically displaced by the global Godzilla, who was now reordering the whole earth.[7]

Of course, if we compare skyscrapers to this famous Japanese monster, you may automatically feel like relating this metaphor to the awful terrorist attack on September 11, 2001. Nevertheless, what I would like to emphasize here is that, as Mark Jacobson suggested, Godzilla's color is exactly the greenness of the whole earth radically refigured as a global theme park, and that the "Godzilla Towers," as Don DeLillo named them, perfectly symbolize the nodal point of the chaotic negotiations between postorientalism and hyperoccidentalism, which undoubtedly point toward the narratives to come.

APPENDIX 1 Toward the Frontiers of "Fiction": From Metafiction and Cyberpunk, through Avant-Pop

The Correspondence between Takayuki Tatsumi and Larry McCaffery

August 17, 1992

Dear Larry,

In retrospect, meeting with you for the first time at a conference in San Diego in the summer of 1986 was a great incident for me, and had a tremendous impact upon my later literary critical career. Of course, before I met you then, I had been familiar with your works. But, what attracted me most was the publication in 1983 of your first collection of essays based on your Ph.D. dissertation, "The Metafictional Muse: The Works of Robert Coover, Donald Barthelme, and William Gass," which I remember reviewing in the same year for a literary journal in Japan, because at that time I was very interested in the aesthetics of postmodern fiction. Around 1980, I could find numerous critics trying to aptly describe the characteristics of contemporary fiction; Robert Scholes invented the term "fabulation," Raymond Federman "surfiction," Linda Hutcheon "narcissistic narrative," Masu'd Zavazadeh "transfiction," Jerome Klinkowitz "post-contemporary fiction," and so on. They seemed to be interested in weird coinages, but in fact most of them were involved with the fate of metafiction—fiction self-criticizing/deconstructing/metaphoricizing fiction itself—which your book explored further than anyone else.

But what happened to metafiction in the mid-80s? Metafiction got so largely disseminated between the 1960s and the 1980s, that its conventional gimmicks like the play of floating signifiers, self-reflexive obsession, Chinese-box structure have become self-evident completely. Post-Pynchon postmodern writers like William Vollmann, Kathy Acker, Steven Millhauser, Julian Barnes, and Peter Ackroyd all seem to take for granted those metafictive devices. But, did those devices actually get dated, or institutionalized?

Here it is very symptomatic that when we got together first at that conference in 1986, a lot of participants discussed the rise of cyberpunk literature represented by William Gibson and others. Theirs was so heated a controversy over cyberpunk itself that it kept most of us from speculating on the literary relationship between cyberpunk SF and postmodern experimental fiction. Of course, you and I have continued to exchange opinions on this topic—in correspondence, in collaborations like your edited *Storming the Reality Studio* (1991), and even at some conferences, including one held in Tokyo in 1987; and it's turned out that it is cyberpunk that let us know of our being surrounded by a metafictive network of advanced capitalist ideology, our own subjectivities constructed as a sort of "cyborg," in Donna Haraway's term. Good old metafictionists in the late 60s narrated the fate of metacharacters in the Chinese-box-like structure of fiction-within-fiction, whereas in the late 80s we have come to live the life of the metacharacters ourselves, with our own identities as the very narrative effects of hypermedia that we invented and have been talking about. Metafiction made us aware that what fiction can tell us is not reality itself but a narrative version of reality, but in the post-Foucauldian hyperreal age we have come to realize that our contemporary lives are all ideological versions of reality, with us characters within narratives. Thus, it is not that metafiction has become out-of-date now, but it is just that whereas metafiction used to be at work as an avant-garde literary device, it has already become part of the popular life we are leading now.

At this point, I find my present vision of metafiction overlapping your theory of "avant-pop." In your inspiring essay "Everything is Permitted: The Post-Pynchon Postmodern American Fiction" (*Positive*, no. 1), you stated: "for most critics of postmodernism, this blurring of the traditional distinctions between 'high' and 'pop' art becomes a central, defining features of postmodernism itself. Today such distinctions are, if anything, even more difficult to maintain. Should rock videos by Madonna, Peter Gabriel, or Laurie Anderson be considered mainstream simply because they are enormously popular—even though they employ visual and poetic techniques that 25 years ago would have certainly been considered highly experimental? Is William Gibson's 'cyberpunk' novel, *Neuromancer*, 'avant-garde' since it employs unusual formal techniques (the use of collage, cut-ups, appropriation of other texts, the introduction of bizarre new vocabularies and metaphors)? Or does its publication by the genre science fiction industry establish it as pop? Are television shows like *Max Headroom*, the early *Saturday Night Live*, or David Lynch's recent *Twin Peaks* series 'underground' works because they utilize so many features associated with postmodern innovation—or as 'pop art' because they were in fact 'merely' television shows?"[1]

August 18, 1992

Yo, Takayuki,

Good to get your note. Or, since I just read your "note" on the MacIntosh word processor computer screen that you loaned me (thanks!), maybe I should not be referring to your "note." I mean, what should we call a note that has no hard copy? Is it still a note, or something else? Or, to be more precise, what about a "note" that is "written" by someone (you and me) who knows in advance that there never will be any hard copy at all (i.e., you and I both know that we'll be reading each other's "notes" on this same computer screen and that these "notes" will eventually be turned over to the people at on discs, which will be used not to create even a single hard copy of our "original" notes but thousands of simulated copies of these "originals"—originals that, in fact, never existed at all and were never intended by either of us to ever exist)? It's a question so mysterious and so complex that perhaps only Baudrillard or Walter Benjamin could answer it, don't you agree?

Likewise, I've begun this "note" to you with this seeming digression about the meaning of the word "note" as a way of suggesting from the outset how strange and ambiguous I think "reality" is today, how difficult it is to speak precisely about "reality" anymore (it never was easy to do this, but one of the main premises underlying my recent thinking about postmodernism is that thinking and speaking about "the real" has become much more difficult and problematic today than it was only twenty years or so ago—and working out in my own mind why this is).

I mean, back when people wrote each other *real notes written in pen and ink*, that whole long digression about "notes" and "originals" and "hard copies" etc., wouldn't have been necessary! You and I would have both known that 1.) there were real notes written in pen on paper by you and me, actual human beings; or 2.) for some reason, you and I had written notes which appeared to be real but which were in fact fictional notes, impostor notes masquerading as real (we might have created such notes as a joke or as part of a novel, or perhaps as part of some elaborate hoax or crime for which such fabricated notes would be necessary or useful, etc.); 3) someone *other* than you or I had created counterfeit versions of notes allegedly written by you and me (again, there are various reasons someone might have done this, but these need not concern us now. The point is that thirty or fifty or 100 or 1000 years ago, the ontological status of any note that you or I or our readers might be reading would be very limited.

Clearly, as this simple, reflexive, metafictional, metalinguistic discussion of the word "note" indicates, those limitations have vanished. And more and more, I'm starting to think that 1.) postmodernism is a term that has to do with this vanishing of clear distinctions among things that used to seem (more or less) clearly distinguishable (some of these things include truth/illusion, past/present, reality/non-reality, Japan/non-Japan, male/female, original/copy); 2.) although there are many different and complex reasons why distinctions formerly made have vanished, the most important reason has to do with the evolution of technology generally and the evolution of information and reproductive technologies in particular.

In a sense, I think that this letter's "digression" about the meaning of "note" is probably the best way I can reply to the many provocative and important questions you raised in your "note" to me. And since time is running out on my visit here to Japan, perhaps I should send you this note and see what you think about the meanings of "note" and notes.

August 19, 1992

Dear Larry,

I have examined your "note" and thought about what you are saying. It seems to me that you have found a very useful way to point out one of the main sources of postmodern life. Yes, the technologies of *re*-production do seem to confuse things because they are able to add "realities" to our world—hyperrealities that frequently resemble previous realities (as in Baudrillard's notion of "simulacra") and which (as you have pointed out in many of your essays and in your *Storming the Reality* casebook) often tend to *replace* previous realities.

But even though I have enjoyed reading your "note" to me (a "note" which I also have read only on my word processor screen and which therefore is just as unreal as my "note" to you), I would still like to "hear" what you have to say about metafiction, cyberpunk, and postmodernism. If it would somehow make you more comfortable to reply to me in a *real note* (i.e., on a handwritten or typed note), feel free to do so.

Cordially,
VT (Virtual Takayuki)

Aug. 20, 1992

Yo, VT,

Okay, let me have a go at responding more directly about what you were talking about in your "note" to me of 8–17. I've decided against relying on pen, ink, real paper, hard copies, and other High Modernist (and antiquated) methods of information-dissemination. Let's continue exchanging "notes" through the rest of this mutual correspondence.

Of course I'm flattered that you feel our accidental meeting back in 1986 has resulted in having an impact on your own critical thinking. Actually it was around 1986 that I was beginning to rethink a lot of my ideas about postmodernism generally and metafiction in particular. I'd say the three most important areas I was rethinking all turn out to be areas you are touching on in your "note" to me:

1.) The work I was completing in 1986 for my book of interviews with science fiction writers (*Across the Wounded Galaxies*) had begun to convince me that SF and "mainstream" po-mo fiction had been evolving more or less along parallel tracks, with the two forms (which previously had not had much direct influence on each other) often sharing many of the same formal and thematic tendencies. What was becoming increasingly obvious to me by 1986 was that these two forms were increasingly beginning to directly interact and influence each other. This conviction was the basis of the two anthologies I wound up editing in the next couple of years (*The Cyberpunk Controversy* special issue of the *Mississippi Review* that appeared in 1988 and the *Storming the Reality Studio* casebook that Duke U. Press published in 1991). Putting together those two anthologies also put me in touch with several other critics whose opinions I greatly respect (Brooks Landon, Brian McHale, Fredric Jameson, Scott Bukatman, etc.) and who had independently made many of the same conclusions about this that I had.

2.) I was also already feeling uncomfortable with my earlier tendency (in, say, *The Metafictional Muse*) to focus my critical attention so much on po-mo's aesthetic features rather than on the social and political circumstances giving rise to the features. Partially to defend myself, let me just say that back in the early to mid 70s, critics like myself and others trying to analyze and define the new forms of art that had begun appearing so regularly in post-JFK-Assassination America felt we were exploring strange and often bewilderingly new territories. To us, the works of people like Coover, Jimi Hendrix, Barth, Pynchon, Velvet Underground, Federman, Woody Allen, Patti Smith, Philip Dick, Kubrick, and so on probably seemed a lot more *weird* and intimidating than they do today. And the first thing for us to do seemed to be to try and map out the territory—describe what it seemed like, how it was different from what we had encountered in our previous aesthetic journeys, and so on. Analyzing effectively the underlying ideological implications of this stuff was more difficult because, after all, we were living in the midst of all these things—the rise of the Media Culture and of Postindustrial Capitalism generally, Watergate, Vietnam and all the other the social/sexual/political upheavals of the period—that had never before even been noticed, much less theorized, previously (and those people who were theorizing about these things—Guy Debord, Barthes, Foucault, Lyotard, and so on—hadn't been translated as yet).

Anyway, if you look carefully at my early articles and books, you'll see that I wasn't entirely unaware of the ideological and political implications underlying, say, metafiction—implications which I've always felt are basic and profound. Although my Ph.D thesis dealt with the "metafictional" aspects of Robert Coover's work, I tried to make it clear that metafiction nearly always has very direct and relevant implications for our daily lives. After all, if you control people's words and fictions, you control their minds and their lives—and in our own "Information Age" this dictum is if anything, even more apparent (Orwell was certainly aware of this, and even Nabokov's fiction, so often seen as being "escapist" or reactionary, had a hell of a lot more to say about politics than he and most of his critics ever acknowledge). That's why I can't completely agree with your conclusions that metafiction in the 80s should be seen as some kind of "ultraconservative ideology." Sure, if you define metafiction very narrowly as being fiction-about-fiction—as opposed, I suppose, to fiction-about-reality—then it seems escapist and of little ideological or political interest. But broaden metafiction just slightly to include fiction-about-fictions and about fictions'-relationship-to-reality, then metafiction becomes inevitably and centrally concerned with matters of meaning, power, language, semiology, metaphor, lies, model-making, realism, illusion, truth interpretation, insanity, solipsism, world building—in short, the concerns of metafiction begin to overlap increasingly with issues associated with postmodernism itself.

On the other hand, I suppose you could argue something analogous to what Jameson says about avant-garde formal innovations—that when they first appear, they have a certain subversive power to shock and amaze people, but that in the age of hyperconsumerism (i.e., postmodernism) these innovations begin to be appropriated by Capitalism as a commodifiable *style*. That's what happened, I think, to the genuinely subversive and "shocking" features of cyberpunk (and punk before it, and rock before that, and jazz before that, and . . .). Inevitable, I suppose.

But unfortunately, I also agree with you that metafiction, together with its philosophical cousin, deconstruction have both often tended to be (mis?)perceived and (mis?) used as rationalizations for certain trendy brands of nihilism, relativism, and passivity—and hence as excuses to avoid making political, moral and ethical judgments. These rationalizations and excuses themselves undoubtedly have political and ideological sources (chiefly, the failure of the 60s idealism and revolutionary spirit, the ongoing betrayal of communist ideals by the totalitarian regimes in the USSR and China, and the widening cynicism and willful blindness characterizing both the Baby Boomer generation of American Reaganites and Japanese Salarymen and (significantly) their children—that is, the next generation of youths who have been raised in an atmosphere of resignation hyperconsumption and me-tooism, kids whom I sense are longing for idealism but have been given nothing substantial to justify such feelings.

Based on what I've seen here in Japan these past few months, the above may perhaps apply even more strongly over here than in the States. In the absolute state of devastation experienced by Japan in the post WWII period of U.S. occupation, the Japanese understandably embraced the only alternative available to them—capitalism, a U.S.-style notion of democracy, etc., etc. But after that phase of radical resistance to The Inevitable by both the right (Mishima, etc.) and the left (the student uprisings of the late 60s, the Narita Airport affair a bit later), the Japanese now seem to be left with almost no options. Certainly you guys have no options at all politically—and as Jerry Brown kept saying earlier this year, the U.S. is almost in the same situation. I mean, yeah, let's hope Clinton wins, but the Democrats are as waist deep in the big muddy (as Springsteen puts it) as the Republicans. And I don't see anybody on the horizon with the kind of clean hands and resolve to rescue us. Maybe later I can say something more about the conclusions I'm (tentatively) drawing about Japan, but for now let me just say that the writers and artists I've interviewed and talked with over here seem very concerned about this Situation where genuinely radical and even anarchistic art becomes just another trendy fad that is temporarily and mindlessly consumed (with relish or soy sauce) by citizens of our respective daydream nations before they move on to ordering the next trendy item. *surely your salarymen and ours must feel some sense of guilt and unease* about this? Is this why masochism and S&M seem like such dominant images of style and sexuality over here and over there?

Hey, this is bumming me out. I'll take a break for now and read one of those mangas that all the salarymen and schoolkids seem to be staring at on the trains—the ones with the uniformed but sexy girls and the drooling guys standing around. Let me know what you think.

Missionary of S&M,
Lars

PS. I'd like to add that not all of the late 60s metafiction was primarily concerned with metacharacters living out their metaexistences within fictions-within-the fiction. A great deal of the metafiction from that period concerned "real" authors shown to be inventing characters and stories (Sukenick, Federman, Barth, Vonnegut, Katz, the later Dick), Hunter Thompson, Mailer)—and even the ones where the meta-or-purely-invented nature of the metacharacters is foregrounded (Coover, early Dick, Borges, Nabokov, etc) use this structure (often playfully) to talk about *real people* and the *real world*. Or, to put it different, I think that *all* of the significant metafiction from all periods always uses this fiction-about-fictional characters as a device whereby readers are supposed to recognize that the fate of these metacharacters resembles our own in basic ways.

But, again, the basic point you're driving at seems important—we're a lot more likely today to accept the idea that our minds and lives and memories and sexual desires are artificial, that we're all metacharacters living in some weird script being created for us by Somebody Else. And I absolutely agree with your conclusion that "whereas metafiction used to be at work as an avant-garde literary device, it has already become part of the popular life we are leading now." All I'd say, is that we were *always* metacharacters—we just didn't know it before.

Aug 22, 1992

"Yo," Larry,

Such a formulation helped me recognize the critical difference between *Blade Runner* (1982) and *Twin Peaks* (1991–92), that is to say, the typical discourse of the early 80s and that of the early 90s. In the former, we used to get infatuated with the portrait of the replicant Rachel, for whom to become human it is necessary to input fake memory into her artificial brain, while in the latter, we get more interested in the videographic way Sarah Palmer, the mother of the dead Laura Palmer, recalls, reverses or replays what she saw the morning her daughter was murdered—a video replay of her memory as she tries to recall if she may have seen the murderer. This is the effect of what I would like to designate "videographic memory." *Blade Runner* started with the rigid distinction between fake memory and real memory, whereas *Twin Peaks* describes the "real" subjectivity of Sarah herself being immersed and constructed within "hyperreal" videographic culture. Thus, as I suggested in my recent essay "Comparative Metafiction: Somewhere between Ideology and Rhetoric," it is time to discuss not the aesthetics of metafiction but the metafictive ideology of hyper-capitalistic life, which cannot but render our identities more Sarah Palmer-like. For now, you do not seem much concerned with ideological implications of post-metafictional discourses, but I believe it is this aspect of contemporary representation that the "avant-pop" theory should head for. Let us take an example of David Blair's brilliant videographic narrative *WAX, or The Discovery of Television among the Bees* (1991), which I and you have admired very much and spent much time discussing lately. Indeed, in producing this high-tech revenge narrative Blair was so conscious of post-Pynchonesque representational modes that he reappropriated a variety of Western myths like "Cain and Abel," "The Tower of Babel," and the "Atomic Bomb." But, by reconstructing them on the hyper-resolutional Bee TV through the collective unconscious of bees, and with the hero as a sort of "thanatoid" who establishes a consensual relationship with the bees, he radically criticizes Western humanistic/ethnocentric ideology, and tries to go beyond the

Fig. 24 *Wax* as a post-Pynchonesque cinema. Videocassette cover. © David Blair. Tatsumi/*Full Metal Apache*

horizon of human perception. In this respect, what makes his video really conspicuous in the post–Gulf War age might be his incorporation of the Christian Cain-Abel text into the interethnic relationship between an Anglo-Saxon hivephilia and his Arabian brother-in-law. Hence the possibility of ethnographic metafiction in the hyper-capitalistic age.

Here lies another aspect that you seem to have ignored, but which the "avant-pop" theory may well investigate more deeply. For instance, in the wake of cyberpunk, literary representations of "Japan," which in most cases signified advanced capitalism, became very popular in Anglo-American writings. You can easily witness its latest examples in Thomas Pynchon's latest "post-sixties" novel *Vineland* (1990), William Gibson and Bruce Sterling's "steampunk" collaboration *The Difference Engine* (1990), or even Michael Crichton's "Japan Bashing" fiction *Rising Sun* (1991). Insofar as Japan as the "Empire of Signs" helped make writers' (mis)representation more avant-garde and more popular at once, it may be the sign of "Japan" that has persistently promoted the ideology of avant-pop. But, since you have spent almost a couple of months here in Tokyo doing research, reading Japanese postmodern fictions, and interviewing Japanese artists, your images of Japan may have been largely revolutionized. I would be very pleased if you have discovered here discourses, if any, which totally blow up your basic concept of ethnicity, and encourage both of us to inaugurate what might be called "comparative postmodernism" with the avant-pop theory as its background.

Takayuki Tatsumi
Keio University

LM: I'm not sure I agree with the distinction you made in your "note" to me about the "fake memories" that Rachel (the replicant "woman" in *Blade Runner*) has versus the presumably more "real" subjectivities involved in Sarah Palmer's experiencing of the morning she last saw her (now) dead daughter, Laura. Yes, I agree that Lynch is literalizing for us the radical subjectivization of our experience today—the way our past (and those of others, of history itself) becomes a commodifiable object that we can sample, cut-and-mix, colorize, and otherwise re-experience (it's crucial, of course, to recognize that *other people* and other systems—business systems, political systems, and the system of mind-and-body control that are now firmly in place—now often have access to "our" memories and to "our" collective past, and that *they* are likewise free to remix these and create whatever versions of "our" past they wish to; Ronald Reagan's election, and its underlying appeal to a nostalgic, illusory, media-constructed American "past," are good examples of this). But I don't feel the discourses around Rachel and Sarah Palmer are nearly so radically different as you imply—partly because I don't feel that Philip Dick and Ridley Scott were creating the "rigid distinction" between "real memory" and "fake memory" that you feel they were. (Incidentally, I don't think it's a coincidence that so many interesting recent films and books—think of *Videodrome*, *Til the End of the World*, *Total Recall*, *Tokyo Decadence*, nearly all cyberpunk works, as well as those of Kathy Acker, Bill Vollmann, and most of the other writers I included in *Storming the Reality Studio*—are dealing so recurrently with this issue of the "commodification and literalization of memory, or the more generally transformation of what used to be "internal," effanescent "feelings" and "sensations" into *externalized* images. I mean, people have probably always had a sense of nostalgia for the past and a desire for revolution, but only recently could such desires be "captured" and "replayed" for us—say, in the sampled video and audio images of John Lennon singing "You Say You Wanta A Revolution" used so cunningly by Nike in its tennis shoe ads.)

But I agree that David Blair's remarkable new film, *Wax*, is probably the most interesting new treatment of the topic of memory—and that its presentation of consciousness as this eerie blend of "documentary" and "real" images, myths and images of multi-ethnic origins, and so on is compelling.

It's also disturbing, because of course the "consciousness" of the narrator in Blair's film—for all its multi-ethnic origins and different layerings, its undeniable poetic gifts, its sense of humor and of poignancy at the irreconcilability of memory, loss, change and death—is in fact a weapon, a construct which carries out its mission with the same determination and unswerving "can do" spirit as American jet fighter pilots did in the Gulf War.

Like Kubrick's Hal, then, and Rachel, and Arnold, and so on, Blair's narrator may be undeniably "other" but is just as undeniably "us." So, for that matter, was the murderer of Laura Palmer.

Okay, all this talk of replicants and murder is making me nervous. I'm closing this for now. I'm wondering if there is something about the Japanese appropriation of American pop culture myths and archetypes that makes these figures and structures both "us" (American) and them (Japanese)—or is there something about the particular way that the Japanese appropriate these and enter into them that makes them, for all their seeming connection to "us," undeniably more "them"?

Just a thought.

One of us,
Larry

August 29, 1992, 8 A.M. (day of my departure from Tokyo)

Yo, Takayuki,

A day of nostalgia for Sinda and I as we get ready to depart. I finished packing my share of our stuff last night, leaving this morning to finish up our mutual correspondence. Maybe this last note is the most important one because it deals with my evolving conception of "avant-pop," which has turned out to be the focus of most of my lectures over here. You've indicated to me that Japanese editors have seemed to find the idea of "a-p" really catchy, and I've felt all along that I like the sound of the term—maybe it can eventually become the "cyberpunk" of the 90s.

This is where my idea of the evolution of avant-pop (hereafter "A-P") comes into play (or at least I hope it does). As you mention in your "note," when I first developed the concept of A-P for that essay I wrote for *Positive* magazine back in 1989 or 90, I wasn't interested in the ideological implications of the phenomenon. Mainly I was just trying to identify what seemed to be a significant tendency in recent American art and culture—namely, the growing popular acceptance of art whose radical formal features would have likely have relegated it to the fringes of public awareness. I had in mind works by artists like Warhol, Laurie Anderson, the Sex Pistols, cyberpunks, David Lynch, William Burroughs, Sonic Youth, Mark Leyner—artists of genuinely "underground" or "avant-garde" aesthetic sensibilities who were during the 80s very much "above ground" in terms of popularity.

Well, partly due to your prompting—and those of other Japanese friends I've been meeting with here in Tokyo during the past two months—I've decided to shift the whole orientation of my "A-P" concept so that its ideological implications are unmistakable. I want to do this by italicizing or otherwise semiotically emphasizing the "avant" part of the term.

As in <u>Avant</u>-Pop or *Avant*-Pop, or better still, **Avant**-Pop—anything to foreground the connection between A-P and the avant-garde art movement, a movement which hoped to use its radical aesthetic orientation to confuse, confound, bewilder, piss off and generally blow the fuses of ordinary citizens exposed to it. The idea being that sense it's now useless to try to create change via political institutions (useless because they are so infused with corruption, stagnation, and blind adherence to the tautologies that create and protect their existence), so artists need to try and work directly on peoples' consciousnesses *directly*. Radical formal devices are one means of trying to swerve peoples' consciousness off of the daily "grooves" of normalcy—the kind of "tracks" of response, desire, intuition, beliefs, etc. that have been laid down for us by our governments, advertisers, and schools (they're interlocking systems, at this point, don't you agree?), and to steer people *away* from the predictable places (dull, boring places, mostly that most of us try and escape as often and as forcibly as we can—ask any salaryman after work in a bar sometime about this), to maybe discover "tracks" that are more interesting. Maybe even more *appropriate* for our *own* tastes and desires (if we could only discover *for ourselves* what these actually *are*, for a change).

What makes A-P different from works by earlier avant-garde artists is its emphasis on pop-culture—the fact that its principle characters, plot lines, archetypes, conventions, etc. etc. are drawn from the pop cultural realm that is the world we live in today. As I tried to explain in the "A-P manifesto" I wrote for *SF Adventure* (its September issue is going to be devoted to A-P, but not necessary A-P), A-P art is a kind of subversive, guerilla-art created by artists who recognize the banalizing effect that pop culture's hold over our collective imaginations is having on people today.

Now here, I want to make a distinction between pop culture—which I'm identifying with the mass culture that has arisen only recently and which has prodigiously expanded into a mass-or-pop culture industry only since WWII—and popular culture, which has been around ever since culture has been around. Some popular culture rivals "high art" in terms of the degree of its thematic and aesthetic sophistication (American jazz and blues and Japanese wood block prints are examples of popular culture—so was Kabuki theater until its gradual appropriation by "high culture" as a kind of simulated, nostalgic and highly expensive version of Japan's past popular culture; so, too, were the works of Shakespeare, Dickens, and probably Homer).

The point is: the almost unbelievable expansion of the pop culture industry has changed the world—not only has pop culture "colonized" the physical space of nearly every country on earth, but (just as importantly) it has begun to colonize even those realms that nearly everyone once believed were inviolable—like, for instance, our *unconscious*, our sexual desires. And in order to expel the colonizers, in this case I don't think passive resistance will work. In fact, passivity is precisely what pop culture thrives on, feeds on. The more passively resistant we are, the better it likes it. What we need isn't passive but very *active* resistance.

Yeah, Takayuki, *active resistance*.

You, the Japanese Guru and Missionary of Cyberpunk, know exactly what I'm talking about here: I'm talking about *attacking* pop culture on its own ground. I'm talking about being sick and tired of having 57 *channels and nothing's on*! I'm talking about strategies related to cyberpunk's strategy of taking on technological change on its own ground, seizing control of it for our own purposes rather than sitting around like aging 60s hippies and bitching about how ugly the concrete around our homes is.

I mean, you don't bitch about Madonna or Rambo or all those awful sexist, violent/racist television shows, you *colorize em, re-narratize em, given 'em a new sound track, you supply a new non-sexist, non-racist ending that won't offend you.*

You *sample* the parts you like, you *lay down a drumtrack* (literal or narrative), you *become your own conductor*. The technology's already out there if people will only learn to start using their own imaginations rather than relying on other people's.

Why be a slave to somebody else's boring sexual formulas and images when you can make your own porn videos (this can be seen as a metaphor).

Or, *you rev everything up, turn up the dials and knobs of your system so that all the hidden "noise" of racism and sexist and political control can (finally) be heard clearly, and you play it loud so that everyone can hear it.*

In other words, you *storm the reality studio. and retake the universe.*

In this sense, Avant-Pop turns out to be a radical, ideological critique of what the avant-garde and pop culture are—and what they can and should be during the age of po-mo and hyperconsumption.

How does this sound? "Writing" up these thoughts on all this has been fun and interesting—hope it has been for you as well. Right now, it is 11:00 A.M. on 8–29, and I'm waiting for your phone call about my ride to Narita Airport—the scene of my most vivid memories of Japanese resistance to The System (students in the States couldn't believe that the Japanese students actually were able to shut that sucker *down*—and for several years!!). So I'm concluding this last "note" for now—while leaving open the possibility of reconnecting someday? What do you say?

Sayonara (for now),[2]
Larry-San

APPENDIX 2 A Dialogue with the Nanofash Pygmalion: An Interview with Richard Calder

Portrait of the Nano-Artist as a Young Man

Tatsumi: I wanted to meet you—whether in Thailand or in England—since reading your short story "Mosquito" in the fall of 1989, but circumstances have always prevented us from getting together. And despite the strong appeal of your postcyberpunk nanotech science fiction to Anglo-American and Japanese audiences, you have remained something of a mysterious recluse in general, like J. D. Salinger, Thomas Pynchon, or the late James Tiptree Jr. In fact, for a long while now you've detached yourself even from your homeland by living in Thailand. Could you therefore start by talking a little about your biographical background?

Calder: The first book I ever read, if I remember correctly, was a textbook on astronomy. For many years I think it was the only book my parents had in their house. I was enchanted by it, and from that time onwards was eager to find out all I could about the planets, the stars, and the space program, which I am just old enough to have been able to have followed from the launch of Sputnik. Later, astronomy became a hobby, and, after school, I'd spend my evenings in the back garden looking at the moon through a six-inch reflector. It was logical, I suppose, that I should seek out science fiction books. (Less logical, perhaps, that my published fiction should not exploit, at least in any obvious fashion, that early obsession with things astronomical.) Science fiction complemented my hobby and provided an extension to the television serials I was addicted to. If I'm just old enough to remember the newspaper reports of Sputnik and Gagarin, I'm also of an age that I can vividly recall the first episode of *Doctor Who* on British television in, I think, November 1963. That seven-year-old boy was knocked sideways! Those early black-and-white episodes were strange indeed, and frightening. I loved them. There was also *Out of the Unknown*, a series of television adaptations of writers such as Ballard, Sheckley, Brunner, Simak, and many others. It was transmitted on BBC2, a fairly new channel, then. We didn't have the right kind of aerial to receive BBC2 in our house, so I would watch each episode through a cloud of static and interference—which, for me, made the program all the more weird and exciting. I particularly remember a wonderful dramatization of E. M. Forster's "The Machine Stops"—that really *did* scorch my brains. Along with the science fiction books I was reading (I became a great fan of Jules Verne) my taste for fantastic literature in general was becoming finely honed. I read Asimov, Heinlein, Clarke, but then, growing a little older, soon discovered Tolkien and Peake.

But I was reading blind, without a sense of direction, with no real literary map. I've indicated that I grew up in a house without books. I instinctively knew that the arena of the "fantastic imagination" had a wider compass, but apart from the usual children's books, such as *Alice in Wonderland*, I was lost, and did not know that the imaginative worlds I had intimations of and were groping for, worlds, in many ways, but palely represented in all but the very best science fiction, existed, also, in the mainstream of English literary tradition. It was not until I was in my early teens that I began to read more widely. But my imagination has always been underpinned by those early readings and exposures to science fiction, though the reason that science fiction, or the "fantastic" became important to me as I grew up is, perhaps, as much to do with a need I have to recreate patterns of childhood inner life as it is with the inspiration provided by the texts themselves.

Tatsumi: Well, this is how you came to choose English as your major. What was the topic for your B.A. thesis at the University of Sussex?

Calder: Ben Jonson's tragedies. To quote Aubrey Beardsley, I have often felt, about my own work, that it is "nothing, if not grotesque." Jonson's work is full of grotesquerie—bizarre, absurd—but it is his comedies that people most readily turn to. (For good reason, of course: they are his greatest creations.) But I was interested in how that spirit of the grotesque might be employed in a *tragic* context—that is, a modern context back-reading from the perspective of paranoid black comedy present in the drama of the absurd.

Tatsumi: You said you changed jobs often. Does this mean that you've always wanted to be a writer? If so, what kind of fiction did you write as a child? If not, what motivated you to begin writing fiction?

Calder: The word "vocation" may seem a little portentous, but I felt from early on that I would pursue, if not necessarily writing, then some other discipline—music, art—that would give me the opportunity to construct other worlds, alternate realities to the one in which I existed. I have always had a need to create or else discover another plane of existence, somewhere where I can escape to, somewhere I can feel at home. When I was about ten or eleven I kept a diary—it lasted for quite a few years—but not one which delineated the events of my day-to-day life, but one that recorded the life of my imagination. That diary was populated with all kinds of imaginary friends, imaginary palaces and cities that seemed to be superimposed on the familiar world of school and playing field, but which continually lay just out of full percipience and reach. The diary was certainly important, but at that age I think I was more interested in music and drawing. I had begun to play trombone in a local youth orchestra and, at the same time, became obsessed with copying illustrations from comics and picture books. (I had a voluminous collection of British and American comics.) By the time I came to leave school at sixteen I wanted to either study music or go to art school. I ended up doing neither. A particularly virulent and long-term problem with tonsillitis meant that, for some time, I was unable to play a wind instrument, and thoughts of art school gradually evaporated after I went to a college of further education and then to university to study English. After, at long last, I had my tonsils ripped out I started to play again: trombone, then guitar, then saxophones. But that too, with the demands of work, the complaints of neighbors, evaporated, after a while, and all I was left with were words, words, words. I still dream of being Jimmy Knepper.

Orientalism, Counterorientalism, New Exoticism

Tatsumi: Your second short story, "Mosquito," had a tremendous impact on me when I first read it in the fall of 1989. Having been instrumental in helping Steve Brown start the cyberpunk magazine *SF Eye* in 1987, I was at the time constantly being exposed to postcyberpunk fictions. And yet yours was a radically different story. I still remember a *Locus* reviewer aptly saying that you "out-Gibson[ed] Gibson." Whether postcyberpunkish or not, your literary style appealed to my own literary tastes very deeply. As I suggested in my essay "A Manifesto for Gynoids"[1] your first gynoid trilogy is rooted in what I would call the "Madama Butterfly Syndrome," resonating beautifully with the western cultural heritage of the Pygmalion (My Fair Lady?) complex.

In this respect, your Automaton trilogy—like the Dead trilogy that followed (the novels *Dead Girls, Dead Boys*, and *Dead Things*)—is comparable to David Henry Hwang's queer drama *M. Butterfly*, Gary Indiana's hard-gay, hard-boiled story *Rent Boy*, and even Alan Brown's Japanophilic novel *Audrey Hepburn's Neck*. Of course, in the era of nanotechnology, the figure of an orientalist Pygmalion must sound anachronistically conservative, but what I find most attractive in your work is the dazzling new twist you give to familiar orientalist Pygmalion discourse; you are ambitious enough to disclose and even play with radical difference within the context of typical western orientalist narrative. This is why I characterize your fiction as "counter-orientalist," or simply "postcolonialist," in terms of both ethnology and sexuality.

To begin with, let me ask how you personally came to be "allured" by Asia. As you explained to me in your letter of September 26, 1990, you traveled abroad during the early eighties, mainly in Southeast Asia (teaching English in Yogyakarta, Java) and in Australia. You subsequently made several trips back to Southeast Asia, and in particular to Thailand, where you met your wife. I'm curious to know what seduced you into visiting Southeast Asia. Please describe for me your first encounter with "Asia"—was it a book or a specific person? And what contributed to the development of your orientalist aesthetic subsequently?

Calder: I'm not sure if I was ever seduced by Asia per se; I was rather, I think, seduced at an early age by an intense attraction towards otherness. I liked to read tales of the Far East when I was a boy (I was particularly fascinated by Tibet), and this reinforced my already powerful love of the strange, the exotic, the *different*. But I ended up traveling to Asia by chance, really. At the beginning of the eighties I worked—in a very lowly capacity—for an independent television company. Words cannot describe how much I loathed this job—the duties, the *people*—and one day I simply gave in my notice and, shortly afterwards, bought an airline ticket to Australia. I'd had enough of England; I wanted *out*. The stop over was Jakarta, and it transpired that I ended up stopping over for close to a year, and then, on returning from Australia, another year, doing a little teaching in Indonesia, but also traveling to Singapore, Malaysia, and Thailand. What I discovered in Southeast Asia was a concretization of certain, perhaps central elements of my inner life, a correlation of alienation and the alien. I felt oddly "at home." I was, of course, seeing things through a mist of presuppositions and prejudices about what exactly Asia *was*—the worst kind of romantic prejudices—but the enchantment with Asia has lasted, no matter how much the illusions I have entertained about it have been stripped away by time and experience. My orientalism, or counter-orientalism, is probably a combination of a joy at being immersed in otherness and a less joyful, slow process of disillusionment.

Tatsumi: Although the concept of the gynoid was created by Gwyneth Jones (in her *Divine Endurance*), I suppose you must also have found much literary inspiration in Thailand during your decade there. I once compared your surrealistic description of Bangkok to J. G. Ballard's representation of Shanghai. Is their any nodal point in your imagination where your science-fictional technoscape corresponds with your own postcolonialist psychoscape? For *Dead Things* amazed me not simply with its representation of hyperspatiotemporal and postcyborgian identity, but also with its innovation of a creole "Martian Thai" language, product of a deep transaction between Mars and Bangkok.

Calder: The "technoscape" of the novels reflects, I think, the sense of being an alien in an alien landscape, a stranger in a strange land, if you will—something that constitutes a kind of doubly alienated sense of affect. The *technoscaping* of the alien represents, I think, an intensification of vision, or response, to an Asian city. It's expressionistic rather than scientific. The technology daubed, smeared, and stuck to the outward aspect of Bangkok is like *Merz*, the twentieth-century detritus Karl Schwitters used to nail his paintings together, except that *my** Merz belongs to the twenty-first century. Sex and violence is much evident in these canvases, but the central theme of my work seems not to be sex or violence but rather identity, or the problem of identity, a process in which characters become, learn to become, what they already are, or to disburden themselves of false selfhoods. Sex and violence is, in other words, the crucial way in which people discover themselves and achieve a measure of authenticity. The problem of "Who am I?" is reflected in landscapes that, like the backdrop to a Krazy Kat cartoon, are constantly mutating, as if unsure of themselves. Technoscapes!

Tatsumi: Although Gibson has characterized your fiction as "dark, edgy, and inflected with just the right degree of lyricism" in a wonderful blurb he provided for you, I know you don't want to be too closely tied to cyberpunk. But

I'm very interested in how science fiction writers from the New Wave through cyberpunk have revolutionized the concept of "space." Ballard invented "inner-space," Gibson designed "cyberspace," and you, Richard Calder, have created "the robotic unconscious," which you reinvent as the "fibresphere" in your latest short story, "The Embarkation for Cythera." Has your life in Southeast Asia inspired you to reorganize the conventional western framework of "space"?

Calder: I think my novels are strongly visual affairs, but their sense of space, that is color and line, is informed by my preoccupations with time. Space, in my fiction, exists in a temporal flux, forwards, backwards, sideways; space thus assumes a plasticity, it becomes integral to the timeline of the narrative, the sculptural organization of the novels; it flows, like molten rubber, stretched out along the forking paths of time, to cool into the novel's superstructure. My concern with time is no doubt linked to the fact that all of my novels are, in a certain sense, evocations of the past; in particular, of childhood. My characters all seem unable to escape their childhoods. Are defined by their childhoods. Seek to regress to childhood states. The technological metaphors, say, the "fibresphere" of Cythera, exist as dream areas filled with memories, often distorted, buckled, perverse; they are playpens, rumpus rooms, for the exploration of fundamental fears, desires, loves.

From Nanospace to Fibresphere

Tatsumi: If I'm understanding the Dead trilogy correctly, the first novel, *Dead Girls*, is a typical Romeo and Juliet boy-meets-girl kind of romantic comedy; the second, *Dead Boys*, is an extremely William Burroughsian, linguistic virus–oriented, avant-pop creation; and the third, *Dead Things*, is an atavistically incestuous Emily Brontean/Faulknerian work of technogothic. Frankly speaking, I was a bit disturbed on the publication of the second novel by the stylistic shift between *Dead Girls* and *Dead Boys*; while the former was incredibly readable, the latter seemed too experimental. I wasn't sure why you set up such a radical discrepancy between them, but the publication of *Dead Things* solved the mystery, convincing me that the three novels taken together constitute a carefully and brilliantly designed jigsaw puzzle.

In the third novel, Ignatz-Lord Dagon—now not the lover but the brother of Primavera—has experienced a number of alternative histories that have transformed him into a thousand year-old multiple subjectivity. To exterminate the Meta virus, it became necessary for him to return to the year 1994, and in an effort to erase the existence of Dr. Toxicophilous, and reinvent the spatiotemporal structure by planting a reality bomb. Furthermore, you disclose the metarole that the very trilogy we are reading has performed in the nanofash multiverse. Simply put, *Dead Things* turns out to be a metafiction about the species *Meta*.

Looking back, how do you see the plot structure of the trilogy? Did you have the entire structure in mind before writing *Dead Girls*? Or did you continue to develop and reorganize the structure as you were writing the first two novels?

Calder: It's important for me, when I begin to write, to assume the mask of a first-person narrator. Robert Browning has been a significant influence on the way I work. I like to use dramatic monologues that express what either Lionel Trilling or Harold Bloom has called the "psychological atomism" of Browning's work. (Browning's failed questers and charlatans all have different names, and indeed, different personalities and histories, but they all obviously emanate from the same source, as if the poet's ego had fragmented into a thousand pieces, each piece having its own, demonic autonomy.) I usually have the pattern of a book complete in my mind by the time I'm about halfway through it; until then, I travel hopefully. I had not planned to write a trilogy, but when I had completed *Dead Girls* I found I could not put the narrative voice, that is, the mask of Ignatz Zwakh, to one side. He had more to say to me, and I had to let him say it. A leitmotiv of the whole trilogy, it seems to me, is this notion that fiction—the imagination—can transform reality and that reality, in turn, can transform the imagination—and all, in terms of the trilogy's universe, in a very literal way. But the "reality" that triumphs at the Dead trilogy's conclusion seems, in the end, to be only another kind of fictive universe. And so the process may be expected to continue, imagination fluxing into reality, reality into fiction. The "Dead" books are very much influenced and underpinned by Buddhism, both in the way all "reality" is revealed to be illusory, and in the way desire—sexual desire, greed, envy, the desire for life itself—manifests itself in toy universes, prison universes, which enclose and torment their creators. I dream of a fiction so powerful that its strangeness converts, assimilates, transforms those who encounter it, so that it no longer seems strange, a "supreme fiction" that would be a virtual reality subsuming this world, replacing it with the "world after."

Tatsumi: In my view, forbidden love is the key literary-historical concept linking you with Brontë, Sade, Faulkner, Mishima, Angela Carter, and Steve Erickson. At the same time, your description of a quantum physical multiverse in which nanoinformation helps recreate spatiotemporal structure coincides with the recent novels of Japanese science fiction writers such as Chohei Kambayashi and Koji Suzuki. Do you find it plausible that the development of high technology—for example, cloning and nanotechnology—will transgress the boundaries of traditional ethics, challenging the existing taboos of our society? How do you conceptualize the interaction between technology and morality?

Calder: Yes, the concept of "forbidden love" is central to all my work. My female characters are not real women, they are anima figures, supernatural muses who exist as projections of the narrator's own longings and fears. Since they exist in science-fictional universes, their supernatural aspects are determined, not by magic, or even psychology, but by superscience.

Technology is the enabling force allowing them to fulfill their symbolic roles. In embracing their animas' technosexuality my antiheroes step outside not just conventional morality, but the world-as-it-is. That is the meaning of transgression for me: to become an outlaw—a thief, a murderer, a sexual outlaw—is to take leave of the bright light of the familiar and journey into the dark woods where transcendence of self and society becomes a possibility. My characters transgress, not for gain (though they do their share of stealing and cheating) but to lose themselves so that they may be reborn. To paraphrase Marcuse, *per-*

version expresses rebellion against the subjugation of sexuality under the order of procreation, and against the institutions which guarantee that order. The technology deployed in my novels sometimes reinforces the status quo, but also aids and abets those who rebel. It translates their perverse relationship to the world. And it does so, not by supplying tools, but by offering a reworking of reality. Technology becomes a totem of imaginative power. The theme of "forbidden love," then, for me, has a kind of quasi-religious significance. My antiheroes, if damned, if wholly nasty pieces of work, are vital—like Mr. Punch—and their vitality offers them some hope of redemption. If they hate and kill, they can also love and sing. They are not truly "dead."

Tatsumi: I have always been amused by your references to Japanese pop-cultural phenomena such as "kayokyoku," "karaoke," and Japanimations, or "anime." To what extent are you familiar with Japanese subcultures? What role does Japan play in your imagination?

Calder: I have never visited Japan and, like most westerners, my appreciation of Japanese "subculture" is limited to pop-cultural journalism and anime. Anime is now quite popular in the U.K. When I left for Thailand, eight years ago, nobody seemed to know much about it, but now there are anime seasons on late-night television, which is great. The fast-paced action, the editing techniques, simply the way things look and sound in anime, has certainly influenced the way I write, as has Hong Kong cinema. I have a particular fondness for Alita (but then, you know, she's a robot, and I have this *thing* about robots) and I like Hong Kong "ghost" movies. The "Dead" trilogy has a furious, cartoon-like pacing; its action sequences are screwball-violent; and its characters have the monstrously, fabulously larger-than-life flavor of manga heroes and villains. Hey, the Dead trilogy would make a great anime! In the end, my interest in science fiction is probably mandated by the fact that it seems central to contemporary pop culture, both east and west. I'm thinking of the prominence of video games, comics, fashions, indeed anime. Pop culture today—pop sensibility—is infused with the *feel* of science fiction's stylistics. Are you familiar with the Japanese pop/cabaret girl-duo resident in the U.K., Frank Chickens? I love 'em!

Tatsumi: Explain the basic concept of your next novel, *Cythera*, if you would. Is your latest short story, "The Embarkation for Cythera," a chapter from this forthcoming novel? Or do you plan to incorporate the story into the novel as you did "The Lilim" into *Dead Girls*? Is this novel closely related to the trilogy? How would you differentiate the robotic unconscious and the nanotech multiverse of the Dead trilogy from the fibresphere you have invented for the new novel? As far as the short story is concerned, your brilliant characterization of the artificial pop star Dahlia brings to mind Gibson's *Idoru*. Have you formulated any specific opinions on recent theories of complexity and artificial life? You have recently published a number of book reviews. I found your rereading of Liz Hand and Jack Womack, in particular, to be brilliant. What literary critical standards do you employ as a critic? In what way would you like to be understood to have contributed to science fiction, or postmodern literature, in general?

Calder: "The Embarkation for Cythera," which appeared in *Interzone*, reappears, in a revised, expanded form, as the first chapter of *Cythera*. (*Cythera* will be published in the U.K. by Little, Brown, in April, and simultaneously in the U.S. by St. Martin's.) The novel was written in Thailand, but was to some extent inspired by a certain climate of opinion in the U.K. In Nongkhai, I would listen to the BBC World Service on a daily basis, and U.K. news often seemed dominated by various "moral panics" to do with children—both perceived threats to children and a perceived rash of juvenile crime—and calls for the stricter enforcement of the law and censorship. A moral virtue was being made of fear. It brought to mind something that Aldous Huxley wrote: "Morality is always the product of terror, its chains and strait-waistcoats are fashioned by those who dare not trust others, because they dare not trust themselves, to walk in liberty." Extrapolating from those BBC reports, I found myself in the early twentieth-century world of *Cythera*. The novel stands apart from the Dead trilogy, but can be read as sharing a similar universe (at least the universe of *Dead Girls*). Its time frame precedes that of *Dead Girls* by about fifty years and some characters who appear in the trilogy—Madame Kito and Mosquito—appear in *Cythera*, but half a century younger, at a time when they are just starting out on their illustrious careers. But apart from this, the worlds of the trilogy and *Cythera* pretty much stand apart, though the "fibresphere" is an antecedent to the "robot unconscious" of the trilogy in that it too is a kind of dreamscape, but very much an evolving, unfinished one. *Cythera* is, once again, an evocation of childhood—the novel is populated with cruel, animalistic children with monstrous imaginations and appetites and adults who either worship them or revile them. It is a novel about crimes of the imagination, what the state might call "illegal fantasies." It is about vindictive sanctimony. It is about how reality and the world of the media are becoming indistinguishable.

The novel that will follow *Cythera* is *Frenzetta* (to be published late 1998 by Little, Brown) and will be set in the far future. It is science-fictional, but might be more cogently described as a kind of *fantasy punk*. As for *my* future—as a writer—I see myself as trying to write a science fiction that is not a science fiction; science fiction that becomes something else. Call it simply the "fantastic," perhaps. What I feel the need to do is to pare myself down to a very naked level of authenticity, to rediscover a vision, the original of which I locate in childhood, to fearlessly lay that vision bare, to body it forth using the combined imaginative language of science fiction, horror, the gothic, surrealism, expressionism, and anything else in my ragbag that might contribute to the creation of a place which I will recognize as *home*. As Oscar Wilde said, "One's real life is the one one does not lead."

Conducted through email in February 1998.[2]

NOTES

Foreword

1. In his introduction to the special *Contemporary Japanese Fiction* issue of *The Review of Contemporary Fiction* that we coedited (with Sinda Gregory), Tatsumi defines "Japanoid" as a form of "post-80s hyper-creole subjectivity transgressing the boundary between the Japanese and non-Japanese, and in so doing, naturalizing the very act of transgression" ("The Japanoid Manifesto," 16). If you eat sushi or drive a Toyota, root for Ichiro or Cool Hand Koboyashi, if you're an anime or manga fan, do karaoke or watch sumo, enjoyed William Gibson's *Idoru*, or . . . but you can see where this is going. As Tatsumi states in his introduction to that special issue, in the current postmillennial world, "ethnically Japanese or not, we are all Japanoid."
2. My title appropriates various semiotic elements from the following: Flaming Lips' *Yoshimi Battles the Pink Robots* (2002), an apocalyptic, anime-inspired concept album depicting the way that the transformation of the real into digitalized simulation is leading to the end of the world as we know it; Nicholas Bornoff's 1991 study of sex and gender roles in contemporary Japan, *Pink Samurai: Love, Marriage and Sex in Contemporary Japan*; t.o.L's dystopian postanime feature, *Tamala 2010—A Punk Cat in Space* (2002), which borrows elements from Pynchon, Kubrick, Russian futurism, and Bosch to render an entire "feline galaxy" eerily resembling the paranoid alienated world of contemporary Tokyo; closet Japanoid Bruce Springsteen's classic rocker "Pink Cadillac"; and to Larry McCaffery's *Storming the Reality Studio*, whose title itself borrowed the "reality studio" trope first proposed by William Burroughs in *Nova Express*.

   My title also was generated out of the same process of remixing semiotic elements drawn from disparate sources that Tatsumi employs throughout *Full Metal Apache* to generate such surrealist, hilariously appropriate chapter titles as "Waiting for Godzilla," "Deep North Gothic," and of course "Full Metal Apache" itself. This process is one of the key formal methods used variously by many of the Japanoid writers and artists examined in *Full Metal Apache*.
3. Team Takayuki is the staff of postmodern literary critics and theory experts

that Takayuki Tatsumi began assembling back in the late eighties to assist him in the development of a new sort of critical framework that could be used to analyze and promote the radically new forms of fiction and art being created out of the post-postmodernist paradigm of cultural production he was also developing simultaneously with his concept of Japanoid culture. My own contributions to the framework design that Tatsumi eventually employs in *Full Metal Apache* can be inferred from the series of email exchanges that appears here as appendix 1: "Toward the Frontiers of Fiction: From Metafiction and Cyberpunk through Avant-Pop."

4. Of course, this "barrier" isn't physical but is a cultural construct created primarily out of the mutually supporting systems of clichés, misleading stereotypes, and ideologically based assumptions called "orientalism" and "occidentalism."
5. Prior to this, Tatsumi was probably best known in this country as the author of *Graffiti's Rainbow* (a regular column he wrote from 1987 to 1995 for Steve Brown's legendary SF "prozine," *Science Fiction Eye*) and of "Japanese Reflections of Mirrorshades," which appeared in my *Storming the Reality Studio* anthology; other English translations of materials later appearing in *Full Metal Apache* include "Comparative Metafiction" (in *Critique*), "Creative Masochism" (in *American Book Review*), and our collaborative, epistolary essay, "Toward the Frontiers of 'Fiction': From Metafiction and Cyberpunk through Avant-Pop" (see appendix 1), which appeared in *Science Fiction Eye* and received the 1993 Pioneer Award given annually by the Science Fiction Research Association for the essay making the most important contribution to the study of SF; incidentally, this was the first essay so honored that was published in a fanzine rather than an academic journal.
6. Mari Kotani has collaborated with Tatsumi on a number of major projects, including their enormously influential translation *Cyborg Feminism* (1991) of theoretical essays by Donna Haraway (the influence of her "Cyborg Manifesto" is everywhere apparent in *Full Metal Apache*), Samuel R. Delany, and Jessica Amanda Salmonson. Kotani also coconducted and cotranslated many of the interviews appearing in the recent special issue of *Review of Contemporary Fiction* devoted to new Japanese fiction (22.2 [2002]). She has also published numerous influential critical studies of her own dealing with SF, fantasy, and anime. Among these was her first collection of essays (1994) dealing with various forms of radical postfeminism, *Joseijo-Musishiki* (*Techno-Gynesis*)—a work whose examination of the origins of Yaoi culture (the Japanese equivalent of "slash" culture) greatly increased feminist interests in the female "Otaku," which had been largely ignored in Japan up until then. In 1997, she published *Seibo Evangelion* (Evangelion as the Immaculate Virgin), an enormously popular study of the Japanese anime *Evangelion*.
7. That is, Japanese cars such as the Honda and Subaru, which the narrator of Bruce Springsteen's "Pink Cadillac" implies are too inadequate, too *small*, to symbolize the enormous love he feels for his girlfriend—a love so grand that it is capable of being expressed symbolically only by that enormous, sexually suggestive, American, chrome-plated, air-conditioned guzzler, the original favorite of Elvis Presley, the pink Cadillac:

> But my love is bigger than a Honda, it's bigger than a Subaru,
> Honey there's only one thing, and one car that will do
> Anyway we don't have to drive honey, we can park it out the back
> And have a party in your pink Cadillac.

Readers wishing to pursue a cross-cultural rereading of Bruce Springsteen as "closet Japanoid," are urged to carefully examine the crucial role Japanese references have played in such songs as "57 Channels" (1992) and "The Wish" (1998), as well as in his very earliest Japanoid tune, "Tokyo" (1972), with its classic, proto-Japanoid refrain—"Tokyo, I'm singin' for ya."

8. And, although I have never publicly admitted this before, *so was I*! And in one of those dazzling coincidences that poets love and logicians loathe, it even turns out that Tatsumi and I both began our development as Japanoids at almost exactly the same time—May 1955. This was the month when Tatsumi was born in Tokyo and when I first arrived in Okinawa, where I would spend the next ten years of my life.
9. I say "formerly" because, as Tatsumi demonstrates throughout *Apache*, many of the innovative formal features that were employed by the first wave of postmodern innovators back in the sixties and early seventies were retrofitted by the cultural mainstream during the eighties as flashy *images* of transgression that could be marketed to the "alternative" audiences. The issue of what sorts of options remain for writers and audiences with genuinely subversive sensibilities is one of *Apache*'s most important subthemes.
10. Since we're already on the topic of the value of deconstructing cultural narratives, perhaps I should note that even the master narrative underlying much of Tatsumi's study (i.e., that until recently artistic influences have traveled in a one-way cultural direction, from the West to Japan) could do with some fine-tuning. While this one-way traffic paradigm does generally apply to what has occurred throughout much of the twentieth century, this was not always the case. To the contrary, almost immediately following Commodore Perry's arrival in Yokohama Bay in 1853, Japanese art and culture began to have a major impact on the West, particularly in France and other European countries where the seeds of the great twentieth-century modernist experiments were already nurturing a sense of the need of western art to develop new approaches to cultural production more in keeping with vast transformations that had occurred in Europe during the nineteenth century. Although infrequently remarked upon today, the influences that Japanese art had on, for example, Van Gogh, Gauguin, Degas, and Monet and on various other western innovators can hardly be overstated. Art historians were already noting this widespread recognition and appreciation by European artists of the Japanese artistic achievement at the dawn of the twentieth century. Thus, in a letter announcing a gift of a large number of Japanese prints, painting, drawings, and books to the Library of Congress dated October 17, 1905, the editor and publisher of *The Washington Star*, Crosby Stuart Noyse (1825–1908), described the impact that Japanese wood-block prints was already having in Europe as follows: "It is the art that taught Whistler his exquisite draughtsmanship and brush work, subtle gradations of tone and dainty color harmonies; the art from which Manet and the French school

of Impressionists got their inspiration, and that, as Hartman [the influential turn-of-the-century German critic] declares, has influenced the several lines of work of Whistler, Manet, Degas, Skarbina, the German Secessionists, Puvis de Chavannes, D. W. Tryon, Steinlein, and Monet; and [Hartman] added that 'nearly two-thirds of all painters who have become prominent during the last twenty years have learned in one instance or another from the Japanese' " (quoted in Lee, "Introduction," 9).

11. As many commentators within and outside of Japan have noted, this sense of brooding vulnerability and inferiority is no doubt rooted in Japan's position as an island nation whose culture and national identity have constantly been threatened due to its proximity to nations such as Korea and especially China.

12. The origins and evolution of the term *Otaku* are intriguing. Tatsumi notes that this second-person pronoun was already being used to refer to any person who owned rare books back in the late sixties; by 1984, Nakamori Akio, former spokesman of "Shinjinrui" (the eighties equivalent in Japan of our Gen X), named the whole strange tribe of Japanese SF fandom "Otaku." (See Tatsumi's "Editorial Afterword: A Soft Time Machine," 483.) For American readers, the best study of the Otaku phenomenon during the late eighties and early nineties period is Karl Greenfeld's *Speed Tribes*, which provides the following definition of the term: "The *Otaku* came of age way back in the eighties with Paleolithic 186 computers and Neanderthal Atari Pac-Men as playmates. They were brought up on junk food and educated to memorize reams of contextless information in preparation for multiple-choice high school and college entrance examinations. They unwound with ultraviolent slasher comic books or equally violent computer games. And then they discovered that by interacting with computers instead of people, they could avoid Japanese society's dauntingly complex Confucian web of social obligations and loyalties. The result: a generation of Japanese youth too uptight to talk to a telephone operator but who can go hell-for-leather on the deck of a personal computer or workstation" (174–175).

13. Tatsumi provides a fascinating insider's look at the Japanese SF scene he entered as a junior high student in the late sixties in chapter 5, "Which Way to Coincidence?"

14. Tatsumi provides a more extended description of his immersion in Tokyo's SF fandom in "A Soft Time Machine," his editorial afterword to the *Science Fiction Studies* issue devoted to Japanese science fiction.

15. I have borrowed from the following "original" sources in developing my haiku and poetry:

The ancient pond
A frog jumps in
The sound of the water.
—The famous haiku by Basho, trans. Donald Keene
(Keene, *Japanese Literature*, 39)

The screen door slams
Mary's dress waves
—Opening lines to Bruce Springsteen's "Thunder Road"

On the young shoots of the leaves
A spider's web lies suspended.
—Haiku by Basho disciple Kikaku, trans. Donald Keene
(Keene, *Japanese Literature*, 41)

To what shall I compare
This world?
To the white wake behind
A ship that has rowed away
At dawn!
—Early poem by the priest Mansei (ca. 720), trans. Arthur Waley
(Keene, *Japanese Literature*, 133)

The cries of the insects
Are buried in the roots of
The sparse pampas grass—
The end of autumn is in
The color of the last leaves.
—Early poem by the priest Jakuren (d. 1202), trans. Donald Keene
(Keene, *Anthology of Japanese Literature*, 96)

To bird and butterfly
it is unknown, this flower here:
The autumn sky.
—Basho haiku, trans., Harold D. Henderson
(Keene, *Anthology of Japanese Literature*, 384)

Introduction

1. Bester, foreword to his translation of Doi, *Amae no Kozo* (Anatomy of Dependence), 7.

Chapter 1. Mikadophilia

1. My earliest analysis of the talented playwrights Hideki Noda and Yoji Sakate was published in Hayakawa's monthly *Higeki-Kigeki* (Tragedy and Comedy), no. 595 (May 2000). Although my literary interest lies in fiction, I found this discussion of Noda and Sakate highly useful for representing cyberpunk Japan.
2. The origin of "comparative avant-pop" can be located in my article "Creative Masochism as an Approach to Comparative Avant-Pop," in *In Memoriam to Postmodernism*, ed. Mark Amerika and Lance Olsen.
3. My project of establishing a new theoretical framework of exoticism started on August 2, 1996, at the Kyoto American Studies Summer Seminar held at Ritsumeikan University, where I delivered a paper entitled "New Exoticism in American Literary History of the 1990s, or Independence Day" in response to Emory Elliott's keynote lecture, "Writing a History of American Literature at the End of the Twentieth Century: Mission Impossible."

Chapter 2. Comparative Metafiction

An earlier version of chapter 2 was published in *Critique* 39.1 (fall 1997): 2–17.

1. Also see McHale, *Postmodernist Fiction*.
2. Spinrad, "North American Magic Realism," 177–190; Sterling, "Slipstream," 77–80; McCaffery, "The Post-Pynchon Postmodern Fiction," 248–267.
3. Waugh, *Metafiction*, 148.
4. Federman, "Self-Reflexive Fiction," 1148–1149.
5. Barth, "The Literature of Exhaustion," 62–76.
6. Foucault, *Language, Counter-Memory, Practice*, 366.
7. Baudrillard, *La Guerre du Golfe N'a Pas Eu Lieu*.
8. Porush, *Soft Machine*.
9. McCaffery, "The Fictions of the Present," 1164.
10. Sterling, preface, vii–xiv.
11. Cf. Kojève, *Introduction à la lecture de Hegel*.
12. Schvelbusch, *The Railway Journey*, 136.
13. Cf. Beasley, *The Modern History of Japan*, 140.
14. Tsutsui, "Kyoko-Riron ni Tsuite."
15. Coover, "The End of Books," 24.
16. Numa, "Afterword," *Yapoo the Human Cattle*, 2:654.
17. Michaels, *The Gold Standard*. Michaels writes: "But if [the] masochist's desire to be owned is perverse, it is nevertheless a perversion made possible only by the bourgeois identification of the self as property. . . . What the masochist loves is only the freedom to be a slave. . . . To put it another way, the masochist loves what the capitalist loves: the freedom to buy and sell, the inalienable right to alienate. In this respect, the masochist embodies the purest commitments to laissez-faire" (124, 132–133).

Chapter 3. Virus as Metaphor

1. Stableford, "H. G. Wells," 1313.
2. For this fascinating concept of "sequelology," see Westfahl, "The Sequelizer."
3. I. F. Clarke, "The Future-War Fiction," 387.
4. Franklin, *War Stars*, 10.
5. Ibid., 13.
6. Vevier, "Yellow Peril," 356–357.
7. Note that the way Dupin comes to determine the identity of the murderer's "voice" is extremely enigmatic, especially in our context: "Murder, then, has been committed by some third party; and the voices of this third party were those heard in contention. . . . The witnesses, as you remark, agreed about the gruff voice; they were here unanimous. But in regard to the shrill voice, the peculiarity is—not that they disagreed—but that, while an Italian, an Englishman, a Spaniard, a Hollander, and a Frenchman attempted to describe it, each one spoke of it as that *of a foreigner*. . . . You will say that it might have been the voice of *an Asiatic—of an African*. Neither Asiatics

nor Africans abound in Paris" (Poe, "The Murders in the Rue Morgue," in *Collected Works of Edgar Allan Poe*, 2:549–550, emphasis mine).

8. In the last sequence of *The Yellow Danger*, Shiel invents "the new Black Death" as an ethnic weapon for countering Chinese power in Europe. "As soon as an idolless Chinaman was griped by the malady, or even saw the black spot on a neighbour's cheek, his first instinct was to rush toward the one place of hope—the temple at Paris. And as he rushed, he went spreading far and wide that winged plague, that more putrid Cholera, dissipating it among thousands, who, in their turn, rushed to infect wide millions" (342).

9. This story is uncannily prophetic in its anticipation of the possibilities of bacteriological warfare. Jack London describes the superweapon storming China: "Had there been one plague, China might have coped with it. But from a score of plagues no creature was immune. . . . For it was these bacteria, and germs, and microbes, and bacilli, cultured in the laboratories of the West, that had come down upon China in the rain of glass" ("The Unparalleled Invasion," 118). Also see Franklin, *War Stars*, 36–37. He also explains that the yellow and black perils are sometimes closely intertwined (35), as we can see in William Ward Crane's "The Year 1899" (1893).

10. In "Flies and Russians" Twain states: "If we combine these three (the rabbit, the mollusk and the idiot) and add the bee, what do we get? A Russian. . . . The captive rabbit spends its whole life in meek submission to whatever master is over it; the mollusk spends its whole life asleep, drunk, content; the idiot lives his days in a dull and cloudy dream, and reasons not; *the bee* slaves from dawn to dark storing up honey for a robber to live on" (*Mark Twain's Which Was the Dream?*, 422, emphasis mine). In "The Fable of the Yellow Terror," the same author compares Americans to butterflies, and Asians to bees: "They (the Butterflies) said that those fat and diligent and contented *Bees*, munching grass and cabbage, ignorant of honey, ignorant of civilization and rapacity and treachery and robbery and murder and prayer and one thing and another, and joying in their eventless life and in the sumptuous beauty of their golden jackets, were a *Yellow Peril*" (427, emphasis mine). These two fables, written in almost the same year, are Twain's critique of the racial prejudice inherent in the notion of the yellow peril, which is allied, in the author's idiosyncratic figuration of the bee, with the red menace. Note that chap. 28 of Shiel's *The Yellow Danger* is entitled "The Yellow Terror," which very likely inspired Twain to compose the second fable.

11. For further details, see Franklin, *War Stars*, 41.

12. Cf. Renzi, *H. G. Wells*, 119–147.

13. Clarke, *3001*, 265.

14. Page numbers referred to are based on Arthur C. Clarke's *2001*, *2010*, and *2061*. For a more detailed analysis of Monolith, see my article "Post-Human, Post-Monolith," 46–50, and my book *Nisenichinen Uchu-no Tabi Kougi*. Also see http://web.mita.keio.ac.jp/~tatsumi/html/zensigoto/2001cb.htm.

Chapter 4. Deep North Gothic

1. The earliest version of this chapter was first prepared for my seminar on the American influence on Japanese cinematography at the Japan Society in New York City on March 15, 1996. The audience included a large number of high school teachers of New York required to teach some aspects of Japanese culture.
2. This account of the life of Kunio Yanagita, the founder of Japanese folklore studies, is loosely based on Morse's article "Yanagita Kunio" in the *Kodansha Encyclopedia of Japan*.
3. "Translator's Introduction," by Morse, in Yanagita, *Tono Monogatari*, xxiii–xxiv.
4. Ivy, *Discourses of the Vanishing*, 39, 59.
5. Quoted in ibid., 129.
6. I still remember the tremendous impact of the topic of "impossible intercourse" between "human beings and other species" on most of the participants of my seminar. Some of them seemed extremely disturbed by the concept.
7. Ivy, *Discourses of the Vanishing*, 123. On kappa, see Kazuhiko Komatsu, *Ijinron*.
8. Ivy, *Discourses of the Vanishing*, 126.
9. I can mention in passing that Hollywood released a number of alien encounter films that roughly coincided with the 1982 release of Murano's *The Legend of Sayo*, including Ridley Scott's *Alien* (1979), Steven Spielberg's *Close Encounters* (1980), and *E.T.* (1982). This coincidence may bring to mind my analysis in chapter 2 of Shozo Numa's reinterpretation of kappa in *Yapoo the Human Cattle*, in which I examined the influence on Numa of Arthur C. Clarke's masterpiece *Childhood's End*. Whereas Clarke considered Satan as an overlord, Numa considered the kappa as a Yapoo.
10. Hirakawa, *Yakumo Koizumi*, 407–410.
11. Cott, *Wandering Ghost*, 84.
12. Ibid., 145.
13. Hearn, *Interpretations of Literature*, 50–55.
14. In February 2004 I was able to meet Bon Koizumi, a great-grandson of Lafcadio Hearn; Koizumi was born in Tokyo in 1961, but since the 1980s he has lived in Matsue, Shimane Prefecture, where he directs the museum of Koizumi Yakumo. He pointed out that Hearn was very familiar with Sir George James Frazer's preanthropological canon *The Golden Bough* (1890–1915), and that Colonel Bonner Fellers, an avid reader of Lafcadio Hearn, taught General Douglas McArthur the significance of the Japanese emperor. Accordingly, we could well reinterpret Hearn not simply as the precursor of nativist ethnology and structuralism, but also as the popularizer of the emperor system peculiar to Japan. In this sense, Hearn must have witnessed the miraculous intersection between the universal and the particular around the turn of the century.

Chapter 5. Which Way to Coincidence?

1. An earlier and longer version of this chapter was originally written as the introduction to the Japanese edition of *Crash*, published in 1992. That version focused more attention on the interaction between postmodernism and science fiction.
2. For more details about my own sentimental journey toward science fiction, see my article "Editorial Afterword."

Chapter 6. A Manifesto for Gynoids

1. An earlier version of this chapter appeared as the introduction to the original Japanese edition of Calder's short story collection *The Allure* (Tokyo: Treville, 1991). Note that in his latest film *Innocence* (2004), the sequel to *Ghost in the Shell* (1995), one of the most influential anime artists, Mamoru Oshii, made skillful use of the concept of "gynoid," intertwining it with Donna Haraway's "cyborg feminism."
2. While the term "gynoid" was coined in 1984 by Gwyneth Jones in her novel *Divine Endurance*, there is a critical difference between Jones's gynoid and Calder's one: while the former is constructed as the angel doll chosen among the beautiful in a near-future Chinese palace, the latter is reconstructed as a hi-tech transvestite and/or transsexual cyborg. Jones's gynoid vividly recalls Bernardo Bertolucci's film *The Last Emperor* (1987), while Calder's story recalls Hwang's *M. Butterfly* (1986). For a more detailed analysis, see Mari Kotani's collection of essays *Alien Bedfellows*.

Chapter 7. Semiotic Ghost Stories

1. Although the earliest version of the chapter was first published in the first issue of *Science Fiction Eye* in March 1987, it was the International Conference on Japan and the United States, "Perceptions, Misperceptions, Counterperceptions between Two Cultures," May 13–15, 1989—especially the literature section panel moderated by Iwao Iwamoto on May 14—that inspired me to radically reconstruct my argument. My fellow panelists, including William Gass, Kenzaburo Ohashi, and Norma Field, gave me many insightful suggestions.

   Bruce Sterling's introduction is published in *ArmadilloCon 8 Program Book* (quotation on p. 7). ArmadilloCon 8 was the annual convention of the Fandom Association of Central Texas, held in Austin Texas, October 10–12, 1986.
2. Disclave 86 was the annual convention of the Washington Science Fiction Association, held in Washington, D.C., May 23–25, 1986.
3. Regarding "the postmodernist paradox" that "the perceiver literally becomes the perceived," the American philosopher Geoff Waite quotes the last two sentences of this penultimate section and gives the following highly provocative comments: " 'Nietzsche' can be substituted for 'Gibson' in Tatsumi's argument—and likely for 'Tatsumi' himself—and 'Nietzscheanism' for 'Japan.' And Nietzsche was well familiar with an earlier form of this ar-

gument, developed by Schopenhauer, to the effect that when we transcend the strictures of the principle of sufficient reason (i.e., for everything there is, there is a reason or ground why it is) 'we no longer consider the where, the when, the why, and the whither of things, but simply and solely the *what*. . . . [I]t is as though the object alone existed without anyone to perceive it, and thus we are no longer able to separate the perceiver from the perceived' " (*Nietzsche's Corpse*, 172).

4. The term "ghost" in the sense of "ghost writer" was first used in 1884. The *Oxford English Dictionary* defines this "ghost" as "one who secretly does artistic or literary work for another person, the latter taking the credit." See Leah Price's fascinating article "From Ghostwriter to Typewriter." It is interesting that some hundred years after the coining of the term, the rise of cyberpunk came to revolutionize "ghost" by exploring the frontier of digital technology, cyberspace, and artificial life.

Chapter 8. Junk Art City

1. Polledri, *Visionary San Francisco*, 19–20.
2. Starr, Preface to *Visionary San Francisco*, 14–15.
3. Gibson, "William Gibson: New Futures, Just on the Horizon," 4.
4. When I published my first review of *Virtual Light* in the September 11, 1993, issue of *Tosho-Shinbun* (Book Review Press), at the request of the editor Shu Fujisawa, I did not notice the similarity between Gibson and Süskind. Hiroshi Takayama of Tokyo Metropolitan University read this review and suggested I read Robert Isherwood's theory of bridge culture (as developed in Isherwood's *Farce and Fantasy*); Isherwood's book led me in turn to the work of this German author.
5. Nelson, *Treehouses*, 125–126.
6. Akasegawa, *Geijutsu Genron*, 249–259.
7. The terms come from Tsuru, *Japan's Capitalism*, and Tatsumi, "Creative Masochism," respectively.
8. Emory Elliott commissioned Larry McCaffery to contribute the chapter "The Fictions of the Present" to *The Columbia Literary History of the United States*, from which I quoted McCaffery's appreciation of cyberpunk in chapter 2. Here I show you how he characterized Gibson in the same chapter: " 'Realism,' of course, had never been so rigid, naïve, and monolithic a notion as postmodernist apologists had implied. During the 1970s the various impassioned debates about 'The Death of the Novel,' 'Moral versus Immoral Fiction,' 'The Literature of Exhaustion,' 'Self-reflexive versus Mimetic Fiction' gradually lost their energy, but these discussions had established widespread acceptance of the view that 'realism' encompasses many different stylistic approaches and that even seemingly anti (or non) realistic fictional methods express a vision of external reality. Thus Walter Abish's *How German Is It* (1980), with its sharply etched descriptions of contemporary Germany, was a 'realistic depiction' not of Germany (which Abish had never visited) but of the Germany existing in the American public's imagination. William Gibson's futuristic 'cyberpunk' novel, *Neuromancer* (1984), describes

a punked-out, high-tech world of cyber realities, tribal jungles operating on society's marginalized fringes, and dizzying labyrinths of images reflecting human desires that are endlessly replicated in mirrors and computers; yet for all its exoticism, *Neuromancer* offers a compelling vision of the way technology has *already affected* our lives" (1164).

9. The self-effacing text of "Agrippa" is now easily available on William Gibson's official Web site (http:/www.williamgibsonbooks.com/source/source.asp). As we learn from Gibson's autobiographical essay "Since 1948," his father became involved with the Manhattan Project, and that without this personal history Gibson could not have meditated upon a variety of catastrophes, natural or artificial, so deeply. In this respect, the San Francisco earthquake as depicted in *Virtual Light* could be reconstrued as a prelude to the 9/11 terrorist attacks as narrativized in *Pattern Recognition*.

Chapter 9. Pax Exotica

1. The earliest version of the chapter was first presented on June 16, 1996, at the thirtieth annual meeting of the Japanese Association for American Studies. A revised version was published in *Science Fiction Eye*, no. 15 (1997), and delivered in an abridged version on August 22, 1997, at the conference "Endings and Transformations: Cultural Studies and the Millennium," Trent University, Peterborough, Toronto.
2. *San Francisco Bay Times*, November 5, 1992, p. 1.
3. "Anna-chan of Green Gables" was published in the Canadian journal *Grain* 24.1 (summer 1996): 116–128. I first met Michael Keezing at the conference "The American Cultural Impact on Germany, France, Italy and Japan, 1945–1995: An International Comparison," Brown University, April 12–13, 1996. Keezing spent three years in Tokyo from 1997 through 2000, developing good social relationships with Japanese literati, including Yoriko Shono, the winner of many prestigious awards such as the Akutagawa Prize and the Mishima Prize. Without his editorial skill and intercultural knowledge Larry McCaffery, Sinda Gregory, and I could not have edited so carefully "New Japanese Fiction." Keezing now lives in South Hadley, Massachusetts.
4. Davidson, *Reading in America*, 168.
5. For example, Baldwin, *Land of the Red Soil.*
6. As reported in the Japanese edition of *Esquire* (August 1996): 133.
7. Karl Taro Greenfeld, *Speed Tribes*, 272.
8. Keezing's story somehow encouraged William Gibson to describe Japanese subculture in his novel *Pattern Recognition*: "If Keiko were real, would she necessarily have to like Anne of Green Gables? And anything Cayce might ever have known about the Anne of Green Gables cult in Japan has just gone up in a puff of synaptic mist" (151).

Chapter 10. Magic Realist Tokyo

1. When I published the earliest version of this chapter in the fifth issue of *Theater Arts* (Tokyo: Bansei Shobo) in 1996, it lacked a comparative study of

Bartók and Terayama. The present version springs from the paper I delivered on October 19, 1999, at the international Edgar Allan Poe conference commemorating the sesquicentennial of Poe's death, held in Richmond, Virginia. This summary of *The Miraculous Mandarin* is based largely upon Downes's *Everyman's Guide*, 50.

2. Bartók's health declined precipitously during the first part of 1943. In January and February of that year, he experienced such weakness that he could scarcely walk from one room to another, and his temperature frequently ran four degrees above normal. In April he began to experience recurrent periods of lower or higher fever. In May, pain in the joints made walking almost impossible. Bartók was able to deliver only three of a series of lectures that Harvard University had invited him to give during the spring semester of 1943. By the end of June 1943, he felt there was no hope of recovery. Despite the success of his Concerto for Orchestra in 1944, he grew steadily weaker, and although an attack of pneumonia was quickly conquered by antibiotics, he had apparently developed leukemia. When Tibor Serly saw him on the evening of September 21, 1945, Bartók was working on the orchestral score of his Third Piano Concerto. The next day he was taken from his tiny apartment on 57th Street to West Side Hospital, where he died on September 26. See Downes, *Everyman's Guide*, 50; Stevens, *The Life and Music of Bela Bartok*, 98–106.
3. Poe, *The Short Fiction*, 368.
4. Terayama and Caesar, "Enshutsu Shukou," 4.
5. William Whipple and Stuart and Susan Levine focus on General Richard M. Johnson's public persona as the object of Poe's satire. In a dreadful small-scale encounter in a swamp—part of the larger battle of the Thames in 1813—Johnson fought with great bravery, killed Tecumseh, and himself suffered multiple severe wounds. His courage, his stature as a national hero, and his injuries proved to be potent campaign assets. See Whipple, "Poe's Political Satire," and Levine, *The Short Fiction*, 438.
6. Donna Haraway defines "women of color," in particular, as a cyborg identity, a potent subjectivity synthesized from fusions of outsider identities within the complex politicohistorical layerings of her "biomythography." The analogy between the cyborg identity and a multicultural creole subjectivity follows from this assumption. As Ron Eglash explains, pursuing a related argument, "The problems of natural/artificial dualisms encountered by cyborgs are similar to those which plague activists and theorists in the long historical battles against racism. . . . An anti-racist characterization of African influences in cybernetics must be situated in ways which do not merely reverse or refute its claims, but address its historical construction" ("African Influences in Cybernetics," 17).
7. Terayama and Caesar, "Enshutsu Shukou," 4.
8. Terayama's essay is in *Zouki-Koukan Josetsu* [Transplanting Organs], 131–132.
9. Rosemarie Garland Thomson offers the following explanation of the political implications of Barnum's freak show: "By highlighting ostensible human anomaly of every sort and combination, Barnum's exhibits challenged audiences not only to classify and explain what they saw, but to re-

late the performance to themselves, to American individual and collective identity. With bearded ladies, for example, Barnum and his followers demanded that American audiences resolve this affront to the rigid categories of male and female that their culture imposed. With Eng and Chang, the famous 'Siamese' twins, the freak show challenged the boundaries of the individual, asking whether this entity was one person or two. With dwarfs as well as armless and legless 'wonders,' the pitchman charged their audiences to determine the precise parameters of human wholeness and the limits of free agency. The freak show thrived in an era of unbounded confidence in the human ability to perceive and act upon truth. These collective cultural rituals provided dilemmas of classification and definition upon which the throng of spectators could hone the skills needed to tame world and self in the ambitious project of American self-making" (58–59).

10. Poe, *The Short Fiction*, 438.
11. Poe, *The Short Fiction*, 446 (italics mine).
12. As noted in chapter 2, the concept of the reality studio was first proposed by William Burroughs and later reorganized by Larry McCaffery. In the introduction to his *Storming the Reality Studio*, McCaffery explains that "technological systems and artifacts that people can interface with (physically and imaginatively) or that can recreate experiences and 'realize' desires, illusions, and memories have created vast new 'areas' of sensory experience with their own spatial and temporal coordinates, their own personal and metaphysical dimensions. These new realms of experience—theorized by Guy Debord's 'Society of the Spectacle,' Baudrillard's 'precession of simulacra,' and Cook and Kroker's 'hyperreality,' and metaphorized perhaps most vividly by Gibson's 'cyberspace'—have become integrated so successfully into the daily textures of our lives that they often seem more 'real' to us than the presumably more 'substantial,' 'natural' aspects" (6) of reality. The concept of the reality studio clearly coincides with that of the "pseudo-event," as championed by Daniel Boorstin in his magnum opus *The Image*.

Chapter 11. Full Metal Apache

1. *Tetsuo* and *Tetsuo II: Body Hammer*, both directed by Shinya Tsukamoto, hereafter referred to as "the *Tetsuo* series" or "the *Tetsuo* diptych." The program books for these movies gave me very helpful information. The first English version of this chapter was prepared for a lecture on these movies at the Japan Society, March 15, 1996. A revised version of the chapter was published in the *Japanese Journal of American Studies*, no. 7 (Japanese Association for American Studies, September 1996). I have since delivered lectures on this topic at various universities, including Sapporo University, University of Montreal, McGill University, and University of California–Los Angeles. I am not sure whether Hiromu Arakawa's popular manga/anime *Full Metal Alchemist* has something to do with my original paper. Yet the popularity of this kind of manga/anime will doubtlessly confirm that the Japanese people are indeed obsessed with the image of metal.
2. Tatsumi and Tsukamoto, "Cyber-Eros in Full Metal Apache." The Ameri-

can acceptance of *Tetsuo* as a typical cyberpunk is confirmed in *Flame Wars*, a special issue of *South Atlantic Quarterly*, which featured a still from the movie on its cover.

3. Pynchon, *Gravity's Rainbow*. See Gloege, *The American Origins of the Postmodern Self*, 1–103.
4. Mogen, "Wilderness, Metamorphosis, and Millennium," 94–108.
5. Watabiki, *Mono ga Kataru Sekai no Rekishi*, 39–53.
6. Suzuki, "Kikai to Gijutsu-sha," 134–153.
7. Ubukata, *Kaitaiya no Sengo-Shi*, 12–36.
8. Ochi, *Kariforunia no Ougon*, chaps. 1 and 2.
9. Unless otherwise specified, all the "Apache" quotations came from the following: Kaiko, *Nippon Sanmon Opera*; Komatsu, *Nippon Apacchi-Zoku*; and Yang Sok Il, *Yoru wo Kakete*. For Yang Sok Il's novel, I translated its title literally as "Playing Cards for Night," though the movie version produced in 2002 was given the English title *Through the Night*. For the etymology of the Japanese Apache, see Junko Otobe's ambitious and painstaking research report, which traces the first use of "Apacchi-Zoku" (Japanese Apache) to an article in the May 28, 1958, issue of *Osaka Nichi-nichi Shinbun* (Osaka Daily News), 30, where it is the nickname for scrap thieves; the headline reads: "The Japanese Apache Bust: 53 Members of the Tribe Arrested."
10. For the historical survey of the rise of the Japanese Apache, I referred to not only the Apache novels but also Yang Sok Il's nonfictional books, *Shura wo Ikiru* and *Yami no Souzouryoku*.
11. Masaaki Hiraoka skillfully sets up the analogy between the figure of Kim in the novel and that of Malcolm X (*Yang Sok Il wa Sekai-Bungaku de aru*, 89–90).
12. Note that Yang Sok Il's acceptance of Ken Kaiko's *Nippon Sanmon Opera* is ambivalent. While he appreciates the novel as one of Kaiko's masterpieces, Yang reveals that the Japanese Apaches themselves felt very uncomfortable with it: "Kaiko did not succeed in representing the Koreans living in Japan just as they are. . . . But, it is the limitation of Kaiko that motivated me to write *Yoru wo Kakete*, and to disclose what our struggle for life was actually like" (*Yami no Souzouryoku*, 129–131). On the same topic, Masaaki Hiraoka discusses with special emphasis on the critical status of the Korean soldiers who had worked for the Japanese army. They could belong neither to the Japanese society nor to the Korean nation. According to Hiraoka, it is this identity crisis that symbolized the whole Korean situation in Japan most seriously (*Yang Sok Il wa Sekai-Bungaku de aru*, 94–108).
13. Adams, *Geronimo*, 13.
14. The generic discourse of the Indian captivity narrative arose from the literary conventions of Puritan spiritual autobiography, the theocratic sermon, and the American jeremiad in the colonial period. While the captivity narrative started by detailing the WASP captives' predicament and redemption, it has had such a tremendous impact on American literature, that even now we find its residues disseminated over a variety of popular subgenres such as the western, the psycho-thriller, and the splatter horror. See Pearce, "The Significance of Captivity Narrative"; Slotkin, *Regeneration through Violence*;

Vaughan et al., *Puritans among the Indians*; Fitzpatrick, "The Figures of Captivity"; Derounian-Stodola et al., *The Indian Captivity Narrative*.

15. Though very critical about Kaiko's *Nippon Sanmon Opera*, Masaaki Hiraoka praises highly Sakyo Komatsu's *Nippon Apacchi-Zoku*, in which he recognizes the author's deeper fear of Stalinism, more radical commitment to the leftist movement, and more serious comprehension of the Koreans living in Japan (*Yang Sok Il wa Sekai-Bungaku de aru*, 109–111).
16. Komatsu and Kaiko, "Loneliness in the Masses," 257–277.
17. Fukuda, "Kagayakeru Shokuyoku"; Yomota, "Kafuka to Yakiniku."
18. Shozo Numa, *Kachiku-jin Yapoo* and *Kachiku-jin Yapoo: Kanketsu-hen* (The Definitive Sequel to *Yapoo the Human Cattle*, Tokyo: Million Publishers, 1991). The whole Yapoo saga is now available from Gentosha.
19. Fukushima, *Mitou no Jidai*, 145.
20. Mark Driscoll explains: "The operation of *zettai mujunteki jiko doitsu* (absolute contradictory self-identity) puts the abstract machinery of logic as logos into mutually constitutive relation with the body, one that touches on the limit of the other. But Nishida wants to emphasize the disjunctive quality of this relation and in so doing he posits the singular entity (*soku*) as a structure of the trace which gives relation and which is the possibility for any binary opposition. The cyborg as singular trace which Nishida argues can never be thought as such, is that which gives and discloses a binary relation" ("Nishida Kitaro's Jouis(ci)ence: Cyborg Ethics as Interfaciality" [1994, unpublished], 5). For the most revolutionary perspective on the postmodern notion of cyborg, see Haraway, "A Manifesto for Cyborgs."
21. Haraway states: "The founding Japanese primatologists had no difficulty with the fact of evolution, but their questions and resulting explanatory systems were directed to social anthropology, and not to questions of fitness and strategies of adaptation" ("The Bio-Politics of a Multicultural Field," 250).
22. Hanada, "Don Fan Ron," 51.
23. In his conclusion to *Fukkou-ki no Seishin* (The Spirit of Renaissance) Kiyoteru Hanada confesses that discussing the major figures of European Renaissance in the book, he had focused on "how to survive the transition period," keenly aware of the critical reality of wartime Japan in the 1940s (*Fukkouki-no Seishin*, 258).
24. This is why Kaiko, since the mid-sixties, has kept writing about the Vietnam War, feeling greater sympathy with the Vietnamese. Cf. Tateo Imamura, "Vietnam kara itteki no Hikari e."
25. For a detailed analysis of this novel, see Tatsumi, "Creative Masochism," 67–68.
26. Isaiah Ben-Dasan explicates the analogy and the difference between Judaism and Nihonism (Nipponism) as follows: "More than anything else, the *Diaspora* forced the Jews into an intensified sense of identity and, perhaps, excessive consciousness of being part of a particular religious faith. Scattered over many parts of the globe, yet united by the idea of the synagogue and by rabbinical tradition, Jews could not avoid comparing themselves with the peoples among whom they lived. In doing so, they discovered their own

traits, from which evolved an awareness of a unique thing called Jewishness. The Japanese, never having undergone such dispersal, are less aware of the forces that unite them, especially of that great binding faith which I have called *Nihonism*. It has so permeated the minds of its followers that it is taken for granted, a remarkable fact when one considers that it is as valid a religion as Judaism, Christianity, or Islam" (*Nihonjin*, 106–107, emphasis mine).

27. Komatsu, *Nippon Chinbotsu*. However, taking for granted the prophetic nature of the novel, Peter Hartcher seems more amused by Komatsu's acute observation on the conservative sensibility of Japanese bureaucrats in general: "what is particularly striking as an insight from Komatsu's book was the Government's reluctance to act in the face of impending disaster. . . . For the government to act, the scientists are obliged to use a circuitous route of private introductions and personal backdoor contacts. . . . At a time when government white papers are laughable, perhaps it should not be surprising that trash can make sense" ("Trashy Novel was a Sign of Things to Come," 11).

28. Sakaguchi, "Daraku-Ron"; Hanada, *Fukkouki no Seishin*; Tsuru, *Japan's Capitalism*; Yamaguchi, *Zasetsu no Showa-shi* (The Mental History of Failure) and *Haisha no Seishin-shi* (The Mental History of Defeat); Matsuoka, *Furajairu*; Tatsumi, "Creative Masochism"; Masaki, *Venus City*; Besher, *RIM*.
29. Also note that, while the first generation among the New England settlers naturalized the analogy between the Jews and the American Indians, later generations became less sure of the origin of the natives. See Smolinski, "The 'New' Hermeneutics and the Jewish Nation," 23–24.
30. Cf. Fiedler, *The Return of the Vanishing American*, 8.
31. For the postcolonialist as well as primatological feminist redefinition of "orientalism," see Haraway, *Primate Visions*, 10–13; cf. Gewertz and Errington, "We Think, Therefore They Are?" For the relationship between cyborg and imperialism, see Sandoval, "New Sciences"; Gabilondo, "Postcolonial Cyborgs."
32. It is well known that the earliest texts of slave narrative borrowed a great deal from the conventions of Indian captivity narrative. Cf. Sekora, "Red, White, and Black." If we positively "misread" the *Tetsuo* diptych from the perspective of American narrative, the director Shinya Tsukamoto seems to have revived and re-Japanized not simply captivity narrative, in which an ordinary "salary man" gets captivated and brainwashed by the cyborg Apaches, but also diaspora narrative, in which these metallocentric and metallivorous freaks are about to declare their own tribal independence within Japan.
33. Goldberg, "Recalling Totalities."
34. Ian Buruma gives us a most helpful "queer" reading of Japanese films and novels. See his "Weeping Tears of Nostalgia."
35. Larry McCaffery defines "avant-pop" as combining "Pop Art's focus on consumer goods and mass media with the avant-garde's spirit of subversion and emphasis on radical formal innovation" (McCaffery, *After Yesterday's Crash*, xvii–xviii).

Conclusion: Waiting for Godzilla

1. I read the original version of this essay on April 13, 1996, at the conference "The American Cultural Impact on Germany, France, Italy and Japan, 1945–1995: An International Comparison," Brown University, April 12–13, 1996. A revised version was included in *Transactions, Transgressions, Transformations: American Culture in Western Europe and Japan*, ed. Heide Fehrenbach and Uta Poiger (New York: Berghahn, 2000).
2. Delany, *Silent Interviews*, 212–213.
3. Nagayama, *Kindai Nippon no Monsho-gaku*, 185–188.
4. Marc Eliot supposes that it was Walt Disney's obsession with the secret of his birth that led to his involvement with the FBI, in exchange for J. Edgar Hoover's help in tracking down his real origins. Moreover, Disney is known to have attended meetings of the American Nazi Party, though he only wanted to get his productions into Nazi-occupied countries in the period before the war. For more details, see Eliot's biography, *Walt Disney*.
5. Kuspit, "Art and Capital," 478.
6. Hartcher, "Trashy Novel Was a Sign," 11.
7. At this point, the allegory of Godzilla will invite you to disfigure the symbol of the Japanese emperor presented in introduction. Throughout this book the discourse of Godzilla mania helps deconstruct that of Mikadophilia, and vice versa.

Appendix 1. Toward the Frontiers of "Fiction"

1. This correspondence was first published in Japanese in one of the Japanese leading newspapers, *Mainichi Shinbun* (Mainichi News), in August 1992, and later expanded and reprinted in English in the cyberpunk magazine *Science Fiction Eye*, no. 12, in 1993. The English version was honored with the fifth Pioneer Award, given by the Science Fiction Research Association.
2. This "Sayonara (for now)" could be interpreted as a kind of prophesy: after the conclusion of this correspondence, Larry meditated more deeply on the potential of avant-pop, and came up with a couple of anthologies, *Avant-Pop* and *After Yesterday's Crash*. Also see McCaffery, "13 Introductory Ways."

Appendix 2. A Dialogue with the Nanofash Pygmalion: An Interview with Richard Calder

1. Chapter 6 of the present volume is an updated version of this essay.
2. This interview was to constitute part of the introduction to the Japanese edition of Calder's *Dead Things*, to be published in 1998; Mamoru Masuda's translation had already been completed. However, the collapse of the publisher Treville prevented us from printing it. An e-text has been available since 2003 on Richard Calder's own website, "Babylon" http://www.richardcalder.net/tatsumi.html.

WORKS CITED

Abe, Kobo. *Hako-Otoko* (The Box Man). Tokyo: Shinchosha Publishers, 1973.

———. *Tomodachi* (Friends). 1967. Translated by Donald Keene. New York: Grove, 1969.

Adams, Alexander B. *Geronimo: A Biography*. New York: Da Capo, 1971.

Akasegawa, Genpei. *Cho-Geijutsu Tomason* (Hyper-Art Thomasson). 1985. Tokyo: Chikuma Publishers, 1987.

———. *Geijutsu Genron* (The Principles of Art). Tokyo: Iwanami Publishing, 1988.

Akutagawa, Ryunosuke. *Kappa*. 1927. Tokyo: Shueisha Publishers, 1992.

———. *Kappa*. Translated by Geoffrey Bownas, introduction by G. H. Healey. 1970. Tokyo: Tuttle, 1994.

Amerika, Mark, and Lance Olsen, eds. *In Memoriam to Postmodernism: Essays on the Avant-Pop*. San Diego: San Diego State University Press, 1995.

Anon. "Rentertainers." Special issue of *SPA!* April 8, 1993, 87.

Aramaki, Yoshio. "Yawarakai Tokei" (Soft Clocks). 1968–1971. Translated by Kazuko Behrens and Lewis Shiner. *Interzone*, no. 27 (January–February 1989).

Atwood, Margaret. *The Handmaid's Tale*. 1985. New York: Faucett Crest, 1986.

Auster, Paul. *Moon Palace*. 1989. New York: Penguin, 1990.

———. *The New York Trilogy*. London: Faber and Faber, 1987.

Baldwin, Douglas. *Land of the Red Soil: A Popular History of Prince Edward Island*. Charlottetown: Ragweed, 1990 .

Ballard, J. G. *Crash*. 1973. London: Granta, 1975.

———. *Empire of the Sun*. London: Gollancz, 1984.

———. *War Fever*. London: Collins, 1990.

Barrie, J. M. *Peter Pan*. 1911. New York: Penguin/Puffin Classics, 1994.

Barth, John. "The Literature of Exhaustion." 1967. In *The Friday Book*. New York: Putnam, 1984. 62–76.

Barthes, Roland. *The Empire of Signs*. 1970. Translated by Richard Howard. New York: Hill and Wang, 1982.

Bartók, Béla. *Bela Bartok: Essays*. Edited by Benjamin Suchoff. 1976. Lincoln: University of Nebraska Press, 1992.

———. *The Miraculous Mandarin: Music for Strings, Percussion, and Celesta*. Conducted by Pierre Boulez. Deutsche Grammophon, 1996.

Baudrillard, Jean. "Ballard's *Crash*." Translated by Arthur B. Evans. *Science-Fiction Studies* (55) 18.3 (November 1991): 313–320.

———. *La Guerre du Golfe n'a pas eu lieu*. Translated by Fumi Tsukahara. Tokyo: Kinokuniya Publishers, 1991.

Beasley, W. G. *The Modern History of Japan*. 3rd rev. ed. Tokyo: Tuttle, 1982.

Ben-Dasan, Isaiah. *Nihonjin (Nipponjin) to Yudayajin* (The Japanese and the Jews). Translated by Richard L. Gate. 1970. New York: Weatherhill, 1972.

Besher, Alexander. *RIM*. New York: HarperCollins, 1994.

Bester, John. "Foreword." In Takeo Doi, *Amae no Kozo* (Anatomy of Dependence). Tokyo: Kobundo, 1971.

Bhabha, Homi. "Of Mimicry and Man: The Ambivalence of Colonial Discourse." *October* 28 (spring 1984): 125–133. Reprinted in *The Location of Culture* (London: Routledge, 1994), 85–86.

Birnbaum, Alfred, ed. *Monkey Brain Sushi*. Tokyo: Kodansha International, 1991.

Bix, Herbert. *Hirohito and the Making of Modern Japan*. 2000. New York: Perennial, 2001.

Blair, David, dir. *WAX, or The Discovery of Television among the Bees*. 1991. Videocassette. Tokyo: Uplink, 1993.

Boorstin, Daniel. *The Image*. 1962. New York: Vintage, 1992.

Borcherding, David. "Nanofash." *bOING-bOING*, no. 9 (1992): 9–10.

Bornoff, Nicholas. *Pink Samurai: Love, Marriage, and Sex in Contemporary Japan*. New York: Pocket Books, 1991.

Brown, Alan. *Audrey Hepburn's Neck*. New York: Pocket Books, 1996.

Buruma, Ian. *The Wages of Guilt: Memories of War in Germany and Japan*. New York: Farrar Straus Giroux, 1994.

———. "Weeping Tears of Nostalgia." *New York Review of Books* 11.14 (August 12, 1993): 29–30.

Calder, Richard. "The Allure." *Interzone*, no. 40 (October 1990).

———. *The Allure*. Translated by Hisashi Asakura. Introduction by Takayuki Tatsumi. Tokyo: Treville, 1991.

———. *Cythera*. London: Little, Brown; New York: St. Martin's, 1998.

———. *Dead Girls*. 1991. London: Grafton, 1992.

———. *Dead Boys*. New York: St. Martin's, 1994.

———. *Dead Things*. New York: St. Martin's, 1996.

———. "The Lilim." *Interzone*, no. 34 (March–April 1990).

———. "Mosquito." *Interzone*, no. 32 (November–December 1989).

———. "Toxine." In *Interzone 4th Anthology*. 1989. London: NEL, 1990. 110–131.

Card, Orson Scott. "Lost Boys." F & SF (October 1989).

———. *Lost Boys* (novel). 1992. New York: Harper, 1993.

Carrier, James, ed. *Occidentalism: Images of the West*. New York: Oxford University Press, 1995.

Chase, Cynthia. *Decomposing Figures: Rhetorical Readings in the Romantic Tradition*. Baltimore: Johns Hopkins University Press, 1986.

Clarke, Arthur C. *Childhood's End*. New York: Ballantine, 1953.

———. *2001: A Space Odyssey*. New York: Signet, 1968.

———. *2010: Odyssey Two*. London: Grafton, 1982.
———. *2061: Odyssey Three*. New York: Del Rey, 1987.
———. *3001: The Final Odyssey*. New York: Del Rey, 1997.
Clarke, I. F. "The Future-War Fiction: The First Main Phase, 1871–1990." *Science-Fiction Studies* 24.3 (winter 1997): 387–412.
Coover, Robert. "The End of Books." *New York Times Book Review*, June 21, 1992, pp. 1, 11, 24–25.
Corn, Joseph J., ed. *Imagining Tomorrow: History, Technology, and the American Future*. Cambridge: MIT Press, 1986.
Cott, Jonathan. *Wandering Ghost: The Odyssey of Lafcadio Hearn*. Tokyo: Kodansha International, 1990.
Creed, Barbara. "Gynesis, Postmodernism and the Science Fiction Horror Film." In *Alien Zone*, edited by Annette Kuhn. London: Verso, 1990. 214–218.
Creighton, Millie. "Imaging the Other in Japanese Advertising Campaigns." In *Occidentalism: Images of the West*, edited by James Carrier. New York: Oxford University Press, 1995. 135–160.
Crichton, Michael. *Rising Sun*. New York: Alfred A. Knopf, 1992.
Davidson, Cathy. *Reading in America*. Baltimore: Johns Hopkins University Press, 1989.
Delany, Samuel. *Silent Interviews*. Hanover: Wesleyan University Press, 1994.
DeLillo, Don. *Libra*. New York: Penguin, 1988.
———. *Underworld*. New York: Scribner, 1997.
Derounian-Stodola, Kathryn Zabelle, et al., eds. *The Indian Captivity Narrative, 1550–1900*. New York: Twayne, 1993.
Dery, Mark, ed. "Flame Wars: The Discourse of Cyberculture." Special issue of *South Atlantic Quarterly* 92.4 (fall 1993).
Dick, Philip K. *The Man in the High Castle*. New York: Putnam, 1962.
"Ding. Dong. The Witch Is Dead!" *San Francisco Bay Times*, November 5, 1992. 1.
Doi, Takeo. *Amae no Kozo* (Anatomy of Dependence). Tokyo: Kodansha, 1971. Translated by John Bester as *The Anatomy of Dependence* (Tokyo: Kobundo, 1973).
Downes, Edward. *Everyman's Guide to Orchestral Music*. London: Dent, 1976.
Driscoll, Mark. "Nishida Kitaro's Jouis(ci)ence: Cyborg Ethics as Interfaciality." Unpublished essay. 1994. Photocopy in the possession of Takayuki Tatsumi.
Eagleton, Terry. *Ideology: An Introduction*. London: Verso, 1991.
Eglash, Ron. "African Influences in Cybernetics." In *Cyborg Handbook*, ed. Chris Hables Gray. New York: Routledge, 1995. 17–27.
Eliot, Marc. *Walt Disney: Hollywood's Dark Prince*. 1993. New York: Harper, 1994.
Elliott, Emory, et al., eds. *The Columbia Literary History of the United States*. New York: Columbia University Press, 1988.
Elmer, Jonathan. *Reading at the Social Limit: Affect, Mass Culture, and Edgar Allan Poe*. Stanford: Stanford University Press, 1995.
Erickson, Steve. *Arc d'X*. New York: Poseidon, 1993.
———. *Days between Stations*. 1985. New York: Vintage, 1986.
———. *Tours of the Black Clock*. London: Futura, 1989.
Eurudice. *F/32*. Boulder: Fiction Collective Two, 1990.

———. "Why Clinton's Foreign Policy Shows He Is Good in Bed." *CUPS* (February 1995): 15.

Federman, Raymond. "Self-Reflexive Fiction." In *The Columbia Literary History of the United States*, edited by Emory Elliott. New York: Columbia University Press, 1988. 1148–1149.

Fehrenbach, Heide, and Uta Poiger, eds. *Transactions, Transgressions, Transformations: American Culture in Western Europe and Japan*. New York: Berghahn, 2000.

Fiedler, Leslie A. *The Return of the Vanishing American*. 1968. New York: Stein and Day, 1969.

Fitzpatrick, Tara. "The Figures of Captivity: The Cultural Work of the Puritan Captivity Narrative." *American Literary History* 3.1 (spring 1991): 1–26.

Foucault, Michel. "What is an Author?" 1969. Translated by Josué V. Harart. In *Literary Criticism*, edited by Robert Con Davis and Ronald Schleifer. Fourth edition. New York: Longman, 1998. 364–376.

Franklin, H. Bruce. *War Stars: The Superweapon and the American Imagination*. New York: Oxford University Press, 1988.

Fukuda, Ikuhiro. "Kagayakeru Shokuyoku" (The Brilliant Appetite). Special issue on Ken Kaiko, *Eureka* 22.8 (July 1990).

Fukumoto, Naomi. Review of *Neuromancer. Starlog Japan* (October 1986).

Fukushima, Masami. *Mitou no Jidai* (The Frontier Age of Japanese Science Fiction). Tokyo: Hayakawa Publishers, 1977.

Gabilondo, Joseba. "Postcolonial Cyborgs: Subjectivity in the Age of Cybernetic Reproduction." In *Cyborg Handbook*, edited by Chris Hables Gray. New York: Routledge, 1995. 423–432.

Gewertz, Deborah, and Frederick Errington. "We Think, Therefore They Are?: On Occidentalizing the World." In *Cultures of United States Imperialism*, edited by Amy Kaplan and Donald Pease. Durham: Duke University Press, 1993.

Gibson, William. *All Tomorrow's Parties*. New York: Putnam, 1999.

———. "The Gernsback Continuum." 1981. In *Burning Chrome*. New York: Arbor House, 1986. 28–40.

———. *Idoru*. New York: Penguin, 1996.

———. "Interview." *Spin* (October 1993): 91–93.

———. *Mona Lisa Overdrive*. New York; Bantam, 1988.

———. *Neuromancer*. New York: Ace, 1984.

———. "New Futures, Just on the Horizon" (interview with Walden Books). *Hailing Frequencies TM* no. 8 (August 1993): 1, 3–5, 13.

———. *Pattern Recognition*. New York: Putnam, 2003.

———. "*PW* Interviews: William Gibson" (conducted by Robert J. Kilheffer). *Publishers Weekly* 6 September 1993: 70–71.

———. "Q & A" (interview with David Streitfeld). *Details* (October 1993): 152–154.

———. "Since 1948." 2002. http://www.williamgibsonbooks.com/source/source.asp.

———. "Skinner's Room." In *Visionary San Francisco*, edited by Paolo Polledri. San Francisco: San Francisco Museum of Modern Art, 1990. 152–162.

———. *Virtual Light*. New York: Bantam, 1993.

———. "The Winter Market." In *Burning Chrome*. New York: Arbor House, 1986. 128.

Gibson, William, and Dennis Ashbaugh. "Agrippa." 1992. http://www.williamgibsonbooks.com/source/agrippa.asp.

Gibson, William, and Terry Bisson. *Johnny Mnemonic*. New York: Pocket Books, 1995.

Gibson, William, and Bruce Sterling. *The Difference Engine*. London: Gollancz, 1990.

Gloege, Martin. *The American Origins of the Postmodern Self*. Ph.D. diss., Rutgers, the State University of New Jersey (Ann Arbor: UMI, 1992).

Goldberg, Jonathan. "Recalling Totalities: The Mirrored Stages of Arnold Schwarzenegger." In *Cyborg Handbook* 1, edited by Chris Hables Gray. New York: Routledge, 1995.

Gray, Chris Hables, ed. *Cyborg Handbook*. New York: Routledge, 1995.

Greenfeld, Karl Taro. *Speed Tribes*. New York: HarperCollins, 1994.

Griffin, Robert J., ed. *The Faces of Anonymity: Anonymous and Pseudonymous Publication from the Sixteenth to the Twentieth Century*. New York: Palgrave Macmillan, 2003.

Hamamoto, Kaoru. Review of *Neuromancer. Bunshun Weekly* (September 4, 1986).

Hanada, Kiyoteru. "Don Fan Ron" (A Note on Don Juan). 1949. In *Avangyarudo Geijutsu* (Avant-Garde Art). 1954. Reprint, Tokyo: Kodansha, 1994. 47–62.

———. *Fukkouki-no Seishin* (The Spirit of Renaissance). 1946. Tokyo: Kodansha Publishers, 1986.

Hand, Elizabeth. Review of *Virtual Light. Science Fiction Eye*, no. 12 (August 1993): 93–95.

Haraway, Donna. "The Bio-Politics of a Multicultural Field." In *Primate Visions*. New York: Routledge, 1989. 244–275.

———. "A Manifesto for Cyborgs: Science, Technology, and Socialist Feminism in 1980s." *Socialist Review* 15.2 (1985): 65–108.

———. *Simians, Cyborgs, and Women: The Reinvention of Nature*. New York: Routledge, 1991.

Hartcher, Peter. "Trashy Novel Was a Sign of Things to Come." *Financial Review* (Australia), August 28, 1995, 11.

Hayakawa Publications, ed. *Neuromancer Shohyo-shu* (Collected Reviews of Neuromancer). Tokyo: Hayakawa Publishers, 1986.

Hearn, Lafcadio (Koizumi Yakumo). *Glimpses of Unfamiliar Japan*. 1894. Tokyo: Tuttle, 1976.

———. *Interpretations of Literature*. Edited by Masayuki Ikeda. Tokyo: Hokuseido Publishers, 1981.

———. *Kaidan-Kidan shu* (Kwaidan and Other Stories). Translated by Ryo Mori et al. 1988. Tokyo: Kawade Shobo Publishers, 1991.

———. *Kwaidan: Stories and Studies of Strange Things*. 1904. Tokyo: Tuttle, 1995.

High, Peter. *An Outline of American Literature*. New York: Longman, 1986.

Hirakawa, Sukehiro. *Koizumi Yakumo: Seiyou Dasshutsu no Yume* (Yakumo Koizumi: Dreaming of the Other of the West). 1981. Tokyo: Kodansha, 1994.

Hirano, Kyoko. "Japanese Filmmakers and Responsibility for War: The Case of Itami Mansaku." In *War, Occupation, and Creativity: Japan and East Asia, 1920–1960*, edited by Marlene J. Mayo et al. Honolulu: University of Hawaii Press, 2001. 212–232.

———. *Mr. Smith Goes to Tokyo: Japanese Cinema under the American Occupation, 1945–1952*. Washington, D.C.: Smithsonian Institute Press, 1992.
———. *Tenno to Seppun* (The Emperor and the Kiss). Tokyo: Soshisha Publications, 1998. (This is essentially a Japanese version of *Mr. Smith Goes to Tokyo*, revised and translated by Hirano.)
Hiraoka, Masaaki. *Yang Sok Il wa Sekai-Bungaku de aru* (Yang Sok Il's Is World Literature). Tokyo: Village Center Publishers, 1995.
Hisama, Jugi. *Yaponika Tapesutori* (Japonica Tapestry). Tokyo: Kawade Shobo Publishers, 1992.

Hoffman, Daniel. *Poe Poe Poe Poe Poe Poe Poe*. New York: Avon, 1972.
Hutcheon, Linda. *Narcissistic Narrative*. London: Methuen, 1980.
Hwang, David Henry. *M. Butterfly*. New York: Penguin, 1986.
Imamura, Tateo. "Vietnam kara itteki no Hikari e" (A Note on Ken Kaiko's Vietnam War Narratives), *Eureka* 22.8 (July 1990). 92–102.
Inose, Naoki. *Mikado no Shozo* (Portrait of Mikado). Tokyo: Shogakkan Publishers, 1986.
Inoue, Shoichi. *Kyoki to Oken* (Madness and Sovereignty). Tokyo: Kinokuniya Publishers, 1995.
Irving, Washington. "The Legend of Sleepy Hollow." 1819. In *Concise Anthology of American Literature*, 4th ed., edited by George McMichel et al. Upper Saddle River: Prentice Hall, 1998.
Isherwood, Robert. *Farce and Fantasy: Popular Entertainment in Eighteenth-Century Paris*. New York: Oxford University Press, 1986.
Itoh, Norio. Review of *Neuromancer. Asahi Shinbun*, September 7, 1986.
Ivy, Marilyn. *Discourses of the Vanishing: Modernity, Phantasm, Japan*. Chicago: University of Chicago Press, 1995.
Jacobson, Mark. *Gojiro*. 1991. New York: Penguin, 1992.
Japan: An Illustrated Encyclopedia. Tokyo: Kodansha Publishers, 1993.
Jardine, Alice. *Gynesis*. Ithaca: Cornell University Press, 1985.
Jinno, Yuki. *Shumi no Tanjo* (The Birth of Taste). Tokyo: Keiso Shobo Publishing, 1994.
Jones, Gwyneth. *Divine Endurance*. London: George Allen and Unwin, 1984.
Kagami, Akira. Review of *Neuromancer. Hayakawa's SFM* (November 1986).
Kaiko, Ken. *Nippon Sanmon Opera* (The Japanese Three Penny Opera). 1959. Introduction by Kiichi Sasaki. Tokyo: Shincho-sha Publishers, 1971.
Keene, Donald, ed. *Anthology of Japanese Literature*. New York: Grove Press, 1955.
———. *Japanese Literature: An Introduction for Western Readers*. New York: Grove Press, 1955.
Keezing, Michael Fujimoto. "Anna-chan of Green Gables." *Grain* 24.1 (summer 1996): 116–128.
Kelly, William. "Hollywood and the Media." Panel organized at the conference "The American Cultural Impact on Germany, France, Italy and Japan, 1945–1995: An International Comparison," Brown University, April 12–13, 1996.
Kishida, Shu. *Kanryo-byo no Kigen* (The Roots of Bureaucratic-Mania). Tokyo: Shinsho-kan Publishers, 1997.
Kobayashi, Erika. *Bakudan-Musume no Yuutsu* (Bombastic Melancholy). Tokyo: Tokyo Analog Project, 1999.

———. *Neversoapland*. 2000. Tokyo: Kawade Publishers, 2001.
Koizumi, Bon. *Minzoku-gakusha Koizumi Yakumo* (Lafcadio Hearn as the Nativist Ethnologist). Tokyo: Kobunsha Publishers, 1995.
Koizumi, Bon, and Kenji Zenimoto. *Yakumo no 54-nen* (The 54 Years of Yakumo Koizumi). Matsue: Matsue-Imai Shoten Publishers, 2003.
Kojève, Alexandre. *Introduction à la lecture de Hegel*. 1947. Translated by Tadashi Kozuma et al. Tokyo: Kokubunsha Publishers, 1987.
———. *Introduction to the Reading of Hegel*. 1947. Translated by J. H. Nichols Jr. 1969. Ithaca: Cornell University Press, 1980.
Komatsu, Kazuhiko. *Ijinron* (On the Aliens). Tokyo: Chikuma Publishers, 1985.
Komatsu, Sakyo. *Nippon Apacchi-Zoku*. 1964. Introduction by Takashi Ishikawa. Tokyo: Kadokawa Shoten Publishers, 1971.
———. *Nippon Chinbotsu* (Japan Sinks). Tokyo: Kobunsha Publishers, 1973.
Komatsu, Sakyo, and Ken Kaiko, "Loneliness in the Masses" (A Dialogue). In *Ningen to Shite*, no. 5 (December 1971). 257–277.
Kondo, Masaki et al., eds. *The Bulletin Board of the Witches: Postmodern Japanese Folklore*. Tokyo: Hakusuisha Publishing, 1995.
Kotani, Mari. *Alien Bedfellows*. Tokyo: Shohakusha Publishers, 2004.
———. *Joseijo-Muishiki (Techno-Gynesis)*. Tokyo: Keiso Shobo Publishing, 1994.
———. *Seibo Evangelion (Evangelion as the Immaculate Virgin)*. Tokyo: Magazine House, 1997.
Kuhn, Annette, ed. *Alien Zone*. London: Verso, 1990.
Kurei. Review of *Neuromancer*. *Ascii* (September 1986).
Kuspit, Donald. "Art and Capital: An Ironic Dialectic." *Critical Review* 9.4 (fall 1995): 469–482.
Lazarus, David. "Harrison-San! You're Late for Work!: Gaijin Celebrities in Japanese Ads." *Mangajin*, no. 54 (April 1996): 58–59.
Lee, Sherman E. "Introduction." In *The Sketchbooks of Hiroshige*. New York: George Braziller, 1985.
Letson, Russel. Review of *Virtual Light*. *Locus* (August 1993): 27.
London, Jack. "The Unparalleled Invasion." *Curious Fragments: Jack London's Tales of Fantasy Fiction*. Edited by Dale Walker. Port Washington: Kennikat, 1975.
Long, John Luther. *Madame Butterfly*. 1898. In *Japan in American Fiction*, vol. 7. London: Ganesha, 2001. 1–86.
Lynch, Kevin. *Wasting Away*. San Francisco: Sierra Club Books, 1990.
Masaki, Goro. "Evil Eyes." *Hayakawa's SFM* (December 1987).
———. *Venus City*. Tokyo: Hayakawa Publishers, 1992.
Matsubara, Takatoshi, et al. eds. *Hikaku-Shinwagaku no Tenbo* (A Perspective on Comparative Mythology). Tokyo: Hakusuisha Publishing, 1995.
Matsuoka, Seigo. *Furajairu* (Fragile). Tokyo: Chikuma Publishers, 1995.
McCaffery, Larry, ed. *After Yesterday's Crash*. New York: Penguin, 1995.
———. *Avant-Pop: Fiction of a Daydream Nation*. Boulder: Black Ice, 1993.
———. "The Avant-Pop Phenomenon." *ANQ* 5.4 (1992): 216.
———. "The Fictions of the Present." In *The Columbia Literary History of the United States*, edited by Emory Elliott et al. New York: Columbia University Press, 1988.
———. *The Metafictional Muse*. Pittsburgh: University of Pittsburgh Press, 1982.

———. "Post-Pynchon Postmodern American Fiction." Translated by Takayuki Tatsumi. In *Positive*, no. 1, edited by Emiko Saito. Tokyo: Shoshi-Kaze-no-Bara [Suisei-sha], 1991. 248–267.

———, ed. *Storming the Reality Studio*. Durham: Duke University Press, 1991.

———. "13 Introductory Ways of Looking at a Post-Post-Modernist Aesthetic Phenomenon Called 'Avant-Pop.'" In *In Memoriam to Postmodernism: Essays on the Avant-Pop*, edited by Mark Amerika and Lance Olsen. San Diego: San Diego State University Press, 1995. 32–47.

McHale, Brian. *Postmodernist Fiction*. New York: Methuen, 1987.

Melville, Herman. *Moby-Dick*. 1851. New York: Norton, 2002.

Michaels, Walter Benn. *The Gold Standard and the Logic of Naturalism*. Berkeley: University of California Press, 1987.

Mitsuoka, Kenji, et al. *Za Shibuya Kenkyu* (The Study of Shibuya). Tokyo: Tokyu Agency, 1989.

Mogen, David. "Wilderness, Metamorphosis, and Millenium: Gothic Apocalypse from the Puritans to the Cyberpunks." In *Frontier Gothic: Terror and Wonder at the Frontier in American Literature*, edited by David Mogen et al. Rutherford: Fairleigh Dickinson University Press, 1993.

Montgomery, Lucy Maud. *Anne of Green Gables*. 1908. New York: Skylark, 1948.

Morse, Ronald. "Yanagita Kunio." In *The Kodansha Encyclopedia of Japan*, vol. 8. Tokyo: Kodansha Publishers, 1983.

Mosley, Leonard. *Hirohito, Emperor of Japan*. Englewood Cliffs: Prentice Hall, 1966.

Murai, Osamu. *Nanto Ideorogii no Tanjo* (The Birth of the Ideology of Southern Islands). 1992. Tokyo: Ota Publications, 1995.

Murakami, Ryu. *Coin Locker Babies*. 1980. Translated by Stephen Snyder. Tokyo: Kodansha International, 1995.

Murasaki, Hyakuro. *Kichiku no Susume* (How to Enjoy the Life of a Garbage Guerilla). Tokyo: Data House, 1996.

Nagayama, Yasuo. *Kindai Nippon no Monsho-gaku* (Emblems of Modern Japan). Tokyo: Seikyusha Publishers, 1992.

Nakajima, Azusa. Review of *Neuromancer*. *Hoseki Weekly*, August 8, 1986.

Nelson, Peter. *Treehouses*. Boston: Houghton Mifflin, 1994.

Night, Nancy. "'The New Light': X Rays and Medical Futurism." In *Imagining Tomorrow: History, Technology, and the American Future*, edited by Joseph Corn. Cambridge: MIT Press, 1986. 10–34.

Noda, Hideki. "Pandora no Kane" (Pandora's Bell). *Bungakkai* (January 2000): 86–137.

Notoji, Masako. *Disneyland to iu Seichi* (Disneyland as a Holy Land). Tokyo: Iwanami Publishing, 1990.

Numa, Shozo. *Kachikujin Yapoo* (Yapoo the Human Cattle). Vol. 1 [1970], rev. ed. Tokyo: Sukora Publishers, 1991; vol. 2, Tokyo: Million Publishers, 1991.

———. *Kachiku-jin Yapoo: Kanketsu-hen* (The Definitive Edition of *Yapoo the Human Cattle Saga*). Tokyo: Gentosha Publishers, 1999.

Ochi, Michio. *Kariforunia no Ougon* (Gold Rush Narrative). Tokyo: Asahi Shinbunsha Publishers, 1990.

Ogiwara, Shinko. "Hito to Doubutsu nno Kon-in-tan no Haikei to Henyo"

(Tales of Interspecies Marriage: Its Background and Transformation). In *Hikaku-Shinwagaku no Tenbo*, edited by Takatoshi Matsubara. Tokyo: Hakusuisha Publishers, 1995. 139–156.

Ohara, Mariko. "Mental Female." *Hayakawa's SFM* (December 1986).

Orwell, George. *1984*. 1949. New York: Penguin, 1984.

Otobe, Junko. "Shinbun kara mita Nippon-Apacchi-Zoku no Koro" (The Etymology of the "Japanese Apache" in the Newspapers in the 1950s). *Komatsu Sakyo Magazine*, no. 15 (July 2004): 62–71.

Pearce, Roy Harvey. "The Significance of Captivity Narrative." *American Literature* 19 (March 1947): 1–20.

Piggott, Juliet. *Japanese Mythology*. 1969. New York: Peter Bedrick Books, 1982.

Poe, Edgar Allan. *Collected Works of Edgar Allan Poe*. Edited by F. O. Mabbott. Cambridge: Belknap Press of Harvard University Press, 1969–1978.

———. *The Short Fiction of Edgar Poe*. Edited by Stuart Levine and Susan Levine. Indianapolis: Bobbs-Merril, 1976.

Polledri, Paolo, ed. *Visionary San Francisco*. San Francisco: San Francisco Museum of Modern Art, 1990.

Porush, David. *Soft Machine*. New York: Methuen, 1985.

Poster, Mark. "The Question of Agency: Michel de Certeau and the History of Consumerism." *Diacritics* 22.2 (summer 1992): 94–107.

Price, Leah. "From Ghostwriter to Typewriter: Delegating Authority at Fin de Siecle." In *The Faces of Anonymity: Anonymous and Pseudonymous Publication from the Sixteenth to the Twentieth Century*, edited by Robert J. Griffin. New York: Palgrave Macmillan, 2003, 211–231.

Pynchon, Thomas. *Gravity's Rainbow*. New York: Viking, 1973.

———. "Is it O.K. to Be a Luddite?" *New York Times Book Review*, October 28, 1984, 41.

———. *Vineland*. Boston: Little, Brown, 1990.

Renzi, Thomas C. *H. G. Wells: Six Scientific Romances Adapted for Film*. Metuchen: Scarecrow, 1992.

Roberts, James. "Stubborn Washington Spurred Kingdom." In *The Papers of George Washington*. July 4, 2000. http://gwpapers.virginia.edu/project/news/washington/roberts.html.

Rucker, Rudy. "Cyberpunk." Panel at the North American Science Fiction Convention, Austin, Texas, August 31, 1985.

Sakaguchi, Ango. "Daraku-Ron" (An Invitation to Total Depravity). [1946]. In *Nippon-ron* (On Japan). Tokyo: Kawade Publishers, 1989.

Sakakibara, Natsu. *General MacArthur and the Showa Emperor*. Tokyo: Shueisha Publishers, 2000.

Sakate, Yoji. "Tennou to Seppun" (The Emperor and the Kiss). Tokyo: Komomiru Publishers, 2001.

Sandoval, Chela. "New Sciences: Cyborg Feminism and the Methodology of the Oppressed." In *Cyborg Handbook*, edited by Chris Hables Gray. New York: Routledge, 1995. 407–421.

Saya, Makito. *Yanagita Kunio*. Tokyo: Ozawa Shoten Publishers, 1996.

Sayle, Murray. "Nerve Gas and the Four Noble Truths." *New Yorker*, April 1, 1996. 68.

Scholes, Robert. *Fabulation and Metafiction*. Urbana: University of Illinois Press, 1979.

Schvelbusch, Wolfgang. *The Railway Journey: The Industrialization of Time and Space in the 19th Century*. Berkeley: University of California Press, 1986.

Schwenger, Peter. "Agrippa, or The Apocalyptic Book." *South Atlantic Quarterly* 92.4 (fall 1993): 617–626.

Sekora, John. "Red, White, and Black: Indian Captives, Colonial Printers, and the Early African-American Narrative." In *A Mixed Race: Ethnicity in Early America*, edited by Frank Shuffelton. New York: Oxford University Press, 1993. 92–104.

Shiel, M. P. *The Yellow Danger*. 1898. Edited by George Locke. London: Thoemmes, 1999.

Shimada, Masahiko. *Etorofu no Koi* (Lovers in Iturup Island). Tokyo: Shinchosha Publishers, 2003.

———. *Higan-Sensei* (Master and Discipline). Tokyo: Fukutake Publishers, 1992.

———. *Suisei no junin* (Inhabiting the Comet). Tokyo: Shinchosha Publishers, 2000.

———. *Utsukushii Tamashii* (The Beautiful Soul). Tokyo: Shinchosha Publishers, 2003.

———. *Yume-Tsukai* (Dream Messenger). 1989. Translated by Philip Gabriel. Tokyo: Kodansha International, 1992.

Shunya, Yoshimi. *Toshi no Doramatsurugii* (The Dramaturgy of City). Tokyo: Kobundo Publishers, 1987.

Slotkin, Richard. *Regeneration through Violence*. Hanover: Wesleyan University Press, 1973.

Smolinski, Reiner. "The 'New' Hermeneutics and the Jewish Nation in Cotton Mather's Eschatology." In *The Threefold Paradise of Cotton Mather: An Edition of Triparadisus*, edited by Reiner Smolinski. Athens: University of Georgia Press, 1995.

Spinrad, Norman. *The Iron Dream*. New York: Avon, 1972.

———. "North American Magic Realism." *Isaac Asimov's Science Fiction Magazine* (February 1991): 177–190.

———. "The State of Art." *Isaac Asimov's Science Fiction Magazine* (August 1994): 160–173.

Stableford, Brian. "H. G. Wells." In *The Encyclopedia of Science Fiction*, edited by John Clute and Peter Nicholls. London: Orbit, 1993. 1313.

Starr, Kevin. Preface to *Visionary San Francisco*, edited by Paolo Polledri. San Francisco: San Francisco Museum of Modern Art, 1990. 11–15.

Sterling, Bruce. *Crystal Express*. Sank City; Arkham House, 1989.

———. Introduction to *ArmadilloCon 8 Program Book* (October 1986): 6–7.

———. Preface to *Mirrorshades: The Cyberpunk Anthology*, edited by Bruce Sterling (New York: Arbor House, 1986), vii–xiv.

———. "Slipstream." *Science Fiction Eye*, no. 5 (July 1989): 78–80.

Stevens, Halsey. *The Life and Music of Bela Bartok*. 3rd ed. 1993. Oxford: Clarendon, 1996.

Suikyoshi. Review of *Neuromancer. Hayakawa's SFM* (October 1986).

Sullivan, Andrew. "Counter Culture: All in the Family?" *New York Times Magazine*, September 6, 2000, 24–26.

Süskind, Patrick. *Perfume: The Story of a Murderer*. Translated by John E. Woods. 1985. New York: Washington Square Press, 1991.

Sussman, Henry. *High Resolution*. New York: Oxford University Press, 1989.

Suzuki, Jun. "Kikai to Gijutsu-sha" (The Machines and the Engineers). In *Sangyo-Kakumei* (Industrial Revolution), edited by Naosuke Takamura. Tokyo: Yoshikawa-Kobunkan Publishers, 1994. 134–153.

Takahashi, Ryohei. Review of *Neuromancer. Hayakawa's SFM* (October 1986).

Tanaka, Stefan. *Japan's Orient: Rendering Pasts into History*. Berkeley: University of California Press, 1993.

Tatsumi, Takayuki. "Creative Masochism." *American Book Review* 16.1 (April–May 1994): 6, 9, 27.

———. *Cyberpunk America*. Tokyo: Keiso Shobo Publishing, 1988.

———. "Editorial Afterword: A Soft Time Machine: From Translation to Transfiguration." *Science-Fiction Studies* (88) 29.3 (November 2002): 475–484.

———. "An Interview with William Gibson." *Science Fiction Eye* 1 (March 1987): 6–17.

———. "The Japanoid Manifesto: Toward a New Poetics of Invisible Culture." In "New Japanese Fiction." Special issue of *Review of Contemporary Fiction* 22.2, edited by Takayuki Tatsumi, Larry McCaffery, and Sinda Gregory. Dalkey Archive Press, 2002, 12–18.

———. "Mado kara San Francisco ga mieru" (A wonderful view of San Francisco). *Tosho Shinbun* (Book Review Press), September 11, 1993: 1.

———. "A Manifesto for Gynoids." *Science Fiction Eye*, no. 9 (1991); Japanese version, in Richard Calder, *The Allure* (Tokyo: Treville, 1991).

———. *Nippon Henryu Bungaku* (Slipstream Japan). Tokyo: Shinchosha Publishers, 1998.

———. *Nisenichinen Uchu-no Tabi Kougi (Lectures on* 2001: A Space Odyssey). Tokyo: Heibonsha, 2001.

———. "Overview of Cyberpunk." *Hayakawa's SFM* (January 1986).

———. "Post-Human, Post-Monolith: 2001 or a Cyberspace Odyssey." *Nobodaddies*, no. 1 (spring–summer 1994). 46–50.

———. "Preface." *Future War Novels of the 1890s*. Vol. 1. Edited by George Locke and Takayuki Tatsumi. London: Routledge-Thoemmes, 1998.

Tatsumi, Takayuki, Larry McCaffery, and Sinda Gregory, eds. "New Japanese Fiction." Special issue of *Review of Contemporary Fiction* 22.2 (Dalkey Archive Press, 2002).

Tatsumi, Takayuki, and Shinya Tsukamoto. "Cyber-Eros in Full Metal Apache (A Dialogue)." *Cape X*, no. 4 (October 1995). 36–39.

Terayama, Shuji. *Kikei no Shimborizumu* (The Symbolism of Freaks). Tokyo: Hakusuisha Publishers, 1993.

———. "The Miraculous Mandarin." 1977. In *The Plays of Shuji Terayama*, vol. 9. Tokyo: Shichosha Publishers, 1987.

———. *Zouki-Koukan Josetsu* (Transplanting Organs: An Introduction). 1982. Tokyo: Farao, 1992.

Terayama, Shuji, and J. A. Caesar. "Enshutsu Shukou" (A Note on Direction). *Gekijo*, no. 16 (1977): 4–5.

Thomson, Rosemarie Garland. *Extraordinary Bodies: Figuring Physical Disability in American Culture and Literature*. New York: Columbia University Press, 1997.

t.o.L (tree of Life), dir. *TAMALA2010*. Tokyo: Kinetique, 2002.

Treat, John Whittier. "Beheaded Emperors and the Absent Figure in Contemporary Japanese Literature." *PMLA* 109.1 (January 1994): 100–115.

Tsukamoto, Shinya, dir. *Tetsuo*. Performance by Tomoroh Taguchi, Kei Fujiwara, Naohira Musaka, Nobu Kanaoa, and Renji Ishibashi at the Kaiju-Theater, 1989.

———, dir. *Tetsuo II: Body Hammer*. Performance by Tomoroh Taguchi, Nobu Kanaoa, Sujin Kim, and Hideaki Tezuka at the Kaiju-Theater, 1992.

Tsuru, Shigeto. *Japan's Capitalism: Creative Defeat and Beyond*. Cambridge: Cambridge University Press, 1993.

Tsutsui, Yasutaka. *Bungaku-bu Tadano kyoju* (Hitoshi Tadano, Professor of English). Tokyo: Iwanami Publishing, 1990.

———. "Kyoko-Riron ni Tsuite" (On My Fictional Theory: A Recollection). Unpublished essay. 1991.

———. "Tatazumu Hito" (The Standing Woman). 1974. Translated by David Lewis. *OMNI* (January 1981). http://www.jali.or.jp/tti/prof_e.html.

———. *Tokaido Senso* (Tokaido Wars). Tokyo: Hayakawa Publishing, 1965.

Twain, Mark. *Mark Twain's Which Was the Dream?* Edited by John S. Tuckey. Berkeley: University of California Press, 1967.

Ubukata, Yukio. *Kaitaiya no Sengo-Shi* (Postwar History as Narrated by a Scrap Merchant). Tokyo: PHP Publishers, 1994.

Van Troyer, Gene. "A Report on American Science Fiction." Translated by Hisashi Kuroma. *Hayakawa's SFM* (January 1978): 144–152.

Vaughan, Alden, et al., eds. *Puritans among the Indians: Accounts of Captivity and Redemption, 1676–1724*. Cambridge: Belknap Press of Harvard University Press, 1981.

Vevier, Charles. "Yellow Peril." In *Dictionary of American History VII*. New York: Charles Scribner, 1976. 356–357.

Vogel, Ezra. *Japan as Number One*. Cambridge: Harvard University Press, 1979.

Watabiki, Hiroshi. *Mono ga Kataru Sekai no Rekishi* (Iron and World History). Tokyo: Seibun-sha Publishers, 1994.

Waite, Geoff. *Nietzsche's Corpse: Aesthetics, Politics, Prophesy, or The Spectacular Technoculture of Everyday Life*. Durham: Duke University Press, 1996.

Waugh, Patricia. *Metafiction: The Theory and Practice of Self-Conscious Fiction*. London: Methuen, 1984.

Wells, H. G. *The War of the Worlds*. [1898]. New York: Oxford University Press, 1995.

Westfahl, Gary. "The Sequelizer, or The Farmer Gone to Hell: Book Three in the Chronicles of Westfahl the Critic." *Science Fiction Eye*, no. 11 (December 1992): 23–27.

Whipple, William. "Poe's Political Satire." *Texas University Studies in English* 35 (1956): 81–95.

Wolfe, Alan. *Suicidal Narrative in Modern Japan*. Princeton: Princeton University Press, 1990.

Wolfe, Gary K. "The Dawn Patrol: Sex and Technology in Farmer and Ballard." *New York Review of Science Fiction*, no. 25 (September 1990): 1, 8–10.

Yamaguchi, Masao. *Haisha no Seishin-shi* (The Mental History of Defeat). Tokyo: Iwanami Publishing, 1995.

———. *Zasetsu no Showa-shi* (The Mental History of Failure). Tokyo: Iwanami Publishing, 1995.

Yamamura, Misa. *Mysteries of A Rental Family*. Tokyo: Bungei-Shunju Publishers, 1993.

Yamano, Koichi. "Japanese SF, Its Originality and Orientation." 1969. Translated by Kazuko Behrens, edited by Darko Suvin and Takayuki Tatsumi. *Science-Fiction Studies* 21.1 (March 1994): 67–80.

Yanagita, Kunio. *Tono Monogatari* (The Legends of Tono). Introduction by Takeo Kuwahara. 1910. Tokyo: Iwanami Publishing, 1976.

———. *Tono Monogatari* (The Legends of Tono). Translated and introduced by Ronald Morse, foreword by Richard Dorson. Tokyo: Japan Foundation, 1975.

———. *Tono Monogatari* (The Legends of Sayo). Film directed by Tetsutaro Murano; script by Yukiko Takayama; performed by Yoko Hara, Ryu Daisuke, Tatsuya Nakadai, Kyoko Enami, and Koji Yakusho. Tetsu Production, 1982.

———. *Warai-no-Hongan* (The Real Desire of Smile). 1946. Tokyo: Iwanami Publishing, 1979.

Yang, Sok Il. *Shura wo Ikiru* (Surviving the Hell). Tokyo: Kodansha Publishers, 1995.

———. *Yami no Souzouryoku* (The Imagination of Darkness). Osaka: Kaiho Publishers, 1995.

———. *Yoru wo Kakete* (Through the Night). Tokyo: NHK Publishers, 1994.

Yomota, Inuhiko. "Kafuka to Yakiniku" (Kafka and Roast Beef). Special issue on Ken Kaiko, *Eureka* 22.8 (July 1990). 88–91.

Zavarzadeh, Mas'ud. *The Mythopoeic Reality: The Postwar American Nonfiction Novel*. Urbana: University of Illinois Press, 1976.

Zuk, William. "Bridge." In *Encyclopedia Americana*. Danbury: Grolier, 1993. 1:522–537.

INDEX

Takayuki Tatsumi is a professor of English at Keio University in Tokyo.

Library of Congress Cataloging-in-Publication Data
Tatsumi, Takayuki, 1955-
Full metal apache : transactions between cyberpunk Japan and avant-pop America / Takayuki Tatsumi.
p. cm.—(Post-contemporary interventions)
Includes bibliographical references and index.
ISBN 0-8223-3762-2 (cloth : alk. paper)
ISBN 0-8223-3774-6 (pbk. : alk. paper)
1. Science fiction, Japanese—History and criticism. 2. Science fiction, American—History and criticism. 3. Japanese fiction—20th century—History and criticism. 4. Japanese fiction—Foreign influences. 5. American fiction—20th century—History and criticism. 6. American fiction—Foreign influences. I. Title. II. Series.
PL740.T37 2006
895.6′30876209044—dc22 2005037847